CW00953939

Cb de Chatillon d   H. Moses sc

THE ELEVATION OF THE HOST.

HIERURGIA;

OR,

THE HOLY SACRIFICE OF THE MASS.

WITH NOTES AND DISSERTATIONS

ELUCIDATING

ITS DOCTRINES AND CEREMONIES,

AND NUMEROUS ILLUSTRATIONS.

BY

DANIEL ROCK, D.D.

REVISED BY

W. H. JAMES WEALE.

FOURTH EDITION.

VOLUME I.

LONDON:

THOMAS BAKER, SOHO SQUARE.

1900.

PREFACE TO THE PRESENT EDITION.

———————

THIS work, published in 1833, and now long out of print, has become scarce, and as it appears to be sought after, it has been decided to reprint it in order to meet the growing desire, on the part both of Catholics and Anglicans, for information as to the use and meaning of the ceremonies of the Mass. Both parts of the book have been carefully revised, the references verified, and the quotations, when necessary, corrected and occasionally amplified.

In the first part, especially in the Notes on the Rubrics, a good many alterations have been made. These will, it is hoped, be found to add to the usefulness of the work, by helping those who assist at Mass to enter more closely into the spirit of the Liturgy, and to follow the holy rite in all its details. There can be no doubt that a thorough knowledge of the Liturgy will be found helpful to the devotion of all, whether they follow the office of the day or assist at the Holy Sacrifice by meditation and acts of mental prayer.

Holy Church leaves her children free, when assisting at Low Mass, to follow the bent of their private devotion, only prescribing that they should kneel throughout the whole service, except during the recital of the Gospel of the day, which ought *always* to be listened to, or read in the vernacular. But High Mass is a public act of homage, and here private devotion should give way to public edification. Catholics ought at least to stand, sit, and kneel at the proper times, and when able, join in singing the Kyrie, Gloria, Credo and Responses, and in reading the Collects, etc., proper to the office of the day. The prayers of the Liturgy are incomparably superior to all others, the best of which are after all but the inventions of individuals, and inasmuch as they do not initiate those who use them into the spirit of the Church offices, far from uniting tend to isolate them. The practice moreover of saying the same prayers at Mass Sunday after Sunday often ends by becoming wearisome and destroying devotion. Catholics cannot do better than follow the way marked out by the Church; and in order to derive as much profit as possible, we would strongly recommend them to read some book on the office of the ensuing Sunday, such as the Liturgical Year of the late Abbot of Solesmes, Dom Prosper Gueranger, of which there is an excellent English translation.

PREFATORY NOTICE

TO THE FIRST EDITION.

———

OF the more intelligent and inquiring amongst our Protestant fellow-countrymen, several have occasionally manifested a desire to see a manual which not only contained the prayers, but explained the ceremonies and elucidated the doctrine of the Mass. The purport of these pages is to fill up such a deficiency in the number of those well-composed and highly useful expositions of Catholic doctrine which we already possess.

The work is divided into two parts; the first of which embraces the Ordinary of the Mass, in Latin and in English, to which are appended notes explanatory of the ceremonies and the ritual of the Liturgy. The second part contains dissertations on the doctrine of the Eucharist, as a sacrifice and a sacrament; on the Invocation of Saints; on Purgatory; on Images; on Ceremonies; on the Vestments, and the history of their origin and gradual change to their present form; and on the several points of ritual and disciplinary observance.

The Roman Catacombs are precious and highly interesting to every true believer in the Gospel, from their having been the burial-place of the holy martyrs and primitive Christians—from their still exhibiting the very subterraneous chambers in which the earliest followers of Christ at Rome were accustomed to assemble on the Lord's Day, in order to assist at and partake of the Eucharistic Sacrifice—and from furnishing a residence and refuge to the Popes, the clergy, and the faithful in general, during more than twelve fiery persecutions. The Basilicae erected by Constantine in the old capital of the Roman empire, and by his immediate successors and pious individuals in the same city and in other parts of the Italian peninsula, are also highly valuable. United together, the catacombs and ancient churches of Rome and of Italy in general constitute a wide and fertile field of monuments, both curiously interesting and serviceable alike to the theologian, the ecclesiastical antiquary, and the artist. Over any part of this diversified region the British reader has seldom, perhaps never, been conducted, while making those inquiries, and prosecuting those investigations, on litigated articles of doctrine and discipline, which in every other quarter have been directed in the most masterly and able manner, and display the fruits of long and toilsome research over a widely extended field of erudition. The author has broken up this new and

prolific ground, and has not unfrequently alleged
an inscription from a martyr's tomb, to fortify his
argument in vindication of some tenet of the
ancient faith; and produced a fresco-painting,
or a piece of sculpture, from the subterranean
chambers of the catacombs, and a mosaic from
some ancient church, to explain the origin of our
present sacerdotal vestments, or in illustration of
the rites and ceremonies still practised at the celebration of our holy Liturgy. A repeated inspection
of many of those venerable monuments, during a
college residence of almost seven delightful years,
in the centre of Christianity, convinced the author
of their inestimable value and importance, at the
same time that it awakened a desire to study and
investigate them. Such impressions were more
deeply imprinted on his mind at a second visit to
Rome, in which he was indulged for the improvement of his health, during the winter of 1828–29,
by the liberality of his kind and noble patron, the
Earl of Shrewsbury, who procured and placed at
his disposal, during the composition of the present
volumes, works not only highly interesting, but
necessary, yet so expensive as to be entirely
beyond the author's means of purchase.

Knowing, from self-experience, that the *oculus
fidelis*—the faithful eye—can collect much more
information by a single glance at the drawing of
a pictorial or sculptured monument of antiquity,

than from perusing whole chapters taken up with
the most minute and elaborate descriptions of it,
he was determined to enrich his labours with copies
of those monuments referred to in the text or
accompanying notes. The reader will, therefore,
find these pages embellished with several copper-
plate and wood engravings, executed by Mr.
Moses, and other artists of the first order in the
respective branches of their profession, and whom
the author must congratulate on the able manner
in which they have acquitted themselves of the
task confided to their care.

The reader will, no doubt, detect the absence
of true perspective—remark several obvious faults
in the drawing of the human figure—and notice
other seeming deficiencies in some at least of the
engravings which are scattered through these
volumes. He should, however, bear in mind that
of these graphic illustrations of the text many
were selected from monuments executed at a period
when painting and sculpture, together with the
sister arts and sciences, were sinking into, or
emerging from, that night of ignorance which
darkened Europe during the Middle Ages.[1] As
these monuments were produced to elucidate an

---

[1] No admirer of the fine arts should be without the talented and
elaborate works of Seroux d'Agincourt and Cicognara. The learned
Frenchman employed thirty years in the compilation of his '*His-
toire de l'Art par les Monumens, depuis sa Décadence au 4ème siècle,*

ancient custom, or to corroborate some argument, by noticing the accordance in Catholic belief at the present moment with that of early times, the author considered it a religious duty to exhibit as accurate transcripts of them as he could possibly procure. Hence he solicited those friends who so kindly furnished him with tracings and copies of these ancient monuments, and directed the artists who engraved them, to be as minutely faithful in their respective delineations, and transcribe them with every fault, however glaring. The object, in this instance, was not to improve nor decorate, but to render fac-similes of those curious originals which, notwithstanding their defects, are interesting to the artist and antiquary.

---

jusqu'à son renouvellement au 16*ème;* ' and the patriotic Italian has eloquently advanced the claims of his own Italy as the nurse of all the family of the arts in his ' *Storia della Scultura dal suo Risorgimento in Italia fino al secolo di Canova.*' How deeply it is to be regretted that no Englishman has hitherto been stimulated by the patriotism of Cicognara, or warmed by a love for the arts similar to that which quickened Seroux d'Agincourt, to achieve for Great Britain what these authors, with small fortunes and no patronage, have done for Italy—for Europe. Materials are abundant, since not only are our native productions, especially from the tenth century, most numerous in architecture, sculpture, and painting in illuminated MSS., but many of them still exist in the highest state of preservation. Nothing is wanting but some individual, with sufficient abilities and the necessary acquirements, with the will to collect and arrange those splendid national monuments, to vindicate the honour of Britain, and prove the ancient success with which she cultivated the arts, at least from the tenth up to the commencement of the sixteenth century, and hence demonstrate her actual capability of recovering her former glory, and adding to it new splendours, if animated to such a meritorious enterprise by due encouragement.

CONTENTS OF VOL. I.

———•———

PART I.

THE LITURGY OF THE MASS.

	PAGE
SPRINKLING OF HOLY WATER	I
ORDINARY OF THE MASS	3
BENEDICTION WITH THE BLESSED SACRAMENT AFTER MASS .	64
NOTES ON THE RUBRICS.	67

PART II.

CHAPTER I.

SECTION I.

ON SACRIFICE IN GENERAL.

1. The necessity of interior and exterior worship.—2. Sacrifice offered from the beginning of the world.—3. What sacrifice is.—4. The four ends of sacrifice.—5. The legal sacrifices were of no avail when unconnected with the future death of the Redeemer.—6. A new sacrifice was necessary.—7. The sacrifice of the Cross a true sacrifice.—8. All the ancient sacrifices comprised in it.—9. The unbloody sacrifice of the New Law 159

SECTION II.

THE MASS A SACRIFICE.

10. The Mass a true sacrifice.—11. Sacrifice of Melchisedech. —12. The sacrifice of Melchisedech elucidated by the

PAGE

writings of the Fathers.—13. Illustrated by an ancient mosaic at Ravenna.—14. The Paschal Lamb a figure of the Sacrifice of the Mass.—15. Accomplishment of the prophecy of Malachias in the Sacrifice of the Mass.—16. Christ announces a new sacrifice.—17. The Sacrifice of the Mass proved from S. Paul 170

SECTION III.

ON THE REAL PRESENCE.

18. The Real Presence.—19. The promise made by Christ that He would give us His Flesh and Blood to eat and drink. —20. Objection answered.—21. Proof from the Institution. Objections explained.—22. The Real Presence proved from S. Paul.—23. Taught by the rest of the Apostles.—24. All the ancient Liturgies attest the Real Presence 192

SECTION IV.

TRANSUBSTANTIATION.

25. What is meant by the term.—26. Transubstantiation proved from Scripture.—27. Attested by S. Cyril.—28. Illustrated by a practice of the modern Greek Church. Objections answered.—29. From S. Paul.—30. Objection to the term Transubstantiation.—31. Recapitulation . 228

CHAPTER II.

SECTION I.

HISTORY OF THE MASS.

1. Christ said the first Mass.—2. Christ directed the Apostles to celebrate Mass.—3. The Apostles said Mass.—4. A ceremonial instituted by the Apostles for offering up Mass.— 5. Attested by S. John.—6. The remarks of some Protestants noticed.—7. The Liturgy indicated by S. Ignatius. —8. Noticed by Pliny.—9. Described by S. Justin . . 246

SECTION II.

LAY COMMUNION.

PAGE

10. Belief of the Church on lay Communion.—11. Communion under one kind of Apostolic institution.—12. When and why generally adopted by the Latin Church.—13. Agreeable to Scripture.—14. Objection from Scripture answered.—15. Unleavened bread used at the Last Supper.—16. Unleavened bread used by the Latin Church, by the Maronites, and Armenians.—17. The Sacrament hinted at in the Apocalypse.—18. The circular form of the Host very ancient 260

CHAPTER III.

ON THE TERM MASS.

1. Meaning of the word Mass.—2. Origin of it.—3. The antiquity of its use 281

CHAPTER IV.

ON THE USE OF LATIN AT MASS.

1. An unknown tongue used in the Jewish Temple.—2. Not blamed by Christ, who prayed in an unknown tongue.—3. Reasons why the Catholic Church uses Latin at Mass.—4. The people not necessarily obliged to understand the language of the Mass.—5. Latin at Mass nowise prejudicial to the people.—6. Greeks, Syrians, Copts, and Armenians use an unknown tongue at Mass.—7. Objection answered.—8. Stricture on the Protestant version of the words of S. Paul 288

CONTENTS.

CHAPTER V.

ON THE INVOCATION OF SAINTS AND ANGELS.

PAGE

1. Immeasurable distance between the worship given to God and the reverence shown to the saints.—2. Religious respect may be rendered to saints and angels.—3. The angels and saints make intercession for men.—4. Inferred from the communion of saints in the Apostles' Creed.—5. From the charity which animates the saints.—6. The invocation of angels proved from Scripture ; from the Psalms ; from Genesis ; from the Apocalypse.—7. The invocation of saints proved from Scripture.—8. Holy men have, even in this life, been invoked by others.—9. Invocation of saints in the primitive Church proved from ancient inscriptions.—10. Invocation of saints in the Anglo-Saxon Church.—11. Contained in all the Liturgies.—12. Objections answered.—13. Charity engages the saints to pray for us.—14. They have the power of doing it.—15. They know what passes upon earth.—16. Their intercession not derogatory to the mediatorship of Christ.—17. Manner of addressing God through the saints.—18. Similarity of Catholic and Protestant prayers.—19. Inconsistency of an objection 302

LIST OF ILLUSTRATIONS.

VOL. I.

1. *Engraving.* THE ELEVATION . . . . . *Frontispiece.*

The lower part represents the Elevation of the Host, immediately after the Consecration. The upper portion of the engraving was suggested by various passages in the Apocalypse, respecting the mystic sacrifice of the Lamb, which S. John saw in vision.

The beautiful passage extracted from the writings of S. John Chrysostom (p. 135) will furnish an appropriate elucidation of the subject of this engraving.

2. *Engraving.* THE CRUCIFIXION . . . *facing page* 1

After Michael Angelo. The original design was in the possession of the Prince of Lucca, and preserved in the ducal palace of that city.

3. *Woodcut.* The painting which usually ornaments the ceiling over the altar, in Greek churches . . *page* 233

During the time that M. de Nointel was ambassador of France at the Porte, he visited many of the churches belonging to the Greeks. Excepting in those which were extremely poor, he invariably observed a lamp suspended and burning before the place in which the Blessed Sacrament was deposited. His attention was attracted by certain paintings representing sometimes an altar on which lay an open volume exhibiting these words, 'Take, eat; this is My Body;' at other times a chalice, out of which Jesus Christ was issuing, under the form of a little infant, having the book of the Gospels opened, and showing the words of consecration on the right, and on the left the Eucharistic bread. In some churches the ambassador observed, over the altar, a painting in which there appeared the chalice, the Host, and the book of the Gospels, with figures on both sides, each holding in his hand a scroll, on which was written, 'O God, our God, who hast sent us Thy celestial bread which is the nourishment of the world.' The pictures that are to be more generally seen are those which represent angels and saints adoring the Host made in the form of a human figure, and the chalice on an altar.—P. LE BRUN, *Explication des Prières et des Cérémonies de la Messe,* tome III, p. 660.

4. *Woodcuts.* Arculae, little boxes used in the first ages of the Church by the faithful for carrying home the Blessed Eucharist after Mass . . . *page* 260

5. *Woodcut.* The various forms of the Host, or Eucharistic bread. 1. Form of the Eucharistic bread in the Latin Church. 2. Its form in the Greek Church. 3. Corban, or Eucharistic bread used by the Copts . . . . *page* 280

Michael Angelo inv.   Ch de Chatillon d.   H Moses fc.

THE CRUCIFIXION.

THE LITURGY OF THE MASS

SPRINKLING OF HOLY WATER.

¶ *Before High Mass on Sundays, the following Antiphon is commonly sung:*

Aspérges me Dómine hyssópo, et mundábor: lavábis me, et super nivem dealbábor.

Miserére mei Deus, secúndum magnam misericórdiam Tuam.

V. Glória Patri, et Fílio, et Spirítui Sancto.

R. Sicut erat in princípio, et nunc, et semper, et in saecula saeculórum. Amen.

Ant. Aspérges me, etc.

Thou shalt sprinkle me, O Lord, with hyssop,[1] and I shall be cleansed: Thou shalt wash me, and I shall be made whiter than snow.

Have mercy on me, O God, according to Thy great mercy.

V. Glory be to the Father, and to the Son, and to the Holy Ghost.

R. As it was in the beginning, is now, and ever shall be, world without end. Amen.

Ant. Thou shalt sprinkle me, etc.

¶ *From Easter to Whitsunday, inclusively, instead of the foregoing Antiphon, the following is sung:*

Vidi aquam egredién tem de templo a látere dextro, Allelúia : et omnes ad quos pervénit aqua ista, salvi facti sunt, et dicent, Allelúia, Allelúia.

I saw water flowing from the right side of the temple, Alleluia : and all to whom that water came, were saved, and they shall say, Alleluia, Alleluia.

Ps. Confitémini Domino, quóniam bonus: quóniam in saeculum misericórdia Eius. Gloria, etc.

Ps. Give praise to the Lord, for He is good : for His mercy endureth for ever. Glory, etc.

¶ *The Priest, having returned to the foot of the Altar, says:*

V. Osténde nobis Dómine misericórdiam Tuam. (*T. P.:* Allelúia.)

R. Et salutáre Tuum da nobis. (*T. P.:* Allelúia.)

V. Dómine exaúdi oratiónem meam.

R. Et clamor meus ad Te véniat.

V. Show us, O Lord, Thy mercy. (*In Paschal time:* Alleluia.)

R. And grant us Thy salvation. (*In Paschal time:* Alleluia.)

V. O Lord, hear my prayer.

R. And let my cry come unto Thee.

V. Dominus vobís-cum.

R. Et cum spíritu tuo.

Oremus.

Exaúdi nos, Domine sancte, Pater omnípotens, aetérne Deus ; et míttere dignéris sanctum Angelum Tuum de caelis, qui custódiat, fóveat, prótegat, vísitet, atque deféndat omnes habitántes in hoc habitáculo. Per Christum Dominum nostrum.

R. Amen.

V. The Lord be with you.

R. And with thy spirit.

Let us pray.

Graciously hear us, O holy Lord, Father almighty, eternal God ; and vouchsafe to send Thy holy Angel from heaven, to guard, cherish, protect, visit, and defend, all who are assembled in this house. Through Christ our Lord.

R. Amen.

THE ORDINARY OF THE MASS.[2]

¶ *Standing at the foot of the Altar, and having bowed to the Cross or the Altar,*[3] *the Priest signs himself with the sign of the Cross from the forehead to the breast, and says with a distinct voice :*

¶ *At Solemn High Mass,*[4] *the Priest is accompanied by a Deacon and Sub-deacon. At High Mass, in churches to which only one priest is attached, and at Low Mass, he is*

attended by clerks in minor orders,[5] *or failing these, by lay individuals.*

In nómine Patris, ✠ et Fílii, et Spíritus Sancti. Amen.

In the name of the Father,[6] ✠ and of the Son, and of the Holy Ghost. Amen.

Then, with his hands joined before his breast, he begins the Antiphon:[7]

Introíbo ad altáre Dei.

R. Ad Deum, qui laetificat iuventútem meam.

Ps. Iudica me, Deus, et discérne causam meam de gente non sancta : ab hómine iníquo, et dolóso érue me.

R. Quia Tu es, Deus, fortitúdo mea: quare me repulísti, et quare tristis incédo, dum affligit me inimícus?

Emítte lucem Tuam, et veritátem Tuam : ipsa me deduxérunt, et adduxérunt in montem

I will go in to the altar of God.

R. To God, who giveth joy to my youth.

Ps.[8] Judge me, O God, and distinguish my cause from the nation that is not holy : deliver me from the unjust and deceitful man.

R. For Thou, O God, art my strength : why hast Thou cast me off, and why do I go sorrowful whilst the enemy afflicteth me?

Send forth Thy light and Thy truth : they have led me, and brought me unto Thy holy mount,

sanctum Tuum, et in tabernácula Tua.

R. Et introíbo ad altáre Dei : ad Deum, qui laetíficat iuventútem meam.

Confitébor Tibi in cíthara, Deus, Deus meus : quare tristis es ánima mea, et quare contúrbas me ?

R. Spera in Deo, quóniam adhuc confitébor Illi : salutáre vultus mei, et Deus meus.

Glória Patri, et Fílio, et Spirítui Sancto.

R. Sicut erat in princípio, et nunc, et semper, et in saecula saeculorum. Amen.

Introíbo ad altáre Dei.

R. Ad Deum qui laetíficat iuventútem meam.

Adiutórium ✠ nostrum in nómine Dómini.

and into Thy tabernacles.

R. And I will go in to the altar of God : to God, who giveth joy to my youth.

I will give praise to Thee on the harp, O God, my God : why art thou sad, O my soul, and why disquietest thou me ?

R. Hope in God, for I will still give praise to Him : the salvation of my countenance, and my God.

Glory be to the Father, and to the Son, and to the Holy Ghost.

R. As it was in the beginning, is now, and ever shall be, world without end. Amen.[9]

I will go in to the altar of God.

R. To God, who giveth joy to my youth.

Our help ✠ is in the name of the Lord.

R. Qui fecit caelum et terram.

R. Who hath made heaven and earth.

¶ *Inclining his head profoundly,*[10] *the Priest says:*

Confíteor Deo omnipoténti, beátae Maríae semper Vírgini, beáto Michaéli Archángelo; beáto Iohánni Baptístae, sanctis Apóstolis Petro et Paulo, ómnibus Sanctis, et vobis fratres : quia peccávi nimis cogitatióne, verbo, et ópere, (*Percutit sibi pectus ter, dicens*) mea culpa, mea culpa, mea máxima culpa. Ideo precor beátam Mariam semper Vírginem, beatum Michaélem Archángelum, beátum Iohánnem Baptístam, sanctos Apóstolos Petrum et Paulum, omnes Sanctos, et vos fratres, oráre pro me ad Dóminum Deum nostrum.

I confess to Almighty God, to blessed Mary, ever Virgin, to blessed Michael the Archangel, to blessed John the Baptist, to the holy Apostles Peter and Paul, to all the Saints, and to you, brethren, that I have sinned exceedingly in thought, word, and deed, (*Here he strikes his breast thrice,*[11]) through my fault, through my fault, through my most grievous fault. Therefore I beseech blessed Mary, ever Virgin,[12] blessed Michael the Archangel,[13] blessed John the Baptist,[14] the holy Apostles Peter and Paul,[15] all the Saints,[16] and you, brethren,[17] to pray to the Lord our God for me.[18]

R. Miserĕátur tui omnípotens Deus, et dimíssis peccátis tuis, perdúcat te ad vitam aetérnam.

R. May Almighty God be merciful unto thee, and forgiving thee thy sins, bring thee to life everlasting.

S. Amen.

P. Amen.

¶ *At Solemn High Mass, the Deacon and Subdeacon, and, at other Masses, the Acolytes, repeat the* Confiteor (I confess, etc.) *with this variation, that they substitute* tibi pater, *and* te pater ("thee, father"), *for* vobis fratres, *and* vos fratres ("you, brethren").

S. Miserĕátur vestri omnípotens Deus, et dimíssis peccátis vestris, perdúcat vos ad vitam aetérnam.

P. May Almighty God be merciful unto you, and, forgiving you your sins, bring you to life everlasting.

R. Amen.

R. Amen.

S. Indulgéntiam, ✠ absolutionem, et remissiónem peccatórum nostrórum, tríbuat nobis, omnípotens, et miséricors Dóminus. R. Amen.

P. May the Almighty and merciful Lord grant us pardon, ✠ absolution, and remission of our sins. R. Amen.

S. Deus Tu convérsus vivificábis nos.

P. Turn to us, O God, and Thou wilt quicken us.

R. Et plebs Tua laetábitur in Te.

R. And Thy people shall rejoice in Thee.

S. Osténde nobis, Domine, misericórdiam Tuam.

P. Show us, O Lord, Thy mercy.

R. Et salutáre Tuum da nobis.

R. And grant us Thy salvation.

S. Dómine, exaúdi oratiónem meam.

P. O Lord, hear my prayer.

R. Et clamor meus ad Te véniat.

R. And let my cry come unto Thee.

S. Dóminus vobíscum.

P. The Lord be with you.[19]

R. Et cum spíritu tuo.

R. And with thy spirit.

¶ *First extending, and then joining his hands, he says :*

Orémus.

Let us pray.

¶ *Then ascending to the Altar, he says secretly :*

Aufer a nobis quaesumus, Dómine, iniquitátes nostras ; ut ad Sancta Sanctórum, puris mereámur méntibus introíre : per Christum Dóminum nostrum. Amen.

Take away from us our iniquities, we beseech Thee, O Lord, that we may be worthy to enter with pure minds into the Holy of Holies : through Christ our Lord. Amen.

¶ *Having arrived at the Altar, he bows down, and kisses it,[20] saying :*

Orámus Te, Dómine, per mérita Sanctorum Tuórum, quorum relíquiae hic sunt, et omnium Sanctorum, ut indulgére dignéris ómnia peccáta mea. Amen.

We beseech Thee, O Lord, by the merits of Thy Saints, whose relics are here, and of all the Saints, that Thou wouldst vouchsafe to forgive me all my sins. Amen.

¶ *Here, at High Mass, the Priest blesses the* Incense [21] *by making the sign of the Cross over it, while he recites the following words:*

Ab illo bene ✠ dicáris, in cuius honóre cremáberis. Amen.

Mayest thou be blessed ✠ by Him in whose honour thou shalt be burned. Amen.

¶ *And afterwards he incenses the Altar. Then turning to the Missal, he makes the sign of the Cross, and reads the* Introit, *which differs according to the day. The following* Introit *properly belongs to Trinity Sunday.*

INTROIT. [22]

Benedícta sit sancta Trínitas, atque indivísa Únitas: confitébimur Ei, quia fecit nobíscum misericórdiam Suam.

Blessed be the holy Trinity, and undivided Unity : we will give praise to Him, because He hath shown us His mercy.

Dómine, Dóminus nos-

O Lord, our Lord, how

ter, quam admirábile est nomen Tuum in univérsa terra.

admirable is Thy name in all the earth.

Glória Patri, et Fílio, et Spirítui Sancto.

Glory be to the Father, and to the Son, and to the Holy Ghost.

Sicut erat in princípio, et nunc, et semper, et in saecula saeculórum. Amen.

As it was in the beginning, is now, and ever shall be, world without end. Amen.

S. Kyrie eléison.[23]

P. Lord have mercy upon us.

R. Kyrie eléison.

R. Lord have mercy upon us.

S. Kyrie eléison.

P. Lord have mercy upon us.

R. Christe eléison.

R. Christ have mercy upon us.

S. Christe eléison.

P. Christ have mercy upon us.

R. Christe eléison.

R. Christ have mercy upon us.

S. Kyrie eléison.

P. Lord have mercy upon us.

R. Kyrie eléison.

R. Lord have mercy upon us.

S. Kyrie eléison.

P. Lord have mercy upon us.

¶ *The Priest goes to the middle of the Altar, where, extending both his arms, he recites the* Gloria in excelsis, *if it is to be said, and bows his head at the words* Deo ; Adoramus Te ; Gratias agimus Tibi ; Iesu ; *and* suscipe deprecationem.[24]

Glória in excélsis Deo. Et in terra pax homínibus bonae voluntátis. Laudámus Te. Benedícimus Te. Adorámus Te. Glorificámus Te. Grátias ágimus Tibi propter magnam glóriam Tuam. Dómine Deus, Rex caeléstis, Deus Pater omnípotens. Dómine Fili unigénite, Iesu Christe. Dómine Deus, Agnus Dei, Fílius Patris. Qui tollis peccáta mundi, miseráre nobis. Qui tollis peccáta mundi, súscipe deprecatiónem nostram. Qui sedes ad déxteram Patris, miseráre nobis. Quóniam tu solus sánctus. Tu solus Dóminus. Tu solus altíssimus, Iesu

Glory be to God on high. And on earth peace to men of good will. We praise Thee. We bless Thee. We adore Thee. We glorify Thee. We give Thee thanks for Thy great glory. O Lord God, heavenly King, God the Father almighty. O Lord, only begotten Son, Jesus Christ. O Lord God, Lamb of God, Son of the Father. Thou who takest away the sins of the world, have mercy on us. Thou who takest away the sins of the world, receive our prayer. Thou who sittest at the right hand of the Father, have mercy on us. For

Christe. Cum ✠ Sancto Spíritu, in glória Dei Patris. Amen.

Thou only art holy. Thou only art Lord. Thou only most high, O Jesus Christ. With ✠ the Holy Ghost, in the glory of God the Father. Amen.

¶ *Immediately after reciting the* Gloria in excelsis *at Low Mass, and at High Mass when the people have concluded singing it, the Priest kisses the middle of the Altar, and, turning with outstretched arms to the people, says:* [25]

Dominus vobiscum.
R. Et cum spiritu tuo.

The Lord be with you.
R. And with thy spirit.

¶ *Afterwards he turns to the Missal, and with uplifted hands* [26] *recites the* Collect, [27] *or Collects for the day, making a slight inclination of the head towards the Cross* [28] *each time he says* Oremus, *or pronounces the holy name of Jesus.*

COLLECT.

Oremus.

Omnípotens sempitérne Deus, qui dedísti fámulis Tuis in confessióne verae fidei, aetérnae Trinitátis glóriam ag-

Let us pray. [29]

O almighty, everlasting God, who hast given to Thy servants to acknowledge in the confession of the true faith,

nóscere, et in poténtia maiestátis adoráre unitátem : quaesumus, ut eiúsdem fídei firmitáte, ab ómnibus semper muniámur advérsis. Per Dóminum nostrum Iesum Christum Filium Tuum : qui Tecum vivit et regnat in unitáte Spíritus Sancti, Deus, per omnia saecula saeculorum.

R. Amen.

the glory, and to adore in the power of Thy majesty, the unity of the eternal Trinity : we beseech Thee, that, by the strength of this faith, we may ever be defended from all adversities. Through our Lord Jesus Christ Thy Son : who liveth and reigneth with Thee in the unity of the Holy Ghost, God, world without end.

R. Amen.[30]

OCCASIONAL COLLECTS.

¶ *From the first Sunday in Advent to Christmas-eve, after the* Collect *of the day, the following is said :*

Deus, qui de beátae Maríae Vírginis útero Verbum Tuum, Angelo nuntiánte, carnem suscípere voluísti ; praesta supplícibus Tuis : ut qui vere eam genitrícem Dei crédimus, eius apud Te

O God, who wast pleased that Thy Word, when the Angel delivered his message, should take flesh from the womb of the blessed Virgin Mary ; grant to Thy suppliants, that we who be-

intercessiónibus adiuvémur.

lieve her to be truly the mother of God, may be assisted by her intercession with Thee.

¶ *From Candlemas-day to Passion-Sunday, and from the third Sunday after Pentecost till Advent, except on those Feasts which are called Doubles, or within Octaves, the following is the second* Collect:

Oremus.

A cunctis nos, quaesumus Dómine, mentis et córporis defénde periculis : et intercedénte beáta et gloriósa semper Vírgine Dei Genitríce María, cum beáto Ioseph, beátis Apóstolis Tuis Petro et Paulo, atque beáto N., et ómnibus Sanctis, salútem nobis tríbue benígnus et pacem ; ut destrúctis adversitátibus et erróribus univérsis, Ecclésia Tua secúra Tibi sérviat libertáte.

Let us pray.

Defend us, we beseech Thee, O Lord, from all dangers of mind and body ; and the blessed and glorious ever Virgin Mother of God Mary interceding for us, together with blessed Joseph, Thy blessed Apostles Peter and Paul, and blessed N. (*the patron of the church is here named*), and all the Saints interceding for us ; graciously grant us health and peace, that all adversities and errors being removed, Thy Church may serve Thee in secure liberty.

¶ *To this is added a third, which is left to the choice of the Priest, who in general selects one of the two following:*

Omnípotens sempitérne Deus, cuius Spíritu totum corpus Ecclésiae sanctificátur et régitur : exaúdi nos pro univérsis ordínibus supplicántes : ut grátiae Tuae múnere, ab ómnibus Tibi grádibus fidéliter serviátur. Per Dóminum nostrum Iesum Christum Fílium Tuum, qui Tecum vivit et regnat in unitáte eiusdem Spíritus Sancti, Deus, per omnia saecula saeculorum.

R. Amen.

O Almighty and everlasting God, by whose Spirit the whole body of the Church is sanctified and governed; graciously hear our supplication for all orders thereof, that by the assistance of Thy grace, all ranks may faithfully serve Thee. Through our Lord Jesus Christ Thy Son : Who liveth and reigneth with Thee in the unity of the same Holy Ghost, God, world without end.

R. Amen.

¶ *Or,*

Deus ómnium fidélium pastor et rector, fámulum Tuum N., quem pastórem Ecclesiae Tuae praeésse voluísti, propitius réspice : da ei, quae-

O God, the pastor and governor of all the faithful, graciously look down on Thy servant N., whom Thou hast been pleased to set over Thy Church

sumus, verbo et exémplo quibus praeest profícere: ut ad vitam, una cum grege sibi crédito, pervéniat sempitérnam. Per Dóminum nostrum Iesum Christum Fílium Tuum: qui Tecum vivit et regnat in unitáte Spíritus Sancti, Deus, per omnia saecula saeculórum.

R. Amen.

as pastor: grant him, we beseech Thee, both by word and example, to benefit those over whom he is set: that, together with the flock entrusted to him, he may attain to life everlasting. Through our Lord Jesus Christ Thy Son: who liveth and reigneth with Thee in the unity of the Holy Ghost, God, world without end.

R. Amen.

EPISTLE.[31]

Léctio Epistolae beati Pauli Apóstoli ad Romános. (XI, 33–36.)

O altitúdo divitiárum sapiéntiae et sciéntiae Dei: quam incomprehensibília sunt iudicia Eius, et investigabiles viae Eius! Quis enim cognóvit sensum Dómini? Aut quis consiliárius Eius fuit? Aut quis prior dedit Illi, et

Epistle of S. Paul to the Romans. (XI, 33–36.)

O the depth of the riches of the wisdom and of the knowledge of God! How incomprehensible are His judgements, and how unsearchable His ways! For who hath known the mind of the Lord? Or who hath been His

retribuétur ei ? Quo-
niam ex Ipso, et per
Ipsum, et in Ipso sunt
omnia. Ipsi honor et
glória, in saecula saecu-
lórum. Amen.

R. Deo Gratias.

counsellor ? Or who
hath first given to Him,
and recompense shall
be made him ? For of
Him, and by Him, and
in Him are all things.
To Him be glory for
ever. Amen.

R. Thanks be to God.

¶ *At Solemn High Mass, the Sub-deacon chants the*
Epistle, *which varies according to the Sunday
or Festival.*

GRADUAL.[32]

Benedíctus es, Do-
mine, qui intuéris abys-
sos, et sedes super
Chérubim.

V. Benedíctus es, Do-
mine, in firmaménto
caeli, et laudábilis in
saecula.

Alleluia, Alleluia. V.
Benedíctus es, Domine,
Deus patrum nostrórum:
et laudábilis in saecula.
Alleluia.

Blessed art Thou, O
Lord, who beholdest the
deeps, and sittest on the
Cherubim.

V. Blessed art Thou,
O Lord, in the firma-
ment of the heaven,
and worthy of praise
for ever.

Alleluia, Alleluia. V.
Blessed art Thou, O
Lord, God of our fathers,
and worthy of praise for
ever. Alleluia.

¶ *Both the* Gradual *and* Alleluia[33] *vary with the Sunday; but from Septuagesima Sunday until the Saturday in Holy Week the* Alleluia *is omitted, and replaced by the* Tract,[34] *consisting of some verses of the Psalms.*

¶ *At High Mass the Priest here blesses the* Incense *with the usual prayer: and standing at the middle of the Altar, inclines his head profoundly, and then with his hands joined before his breast, and his eyes lifted towards heaven, says:*

Munda cor meum, ac lábia mea, omnípotens Deus, qui lábia Isaíae prophétae cálculo mundásti igníto : ita me Tua grata miseratióne dignáre mundáre, ut sanctum Evangélium Tuum digne váleam nuntiáre. Per Christum Dominum nostrum. Amen.

Cleanse my heart, and my ips, O almighty God, who didst cleanse the lips of the prophet Isaiah with a burning coal : and vouchsafe, through Thy gracious mercy, so to purify me, that I may worthily announce Thy holy Gospel. Through Christ our Lord. Amen.

Dominus sit in corde meo, et in lábiis meis : ut digne et competénter annúntiem Evangélium Suum. Amen.

May the Lord be in my heart, and on my lips, that I may worthily and in a becoming manner announce His holy Gospel. Amen.

¶ *In the interim, the Acolytes, bearing their tapers elevated,*[35] *and the Thurifer, with the Incense,*[36] *proceed to the Gospel-side of the sanctuary, where they remain during the chanting or lecture of the Gospel, at which time the whole of the congregation stands up.*[37]

¶ *At Solemn High Mass, the Deacon places the book of the Gospels on the Altar;*[38] *and then recites, upon his knees, before the Altar, the prayer* Munda cor meum (Cleanse my heart), *etc. Having taken the book of the Gospels from the Altar, and received the Priest's blessing, he kisses his hand, and then, accompanied by the Sub-deacon, Thurifer, and Acolytes, goes to the right side of the Altar, where he chants the Gospel.*

GOSPEL

P. Dóminus vobíscum.

R. Et cum spíritu tuo.

✠ Sequéntia (*vel* Initium) sancti Evangélii secúndum N.

R. Glória Tibi, Dómine.

P. The Lord be with you.

R. And with thy spirit.

✠ The continuation (*or* the beginning) of the holy Gospel according to N.

R. Glory be to Thee, O Lord.

¶ *At these latter words, the Priest makes the sign of the Cross,*[39] *first upon the book, and then upon his own forehead, mouth, and breast, and, in this last ceremony, is imitated by the people.*[40]

¶ *At High Mass, he afterwards bows to the book, and incenses it three times.*[41]

Matt. xxviii. In illo témpore : Dixit Iesus discipulis Suis : Data est Mihi omnis potéstas in caelo, et in terra. Eúntes ergo docéte omnes gentes : baptizántes eos in nómine Patris, et Fílii, et Spíritus Sancti : docéntes eos serváre ómnia quaecúmque mandávi vobis. Et ecce Ego vobíscum sum ómnibus diébus, usque ad consummatiónem saeculi.

R. Laus Tibi, Christe.

Matt. xxviii. At that time Jesus said to His disciples : All power is given to Me in heaven and on earth. Going therefore, teach ye all nations : baptizing them in the name of the Father, and of the Son, and of the Holy Ghost : teaching them to observe all things whatsoever I have commanded you : And behold, I am with you all days, even to the consummation of the world.

R. Praise be to Thee, O Christ.

¶ *At the end of the Gospel, which varies according to the Feast, or Sunday, the Priest, while repeating to himself this aspiration:* Per Evangélica dicta deleántur nostra delícta,—May our sins be blotted out by the words of the Gospel,[42]—*kisses* [43] *the book, and the assistant answers,* Laus Tibi, Christe.—Praise be to Thee, O Christ. *At Masses for the Dead, the book is not kissed; lights are not borne; nor is incense used, because every mark of joy and solemnity is omitted. At Solemn High Mass, the Subdeacon carries the book of the Gospels to the Priest to be kissed by him: and afterwards the Deacon incenses him,*[44] *and in his turn, is incensed by the Thurifer.*

¶ *Then the Priest, standing in front of the Crucifix, repeats the* Credo *or Creed:* (*if it is to be said.*) [45] *As he commences, he outstretches his arms,*[46] *but immediately afterwards joins his hands together, while he at the same time makes an inclination of his head* [47] *on pronouncing the word* Deo *or God, and then goes on reciting the Creed, which he concludes by signing himself with the sign of the Cross.*

THE CREED.

Credo in unum Deum, Patrem omnipoténtem, factórem caeli et terrae, visibílium ómnium et invisibílium. Et in unum Dóminum, Iesum Chris-

I believe in one God, the Father almighty, maker of heaven and earth, and of all things visible and invisible. And in one Lord Jesus

tum, Fílium Dei unigé-
nitum. Et ex Patre na-
tum ante ómnia saecula.
Deum de Deo, lumen
de lúmine, Deum verum
de Deo vero. Génitum
non factum, consubstan-
tiálem Patri : per quem
ómnia facta sunt. Qui
propter nos hómines, et
propter nostram salútem
descéndit de caelis.*
(*Hic genuflectitur.*) ET
INCARNÁTUS EST DE SPÍ-
RITU SANCTO EX MARÍA
VÍRGINE : ET HOMO FAC-
TUS EST. Crucifíxus étiam
pro nobis; sub Póntio
Piláto passus, et sepúltus
est. Et resurréxit tértia
die, secúndum Scriptú-
ras. Et ascéndit in cae-
lum : sedet ad déxteram
Patris. Et íterum ven-
túrus est cum glória, iu-
dicáre vivos et mórtuos :
cuius regni non erit finis.
Et in Spíritum Sanc-
tum, Dóminum et vivifi-
cántem : qui ex Patre

Christ, the only begotten
Son of God. And born
of the Father before
all ages. God of God,
light of light, true God
of true God. Begotten
not made, consubstantial
with the Father, by whom
all things were made.
Who for us men, and for
our salvation, came down
from heaven.* (*Here
all kneel.*)[48] AND BECAME
INCARNATE BY THE HOLY
GHOST, OF THE VIRGIN
MARY : AND WAS MADE
MAN. Was crucified also
for us ; suffered under
Pontius Pilate, and was
buried. And the third
day He rose again, ac-
cording to the Scrip-
tures. And ascended
into heaven : sitteth at
the right hand of the
Father. And shall come
again with glory, to
judge the living and the
dead : of whose kingdom
there shall be no end.

Filióque procédit. Qui cum Patre et Fílio simul adorátur, et conglorificá- tur: qui locútus est per prophétas. Et unam sanctam Cathólicam, et Apostólicam Ecclésiam. Confíteor unum baptís- ma in remissiónem pec- catórum. Et exspécto resurrectiónem mortuó- rum. Et vitam ✠ ven- túri saeculi. Amen.

And in the Holy Ghost, the Lord and life-giver: who proceedeth from the Father and the Son. Who with the Father and the Son together is adored and glorified: who spoke by the pro- phets. And one holy Catholic, and Apostolic Church. I confess one baptism for the remis- sion of sins. And I expect the resurrection of the dead. And the life ✠[49] of the world to come. Amen.

P. Dóminus vobís- cum.

R. Et cum spíritu tuo.

P. The Lord be with you.[50]

R. And with thy spirit.

Oremus.

Let us pray.

OFFERTORY.[51]

Benedíctus sit Deus Pater, unigenitúsque Dei Fílius, Sanctus quo- que Spíritus: quia fecit nobíscum misericórdiam Suam.

Blessed be God the Father, and the only be- gotten Son of God, as likewise the Holy Ghost, because He hath shown His mercy to us.

OBLATION OF THE HOST.[52]

¶ *At Low Mass, the Priest here unveils the Chalice, and unfolds the Corporal;* [53] *then taking the Paten* [54] *with the Host,* [55] *elevates it with both hands, reciting, at the same time, the following prayer.*

¶ *At Solemn High Mass, the Chalice is deposited on the Altar by the Sub-deacon, and the Corporal is unfolded by the Deacon.*

Suscipe, sancte Pater, omnípotens aetérne Deus, hanc immaculátam Hóstiam, quam ego indígnus fámulus Tuus óffero Tibi Deo meo vivo, et vero, pro innumerabilibus peccátis, et offensiónibus, et negligéntiis meis, et pro ómnibus circumstántibus, sed et pro ómnibus fidélibus Christiánis vivis atque defúnctis; ut mihi et illis profíciat ad salútem in vitam aetérnam. Amen.

Accept, O holy Father, almighty eternal God, this unspotted Host,[56] which I, Thy unworthy servant, offer unto Thee, my living and true God,[57] for my innumerable sins, offences, and negligences,[58] and for all here present; as also for all faithful Christians,[59] both living and dead;[60] that to me and to them it may be profitable unto life everlasting. Amen.

¶ *Having made the sign of the Cross with the Paten, the Priest places the Host upon the*

*Corporal, the Deacon pours wine, and the Sub-
deacon a small quantity of water* [61] *into the
Chalice, at Solemn High Mass; at Low Mass,
the Priest does it himself. Before the water is
poured, he makes (excepting at Masses for the
Dead) the sign of the Cross over it, and says:*

Deus, ✠ qui humánae substántiae dignitátem mirabíliter condidísti, et mirabílius reformásti: da nobis per huius aquae et vini mystérium, Eius divinitátis esse consórtes, qui humanitátis nostrae fíeri dignátus est párticeps, Iesus Christus Fílius Tuus Dóminus noster: Qui Tecum vivit et regnat in unitáte Spiritus Sancti Deus, per ómnia saecula saeculórum. Amen.

O God, ✠ who hast wonderfully created and dignified human nature, and hast still more wonderfully reformed it: grant that by the mystery of this water and wine, we may be made partakers of His divinity, who vouchsafed to become partaker of our human nature, Jesus Christ Thy Son our Lord, who liveth and reigneth with Thee in the unity of the Holy Ghost, God, world without end. Amen.

OBLATION OF THE CHALICE.

Offerimus Tibi, Dómine, Cálicem salutáris, Tuam deprecántes cle-

We offer unto Thee, O Lord, the Chalice of Salvation, beseeching Thy

méntiam, ut in conspec-
tu divinae Maiestatis
Tuae, pro nostra et totius
mundi salúte cum odóre
suavitátis ascéndat. A-
men.

clemency, that in . the
sight of Thy divine Ma-
jesty, it may ascend with
the odour of sweetness
for our salvation, and for
that of the whole world.
Amen.

*Then the Priest makes the sign of the Cross over
the Corporal with the Chalice, places it in the
middle, and covers it with the pall.*

¶ *At Solemn High Mass, the Sub-deacon here
receives the Paten, which he envelops in the
extremities of the veil with which his shoulders
are mantled, and then goes and stands behind
the Celebrant, holding it up in an elevated position until the conclusion of the* Pater Noster,
when he again deposits it upon the Altar.

¶ *When the Priest bows before the Altar, he
says :* [62]

In spíritu humilitátis,
et in ánimo contríto sus-
cipiámur a Te, Dómine :
et sic fiat sacrifícium
nostrum in conspéctu
Tuo hódie, ut pláceat
Tibi Dómine Deus.

In the spirit of humi-
lity, and with a contrite
heart, let us be received
by Thee, O Lord ; and so
let our sacrifice be made
in Thy sight to-day, that
it may be pleasing to
Thee, O Lord God.

¶ *Here the Priest elevates his eyes towards heaven,*[63] *and outstretching his hands,*[64] *which he afterwards joins, makes the sign of the Cross over the Host and Chalice,*[65] *at the same time that he repeats the following prayer:*

Veni, sanctificátor omnípotens aetérne Deus, et béne ✠ dic hoc sacrifícium Tuo sancto nómini praeparátum.

Come, O sanctifier, almighty eternal God, and bless ✠ this sacrifice, prepared for Thy holy name.

¶ *At High Mass, he then, in the following prayer, blesses the Incense.*[66]

Per intercessiónem beáti Michaélis Archángeli stantis a dextris altáris incénsi, et ómnium electórum Suórum, incénsum istud dignétur Dóminus bene ✠ dícere, et in odórem suavitátis accípere. Per Christum Dóminum nostrum. Amen.

Through the intercession of blessed Michael the Archangel standing[67] at the right hand of the altar of incense, and of all His elect, may the Lord vouchsafe to bless ✠ this incense, and receive it as an odour of sweetness. Through Christ our Lord. Amen.

¶ *Receiving the Thurible, he incenses the Bread and Wine, saying:*

Incénsum istud a Te benedíctum, ascéndat ad

May this incense, blest by Thee, O Lord, ascend

Te Dómine, et descén- to Thee, and may Thy
dat super nos misericór- mercy descend upon
dia Tua. us.

¶ *He then incenses the Altar, at the same time*
saying the following Psalm:

Dirigatur Dómine orá- Let my prayer,[68] O
tio mea, sicut incénsum Lord, be directed as in-
in conspectu Tuo: ele- cense in Thy sight; the
vátio mánuum meárum lifting up of my hands
sacrifícium vespertínum. as an evening sacrifice.
Pone, Dómine, custó- Set a watch, O Lord, be-
diam ori meo, et óstium fore my mouth, and a
circumstántiae lábiis me- door round about my
is: ut non declínet cor lips, that my heart may
meum in verba malítiae, not incline to evil words,
ad excusándas excusati- to make excuses in sins.
ónes in peccátis.

¶ *When the Priest returns the Censer, at Solemn*
High Mass, to the Deacon, at others to the
Thurifer, he recites to himself these words;
and is afterwards incensed [69] *by the attendant*
minister.

Accendat in nobis May the Lord en-
Dóminus ignem Sui a- kindle within us the
móris, et flammam aetér- fire of His love, and
nae charitátis. Amen. the flame of everlasting
charity. Amen.

¶ *The Priest, with his hands joined, goes to the Epistle side of the Altar,*[70] *where he washes the tips of his fingers*[71] *as he recites the following verses of Psalm* xxv, *which, excepting at Masses for the Dead, and during Passion-time, he concludes with the minor Doxology:* Glory be to the Father, etc.[72]

Lavabo inter innocéntes manus meas : et circúmdabo altáre Tuum, Dómine.

Ut aúdiam vocem laudis : et enárrem univérsa mirabília Tua.

Dómine, diléxi decórem domus Tuae, et locum habitatiónis glóriae Tuae.

Ne perdas cum ímpiis, Deus, ánimam meam : et cum viris sánguinum vitam meam.

In quorum mánibus iniquitátes sunt : déxtera eórum repléta est munéribus.

Ego autem in innocéntia mea ingréssus

I will wash my hands among the innocent : and will compass Thy altar, O Lord.

That I may hear the voice of Thy praise : and tell of all Thy wondrous works.

Lord, I have loved the beauty of Thy house ; and the place where Thy glory dwelleth.

Take not away my soul, O God, with the wicked : nor my life with men of blood.

In whose hands are iniquities : their right hand is filled with gifts.

But I have walked in my innocence : redeem

sum : rédime me, et miserére mei.

Pes meus stetit in directo : in ecclésiis benedícam Te, Dómine.

Glória Patri, et Fílio, et Spirítui Sancto.

Sicut erat in princípio, et nunc, et semper, et in saecula saeculórum. Amen.

¶ Returning and standing before the middle of the Altar, the Priest, with his head slightly bowed down, and his hands joined, recites to himself the following prayer :

Suscipe, sancta Trínitas, hanc oblatiónem, quam Tibi offérimus ob memóriam passiónis, resurrectiónis, et ascensiónis Iesu Christi Dómini nostri : et in honóre beátae Mariae semper Vírginis, et beáti Ioánnis Baptístæ, et sanctórum Apostolórum Petri et Pauli, et istórum, et

me, and have mercy on me.

My foot hath stood in the direct way : in the churches I will bless Thee, O Lord.

Glory be to the Father, and to the Son, and to the Holy Ghost.

As it was in the beginning, is now, and ever shall be, world without end. Amen.

Receive, O holy Trinity,[73] this oblation, which we make to Thee in memory of the passion, resurrection, and ascension of our Lord Jesus Christ : and in honour of blessed Mary ever Virgin, of blessed John Baptist, of the holy Apostles Peter and Paul, of these and of all

ómnium Sanctórum : ut illis profíciat ad honórem, nobis autem ad salútem ; et illi pro nobis intercédere dignéntur in caelis, quorum memóriam agimus in terris. Per eúmdem Christum Dóminum nostrum.

Amen.

Saints; [74] that it may be available to their honour and our salvation ; and may they vouchsafe to intercede for us in heaven, whose memory we celebrate on earth. Through the same Christ our Lord.

Amen.

¶ *The Priest kisses the Altar, and then, turning himself towards the people, he says :*

Oráte, fratres, ut meum ac vestrum sacrifícium acceptábile fiat apud Deum Patrem omnipoténtem.

R. Suscipiat Dóminus sacrifícium de mánibus tuis, ad laudem et glóriam nóminis Sui, ad utilitátem quoque nostram, totiúsque Ecclésiae Suae sanctae.

Brethren, [75] pray that my sacrifice and yours may be acceptable to God the Father Almighty.

R. May the Lord receive the sacrifice from thy hands, to the praise and glory of His name, and to our benefit, and to that of all His holy Church.

THE SECRET. [76]

Sanctifica, quæsumus, Dómine Deus noster,

Sanctify, we beseech Thee, O Lord our God,

per Tui sancti nóminis invocatiónem, huius oblatiónis hóstiam : et per eam nosmetípsos Tibi perfice munus aetérnum. Per Dóminum, etc.

by the invocation of Thy holy name, the victim of this oblation : and through it perfect us an eternal gift to Thee. Through, etc.

¶ *The Secret varies according to the Festival or Sunday.*

OCCASIONAL SECRETS.

¶ *Which follow the Rubrics, and correspond with the Collects, etc.*

In méntibus nostris, quaesumus, Dómine, verae fídei sacraménta confírma : ut qui concéptum de Virgine Deum verum et hóminem confitémur ; per Eius salutíferae resurrectiónis poténtiam, ad aetérnam mereámur perveníre laetítiam.

Confirm, we beseech Thee, O Lord, in our minds the mysteries of the true faith : that we who confess Him who was conceived of a Virgin to be true God and man, may, by the power of His saving resurrection, deserve to attain to eternal joy.

Exaudi nos, Deus salutáris noster : ut per huius sacraménti virtútem, a cunctis nos mentis et córporis hóstibus

Graciously hear us, O God of our salvation : that by virtue of this sacrament, Thou mayest defend us from all ene-

tucáris, grátiam tríbuens in praesénti, et glóriam in futúro.

Da fámulis Tuis, Dómine, indulgéntiam peccatórum, consolatiónem vitae, gubernatiónem perpétuam : ut Tibi serviéntes, ad Tuam iúgiter misericórdiam perveníre mereántur. Per Dóminum nostrum, etc.

mies of both mind and body : granting us grace in this life, and glory in the next.

Grant Thy servants, O Lord, pardon of their sins, comfort in life, and perpetual direction ; that, serving Thee, they may deserve ever to obtain Thy mercy. Through our Lord, etc.

Or,

Oblatis, quaesumus, Dómine, placáre munéribus : et fámulum Tuum N., quem pastórem Ecclésiae Tuae praeésse voluisti, assídua protectióne gubérna. Per Dóminum nostrum Iesum Christum Filium Tuum : qui Tecum vivit et regnat in unitáte Spíritus Sancti, Deus :

Be appeased, we beseech Thee, O Lord, with the gifts we have offered, and with constant protection direct Thy servant N., whom Thou hast been pleased to set as pastor over Thy Church. Through our Lord Jesus Christ Thy Son : who liveth and reigneth with Thee in the unity of the Holy Ghost, one God :

¶ *Here he raises his voice, and says in an audible tone :*

P. Per ómnia saecula saeculórum.

R. Amen.

P. Dóminus vobíscum.

R. Et cum spíritu tuo.

P. World without end.[77]

R. Amen.

P. The Lord be with you.

R. And with thy spirit.

¶ *Here he uplifts his hands.*[78]

P. Sursum corda.

R. Habémus ad Dóminum.

P. Lift up your hearts.

R. We have lifted them up to the Lord.

¶ *He joins his hands before his breast, and bows his head, while he says :*[79]

P. Grátias agámus Dómino Deo nostro.

R. Dignum et justum est.

P. Let us give thanks to the Lord our God.

R. It is meet and just.

¶ *He disjoins his hands, and says :*

THE PREFACE.[80]

Vere dignum et iustum est, aequum et salutáre, nos Tibi semper et

It is truly meet and just, right and salutary, that we should always,

ubíque grátias ágere: Dómine sancte, Pater omnípotens, aetérne Deus. Qui cum unigénito Fílio Tuo, et Spíritu Sancto, unus es Deus, unus es Dóminus: non in uníus singularitáte persónae, sed in uníus trinitáte substántiae. Quod enim de Tua glória, revelánte Te crédimus, hoc de Fílio Tuo, hoc de Spíritu Sancto, sine differéntia discretiónis sentimus. Ut in confessióne verae, sempiternaeque Deitátis, et in persónis propríetas, et in esséntia únitas, et in majestáte adorétur aequálitas. Quam laudant Angeli, atque Archángeli, Chérubim quoque ac Séraphim: qui non cessant clamáre quotídie, una voce dicéntes:

and in all places give thanks to Thee, holy Lord, Father almighty, eternal God. Who together with Thy only begotten Son, and the Holy Ghost, art one God, and one Lord: not in the singularity of one person, but in the trinity of one substance. For that which, revealed by Thee, we believe of Thy glory, that same of Thy Son, that same of the Holy Ghost, we hold without difference or distinction. That, in the confession of the true and eternal Deity, distinction in persons, unity in essence, and equality in majesty may be adored. Which the Angels and Archangels, the Cherubim also and Seraphim praise, who cease not daily to cry out with one voice saying:

¶ *Here the Priest lowers the tone of his voice, which, however, still continues audible; and with his hands joined, and his head bowed down, he recites the following hymn,*[81] *while the bell*[82] *is rung by the Acolyte.*

Sanctus, Sanctus, Sanctus, Dóminus Deus Sábaoth. Pleni sunt caeli et terra glória Tua.

Hosánna in excélsis. Benedíctus qui venit in nómine Dómini. Hosánna in excélsis.

Holy, Holy, Holy, Lord God of Sabaoth.[83] Heaven and earth are full of Thy glory.

Hosanna in the highest. Blessed is He that cometh in the name of the Lord.[84] Hosanna[85] in the highest.

¶ *On all Sundays in the year which have no proper Preface, the foregoing is recited.*

The following Preface is said on all Festivals, and other days, which have no proper Preface, and in all Masses for the Dead:

Vere dignum et iustum est, aequum et salutáre, nos Tibi semper et ubíque grátias ágere: Dómine sancte, Pater omnípotens, aetérne Deus: per Christum Dóminum nostrum. Per quem

It is truly meet and just, right and salutary, that we should always, and in all places give thanks to Thee, holy Lord, Father almighty, eternal God, through Christ our Lord. Through

maiestátem Tuam laudant Angeli, adórant Dominatiónes, tremunt Potestátes. Caeli, caelorúmque Virtútes, ac beata Seraphim, sócia exsultatióne concélebrant. Cum quibus et nostras voces, ut admítti iúbeas deprecámur, súpplici confessióne dicéntes,

Sanctus, Sanctus, Sanctus, etc.

whom the Angels praise Thy majesty, the Dominations adore, the Powers tremble. The Heavens, and the Powers of the heavens, and the blessed Seraphim unite in celebrating with common exultation. With whom, we beseech Thee, that Thou wouldest command our voices also to be admitted, with suppliant confession saying, Holy, Holy, Holy, etc.

¶ *The Priest lifts up his eyes and hands towards heaven,*[86] *and after kissing the Altar,*[87] *makes the sign of the Cross three times over the Oblation.*[88]

THE CANON [89] OF THE MASS.

Te ígitur, clementíssime Pater, per Iesum Christum Fílium Tuum Dóminum nostrum, súpplices rogámus ac pétimus, uti accépta hábeas, et benedícas, haec

Thee, therefore, most merciful Father, we humbly pray and beseech, through Jesus Christ Thy Son, our Lord, that Thou wouldst accept and bless these

✠ dona, haec ✠ múnera, haec ✠ sancta sacrifícia illibáta, in primis quae Tibi offérimus pro Ecclésia Tua sancta cathólica: quam pacificáre, custodíre, adunáre, et régere dignéris toto orbe terrárum : una cum fámulo Tuo papa nostro N. et antístite nostro N. et ómnibus orthodóxis, atque cathólicae et apostólicae fidei cultóribus.

✠ gifts,[90] these ✠ presents, these ✠ holy unspotted sacrifices, which, in the first place, we offer to Thee for Thy holy catholic Church,[91] which vouchsafe to maintain in peace ; as also to guard, unite, and govern throughout the whole world, together with Thy servant N. our pope,[92 N. our bishop, and all orthodox believers and professors of the catholic and apostolic faith.

COMMEMORATION OF THE LIVING.

Memento, Dómine, famulórum famularúmque N. et N.

Be mindful, O Lord, of Thy servants and handmaids, N. and N.

¶ *He silently mentions those whom he intends specially to pray for.*

Et ómnium circumstántium, quorum Tibi fides cógnita est, et nota devótio, pro quibus Tibi

And of all here present, whose faith and devotion are known unto Thee, for whom we offer

offérimus : vel qui Tibi
ófferunt hoc sacrifícium
laudis, pro se, suísque
ómnibus : pro redemp-
tióne animárum suárum,
pro spe salútis et inco-
lumitátis suae : Tibíque
reddunt vota sua aetér-
no Deo, vivo et vero.

Communicantes, et
memóriam venerántes, in
primis gloriósae semper
Vírginis Maríae, Geni-
trícis Dei et Dómini
nostri Iesu Christi : sed
et beatórum apostoló-
rum, ac mártyrum Tuó-
rum, Petri et Pauli, An-
dréae, Iacóbi, Ioánnis,
Thomae, Iacóbi, Philíp-
pi, Bartholomaei, Mat-
thaei, Simónis et Thad-
daei, Lini, Cleti, Cle-
méntis, Xysti, Corné-
lii, Cypriáni, Lauréntii,
Chrysógoni, Ioánnis et
Pauli, Cosmae et Dami-
áni, et ómnium Sanctó-
rum Tuórum : quorum

to Thee, or who offer to
Thee this sacrifice of
praise for themselves, and
all their relations, for
the redemption of their
souls, for the hope of
their salvation and wel-
fare, and who pay their
vows to Thee, the eter-
nal, living and true God.
Communicating [93]
with and venerating, in
the first place, the me-
mory [94] of the glorious
ever Virgin Mary, Mo-
ther of our Lord and
God Jesus Christ, as also
of Thy blessed apostles
and martyrs, Peter and
Paul, Andrew, James,
John, Thomas, James,
Philip, Bartholomew,
Matthew, Simon and
Thaddeus : Linus, Cle-
tus, Clement, Xystus,
Cornelius, Cyprian, Lau-
rence, Chrysogonus,
John and Paul, Cosmas
and Damian, and of all
Thy Saints ; by whose

méritis precibúsque con-
cédas, ut in ómnibus
protectiónis Tuae muni-
ámur auxílio. Per eún-
dem Christum Dóminum
nostrum. Amen.

merits and prayers, grant
that we may be always
defended by the help
of Thy protection. [95]
Through the same Christ
our Lord. Amen.

¶ *Spreading his hands over the Oblation, he says:* [96]

Hanc ígitur oblatió-
nem servitútis nostrae,
sed et cunctae famíliae
Tuae, quaesumus Dómi-
ne, ut placátus accípias,
diésque nostros in Tua
pace dispónas, atque ab
aetérna damnatióne nos
éripi, et in electórum
Tuórum iúbeas grege
numerári. Per Chris-
tum Dóminum nostrum.
Amen.

This oblation, there-
fore, of our service, as
also of that of Thy whole
family, we beseech Thee,
O Lord, graciously to
accept; dispose our days
in Thy peace, bid us to
be delivered from eternal
damnation, and num-
bered in the flock of Thy
elect. Through Christ
our Lord. Amen.

Quam oblatiónem Tu
Deus in ómnibus, quae-
sumus, bene✠díctam,
adscrí✠ptam, ra✠tam,
rationábilem, accepta-
bilémque fácere digné-
ris : ut nobis Cor✠pus,

Which oblation do
Thou, O God, vouchsafe
in all things to make
blessed ✠, approved ✠,
ratified ✠, and accept-
able, that it may be made
for us the Body ✠ and

et San✠guis fiat dilectíssimi Filii Tui Dómini nostri Iesu Christi.

Qui prídie quam paterétur, accépit panem in sanctas ac venerábiles manus Suas, et elevátis óculis in caelum ad Te Deum Patrem Suum omnipoténtem: Tibi grátias agens, bene ✠ díxit, fregit, dedítque discípulis Suis, dicens: Accípite, et manducáte ex hoc omnes:

Hoc est enim Corpus Meum.

Blood ✠ of Thy most beloved Son our Lord Jesus Christ.

Who the day before He suffered, took bread into His holy and venerable hands, and with His eyes lifted up towards heaven to Thee, God, His almighty Father: giving thanks to Thee, blessed ✠, brake, and gave it to His disciples, saying: Take, and eat ye all of this:

For this is My Body.

¶ *After pronouncing the Words of Consecration, the Priest kneeling adores,*[97] *and elevates*[98] *the sacred Host: and the Acolyte rings the bell.*

Simili modo postquam coenátum est, accípiens et hunc praeclárum cálicem in sanctas ac venerábiles manus Suas: item Tibi grátias agens, bene ✠ díxit, dedítque discípulis Suis, dicens: Ac-

In like manner, after He had supped, taking also this excellent Chalice into His holy and venerable hands; giving thanks also to Thee, He blessed ✠, and gave to His disciples, saying:

cípite et bíbite ex eo omnes: HIC EST ENIM CALIX SANGUINIS MEI, NOVI ET AETERNI TESTAMENTI: MYSTERIUM FIDEI: QUI PRO VOBIS ET PRO MULTIS EFFUNDETUR IN REMISSIONEM PECCATORUM. Haec quotiescúnque fecéritis, in Mei memóriam faciétis.

Take and drink ye all of this: FOR THIS IS THE CHALICE OF MY BLOOD OF THE NEW AND ETERNAL TESTAMENT: THE MYSTERY OF FAITH: WHICH SHALL BE SHED FOR YOU, AND FOR MANY, TO THE REMISSION OF SINS. As often as you shall do these things, you shall do them in remembrance of **Me.**

¶ *The following is in some churches sung immediately after the Elevation:*

O salutaris Hostia!
quae caeli pandis óstium:
bella premunt hostília:
da robur, fer auxílium.

O saving Victim! opening wide
the gate of heaven to man below!
our foes press on from every side;
Thine aid supply, Thy strength bestow:

Uni trinóque Domino,
sit sempitérna glória,
qui vitam sine término,
nobis donet in pátria.
            Amen.

To Thy great name be endless praise,
immortal Godhead, one in three!
Oh, grant us endless length of days
in our true native land with Thee.
            Amen.

¶ *Here also kneeling, he adores; and elevates the Chalice. The Acolyte rings the bell.*[99]

Unde et mémores, Dómine, nos servi Tui, sed et plebs Tua sancta, eiúsdem Christi Fílii Tui Dómini nostri tam beátae Passiónis, nec non et ab ínferis Resurrectiónis sed et in caelos gloriósae Ascensiónis : offérimus praeclárae maiestáti Tuae de Tuis donis ac datis, Hóstiam ✠ puram, Hóstiam ✠ sanctam, Hóstiam ✠ immaculátam : Panem ✠ sanctum vitae actérnae et Cálicem ✠ salútis perpétuae.

Supra quae, propítio ac seréno vultu respícere dignéris ; et accépta habére, sícuti accépta habére dignátus es múnera púeri Tui iusti Abel, et sacrifícium Patriárchae nostri Abrahae : et quod

Wherefore, O Lord, we Thy servants, as also Thy holy people, mindful of the blessed Passion of the same Christ Thy Son our Lord, as also of His Resurrection from hell,[100] and of His glorious Ascension into heaven : offer unto Thy most excellent majesty, of Thy gifts and presents a pure ✠ Victim,[101] a holy ✠ Victim, a spotless ✠ Victim, the holy ✠ Bread of eternal life and the Chalice ✠ of perpetual salvation.

Upon which, vouchsafe to look, with a propitious and serene countenance, and to accept them, as Thou wast pleased to accept the gifts of Thy just servant Abel, and the sacrifice

Tibi óbtulit summus sa-
cérdos Túus Melchíse-
dech, sanctum sacrifí-
cium, immaculátam Hós-
tiam.

of our patriarch Abra-
ham, and that which Thy
high Priest Melchise-
dech offered to Thee, a
holy Sacrifice, a spotless
Victim.[102]

¶ He profoundly inclines himself:

Supplices Te rogá-
mus, omnípotens Deus:
iube haec perférri per
manus sancti Angeli Tui
in sublíme altáre Tuum,
in conspéctu divínae
Maiestátis Tuae: ut quot-
quot, ex hac altáris par-
ticipatióne, sacrosánc-
tum Fílii Tui Cor✠pus,
et Sáng✠uinem sump-
sérimus, omni benedic-
tióne caelésti, et grátia
repleámur. Per eúm-
dem Christum Dóminum
nostrum. Amen.

We humbly beseech
Thee, almighty God,
command these things
to be carried by the
hands of Thy holy Angel
to Thy altar on high, in
the sight of Thy divine
Majesty: that whosoever
of us, by participation
at this altar, shall receive
the most sacred Body
✠ and Blood ✠ of Thy
Son, may be filled with
every heavenly blessing
and grace. Through the
same Christ our Lord.
Amen.

COMMEMORATION OF THE DEAD.[103]

Meménto étiam, Dómine, famulórum famularúmque Tuárum N. et N. qui nos praecessérunt cum signo fídei, et dórmiunt in somno pacis.

Be mindful also, O Lord, of Thy servants and handmaids, N. and N., who are gone before us, with the sign of faith, and slumber in the sleep of peace.[104]

¶ *Here particular mention is silently made of such of the Dead as are to be prayed for.*

Ipsis, Dómine, et ómnibus in Christo quiescéntibus, locum refrigérii, lucis et pacis, ut indúlgeas, deprecámur. Per eúmdem Christum Dóminum nostrum.
 Amen.

To these, O Lord, and to all [105] who rest in Christ, grant, we beseech Thee, a place of refreshment, light, and peace. Through the same Christ our Lord.
 Amen.

¶ *Here, striking his breast, he says:* [106]

Nobis quoque peccatóribus fámulis Tuis, de multitúdine miseratiónum Tuárum sperántibus, partem áliquam et societátem donáre dignéris, cum Tuis sanctis apóstolis et martyribus:

To us sinners also Thy servants, who hope in the multitude of Thy mercies, vouchsafe to grant some part and fellowship [107] with Thy holy apostles and martyrs; with John, Stephen,

cum Ioánne, Stéphano, Mathía, Bárnaba, Ignátio, Alexándro, Marcellíno, Petro, Felicitáte, Perpétua, Agatha, Lúcia, Agnéte, Caecília, Anastásia, et ómnibus sanctis Tuis : intra quorum nos consórtium, non aestimátor mériti, sed véniae, quaesumus largítor admítte. Per Christum Dóminum nostrum.

Per quem haec ómnia, Dómine, semper bona creas, sanctí✠ficas, viví✠ficas, bene✠dícis, et praestas nobis. Per Ip✠sum, et cum Ip✠so, et in Ip✠so, est Tibi Deo Patri ✠ omnipoténti, in unitáte Spíritus ✠ Sancti, omnis honor et glória.

Mathias, Barnabas, Ignatius, Alexander, Marcellinus, Peter, Felicitas, Perpetua, Agatha, Lucy, Agnes, Cecily, Anastasia, and all Thy saints : into whose company we beseech Thee to admit us, not considering our merit, but graciously pardoning our offences. Through Christ our Lord.

Through whom, O Lord, Thou dost always create, sanctify✠, quicken ✠, bless ✠, and give us all these good things. Through Him ✠, and with Him ✠, and in Him ✠, is to Thee, God the Father ✠ Almighty, in the unity of the Holy ✠ Ghost, all honour and glory.[108]

¶ *Here he raises his voice:*

P. Per ómnia saecula saeculórum.

R. Amen.

P. World without end.

R. Amen.

Oremus.

Praecéptis salutáribus móniti, et divína institutióne formáti, audémus dícere:

Pater noster, qui es in caelis; sanctificétur nomen Tuum: advéniat regnum Tuum: fiat volúntas Tua sicut in caelo, et in terra. Panem nostrum quotidiánum da nobis hódie: et dimítte nobis débita nostra, sicut et nos dimíttimus debitóribus nostris. Et ne nos indúcas in tentatiónem.

R. Sed líbera nos a malo.

P. Amen.

Let us pray.

Admonished by saving precepts, and instructed by divine institution, we presume to say:

Our Father,[109] who art in heaven; hallowed be Thy name: Thy kingdom come: Thy will be done on earth, as it is in heaven. Give us this day our daily bread: and forgive us our trespasses, as we forgive them that trespass against us. And lead us not into temptation.

R. But deliver us from evil.

P. Amen.

¶ *At Solemn High Mass, the Deacon, towards the conclusion of the* Pater noster, *goes to the right hand of the Priest, where he awaits the approach of the Sub-deacon, from whom he receives the Paten, which he puts into the hand of the Priest, who then says:*

Libera nos, quaesumus, Dómine, ab ómnibus malis, praetéritis, praeséntibus et futúris: et intercedénte beáta et gloriósa semper Vírgine Dei Genitríce María, cum beátis apóstolis Tuis Petro et Paulo, atque Andréa, et ómnibus sanctis: da propítius pacem in diébus nostris: ut ope misericórdiae Tuae adiuti, et a peccáto simus semper líberi, et ab omni perturbatióne secúri. Per eúmdem Dóminum nostrum Iesum Christum Fílium Tuum: qui Tecum vivit et regnat in unitáte Spíritus Sancti, Deus.

Deliver us, we beseech thee, O Lord, from all evils past, present, and to come; and the blessed and glorious ever Virgin Mother of God Mary,[110] together with Thy blessed apostles Peter and Paul, and Andrew, and all the Saints interceding for us, mercifully grant peace [111] in our days: that assisted by the help of Thy mercy, we may be always free from sin, and secure from all disturbance. Through the same our Lord Jesus Christ Thy Son: who liveth and reigneth with Thee in the unity of the Holy Ghost, one God.

¶ *Here he elevates his voice, and says*.

P. Per ómnia saecula saeculórum.

R. Amen.

P. World without end.

R. Amen.

P. Pax Dómini sit semper vobíscum.

P. May the peace of the Lord be always with you.

R. Et cum spíritu tuo.

R. And with thy spirit.

¶ *Here the Priest breaks the Sacred Host* [112] *into two parts, from one of which he detaches a little particle; and having deposited the two larger ones upon the Paten, he puts the small one into the Chalice, saying:* [113]

Haec commíxtio et consecrátio Córporis et Sánguinis Dómini nostri Iesu Christi, fiat accipiéntibus nobis in vitam aetérnam. Amen.

May this mingling and consecration of the Body and Blood of our Lord Jesus Christ, be to us who receive it, effectual to eternal life. Amen.

¶ *Then having made a genuflection, striking his breast, he says:*

Agnus Dei, qui tollis peccáta mundi, miserére nobis.

Lamb of God, who takest away the sins of the world, have mercy on us. [114]

Agnus Dei, qui tollis peccáta mundi, miserére nobis.

Lamb of God, who takest away the sins of the world, have mercy on us.

Agnus Dei, qui tollis peccáta mundi, dona nobis pacem.

Lamb of God, who takest away the sins of the world, grant us peace.

¶ *In Masses for the Dead, he says:*

Agnus Dei, qui tollis peccáta mundi, dona eis réquiem.

Lamb of God, who takest away the sins of the world, grant them rest.

Agnus Dei, qui tollis peccáta mundi, dona eis réquiem.

Lamb of God, who takest away the sins of the world, grant them rest.

Agnus Dei, qui tollis peccáta mundi, dona eis réquiem sempitérnam.

Lamb of God, who takest away the sins of the world, grant them eternal rest.

¶ *Standing in an inclined position, with his hands joined and resting on the Altar, and his eyes reverently fixed upon the Sacred Host, the Priest recites the following Prayers, the first of which is omitted in Masses for the Dead.*

Dómine Iesu Christe, qui dixísti apóstolis Tuis: Pacem relínquo vobis, pacem Meam do vobis: ne respícias peccáta mea, sed fidem Ecclésiae Tuae: eámque secúndum voluntátem Tuam pacificáre et coadunáre digneris. Qui vivis et regnas Deus,

Lord Jesus Christ, who saidst to Thy apostles: Peace I leave you, My peace I give you; regard not my sins, but the faith of Thy Church; and vouchsafe to maintain her in peace and unity agreeably to Thy will: Who livest and reignest God, world

per ómnia saecula sae- without end. Amen.
culórum. Amen.

¶ *At Solemn High Mass, the Deacon kisses the Altar at the same time with the celebrating Priest, by whom he is saluted with the kiss of peace,*[115] *accompanied by these words:*

P. Pax tecum.   P. Peace be with thee.

¶ *To which the Deacon answers:*

R. Et cum spíritu tuo.   R. And with thy spirit.

¶ *And then salutes, in like manner, the Sub-deacon, who conveys the kiss of peace to those amongst the clergy who may be assisting at Mass.*

Dómine Iesu Christe, Fili Dei vivi, qui ex voluntáte Patris, coope-ránte Spíritu Sancto, per mortem Tuam mundum vivificásti : líbera me per hoc sacrosánctum Corpus, et Sánguinem Tu-um, ab ómnibus iniqui-tátibus meis, et univérsis malis : et fac me Tuis semper inhaerére man-dátis, et a Te nunquam

Lord Jesus Christ, Son of the living God, who, by the will of Thy Father, with the co-operation of the Holy Ghost, hast by Thy death given life to the world: deliver me by this Thy most sacred Body and Blood from all my iniquities, and from all evils: and make me al-ways adhere to Thy com-

separári permittas ; Qui cum eódem Deo Patre et Spíritu Sancto vivis et regnas Deus in saecula saeculórum. Amen.

mandments, and never suffer me to be separated from Thee: Who with the same God the Father and the Holy Ghost, livest and reignest God, for ever and ever. Amen.

Percéptio Córporis Tui, Dómine Iesu Christe, quod ego indígnus súmere praesúmo, non mihi provéniat in iudícium et condemnatiónem : sed pro tua pietáte, prosit mihi ad tutaméntum mentis et córporis, et ad medélam percipiéndam : qui vivis et regnas cum Deo Patre in unitáte Spíritus Sancti Deus, per ómnia saecula saeculórum. Amen.

Let not the participation of Thy Body, O Lord Jesus Christ, which I, though unworthy, presume to receive, turn to my judgment and condemnation; but through Thy goodness, may it be to me a safeguard and remedy of mind and body: who with God the Father, in the unity of the Holy Ghost, livest and reignest God, world without end. Amen.

¶ *Taking the Host in his hands, he says :*

Panem caeléstem accípiam, et nomen Dómini invocábo.

I will take the bread of heaven, and call upon the name of the Lord.

¶ *Striking his breast in humility and with devotion, he says three times :* [116]

Dómine, non sum dignus, ut intres sub tectum meum : sed tantum dic verbo, et sanábitur ánima mea.

Lord, I am not worthy that Thou shouldest enter under my roof; but only say the word, and my soul shall be healed.

¶ *Taking reverently both parts of the Sacred Host in his right hand, and signing with it the sign of the Cross on himself,*[117] *he says the following prayer, and then receives.*

Corpus Dómini nostri Iesu Christi custódiat ánimam meam in vitam aetérnam. Amen.

May the Body of our Lord Jesus Christ preserve my soul unto life everlasting. Amen.

¶ *After a short meditation on the stupendous mystery, he uncovers the Chalice; adores, genuflecting, the sacred Blood: and then, with the most religious diligence, gathers upon the Paten, or silver Disk, the very smallest atoms* [118] *of the Host which remain upon the Corporal (this is the small linen cloth upon which the species are deposited); these fragments he puts into the Chalice, which he then takes* [119] *in his hands, saying :*

Quid retríbuam Dómino pro ómnibus quae retríbuit mihi? Cálicem salutáris accípiam, et nomen Dómini invocábo.

What shall I render to the Lord, for all He hath rendered to me? I will take the chalice of salvation, and call upon

Laudans invocábo Dóminum, et ab inimícis meis salvus ero.

the name of the Lord. Praising I will call upon the Lord, and I shall be saved from my enemies.

¶ *Receiving the Blood of our Saviour, he says:*

Sanguis Dómini nostri Iesu Christi, custódiat ánimam meam in vitam aetérnam. Amen.

The Blood of our Lord Jesus Christ preserve my soul to life everlasting. Amen.

¶ *Taking the first* Ablution, *he says:*

Quod ore súmpsimus, Dómine, pura mente capiámus, et de múnere temporáli, fiat nobis remédium sempitérnum.

What we have taken with our mouth, O Lord, may we receive with a pure mind, and of a temporal gift, may it become to us an eternal remedy.

¶ *Taking the second* Ablution, *he says:*

Corpus Tuum, Dómine, quod sumpsi, et Sanguis quem potávi, adhaereat viscéribus meis: et praesta, ut in me non remáncat scelerum mácula, quem pura et sancta refecérunt sacraménta. Qui vivis et regnas

May Thy Body, O Lord, which I have received, and Thy Blood which I have drunk, cleave to my bowels; and grant that no stain of sin may remain in me, whom Thy pure and holy sacraments

in saecula saeculórum. Amen.

have refreshed. Who livest and reignest for ever and ever. Amen.

¶ *Then he returns to the Book and reads the* Communion, *which varies with the day.*

THE COMMUNION.[120]

Benedícimus Deum caeli, et coram ómnibus vivéntibus confitébimur Ei : quia fecit nobíscum misericórdiam Suam.

We bless the God of heaven, and will praise Him in the sight of all the living : because He hath shown His mercy to us.

P. Dóminus vobíscum.

R. Et cum spíritu tuo.

P. The Lord be with you.

R. And with thy spirit.

POST-COMMUNION.[121]

Oremus.

Let us pray.

Profíciat nobis ad salútem córporis et ánimae, Dómine Deus noster, huius sacraménti suscéptio : et sempitérnae sanctae Trinitátis eiusdémque indivíduae unitátis conféssio. Per Dó-

O Lord our God, may the reception of this sacrament, and the confession of the everlasting holy Trinity and of the undivided unity of the same, profit us, unto the health of body and soul.

minum nostrum Iesum Christum Fílium Tuum: Qui Tecum vivit et regnat in unitate Spíritus Sancti Deus: per ómnia saecula saeculórum. Amen.

Through our Lord Jesus Christ Thy Son; who liveth and reigneth with Thee in the unity of the Holy Ghost, one God, world without end. Amen.

OCCASIONAL POST-COMMUNIONS.

Oremus.

Mundet et múniat nos, quaesumus Dómine, divíni sacraménti munus oblátum: et intercedénte beáta Vírgine Dei Genetríce María, cum beáto Ioseph, beátis apóstolis Tuis Petro et Paulo, atque beáto N. et omnibus sanctis; a cunctis nos reddat et perversitátibus expiátos, et adversitátibus expedítos.

Let us pray.

May the offered up gift of this divine sacrament, we beseech Thee, O Lord, cleanse and defend us; and the blessed Virgin Mother of God, Mary, interceding for us, together with blessed Joseph, Thy blessed apostles Peter and Paul, and blessed N. and all the saints; render us both purified from all perversities, and freed from all adversities.

Grátiam Tuam, quaesumus, Dómine, méntibus nostris infúnde: ut

Pour forth, we beseech Thee, O Lord, Thy grace into our

qui, Angelo nuntiánte, Christi Fílii Tui incarnatiónem cognóvimus ; per passiónem Eius et crucem, ad resurrectiónis glóriam perducámur.

Líbera, quaesumus, Dómine, a peccátis et hóstibus, fámulos Tuos, Tibi supplicántes : ut in sancta conversatióne vivéntes, nullis afficiántur advérsis. Per Dóminum nostrum Iesum Christum Fílium Tuum : Qui Tecum vivit et regnat in unitate Spíritus Sancti, Deus : per ómnia saecula saeculórum. Amen.

Haec nos, quaesumus Dómine, divini sacraménti percéptio prótegat : et fámulum Tuum N. quem pastórem Ecclé-

hearts, that we, to whom the incarnation of Christ, Thy Son, has been made known by the message of an Angel, may by His passion and cross be brought to the glory of His resurrection.

Deliver, O Lord, we beseech Thee, from all sin, and from all enemies, Thy servants, who offer their humble prayers to Thee; that leading holy lives, they may be attacked by no misfortunes. Through our Lord Jesus Christ Thy Son : who liveth and reigneth with Thee in the unity of the Holy Ghost, one God, world without end. Amen.

May the participation of this divine sacrament protect us, we beseech Thee, O Lord ; and always procure safety and

siae Tuae praeésse volu-
isti ; unà cum commísso
sibi grege, salvet semper,
et múniat. Per Dóminum
nostrum Iesum Chris-
tum Fílium Tuum : qui
Tecum vivit et regnat in
unitate Spíritus Sancti,
Deus : per ómnia saecula
saeculórum. Amen.

defence to Thy servant
N. whom Thou hast ap-
pointed pastor over Thy
Church, together with
the flock committed to
his charge. Through our
Lord Jesus Christ Thy
Son ; who liveth and
reigneth with Thee in
the unity of the Holy
Ghost, one God, world
without end. Amen.

¶ *Proceeding to the middle of the Altar, which he
kisses, the Priest turns round and greets the
People with :*

P. Dóminus vobís-
cum.

P. The Lord be with
you.

¶ *To which the Choir, or the Acolyte, answers :*

R. Et cum spíritu tuo.

R. And with thy spirit.

¶ *Then continuing with his face towards the People,
he announces to them leave to depart.*

P. Ite, missa est.

P. Go, you are dis-
missed.

¶ *To which is answered :*

R. Deo grátias.

R. Thanks be to God.

¶ On those days, however, on which the Angelic Hymn, Glory be to God on high, is omitted; instead of dismissing the people with these words, the Priest, after having turned round towards the Altar, says:

P. Benedicámus Dómino.

P. Let us bless the Lord.

¶ In Masses for the Dead, instead of either of the foregoing salutations, is said:

P. Requiéscant in pace.

P. May they rest in peace.

¶ To which is answered:

R. Amen.

R. Amen.

¶ At Solemn High Mass, it is the Deacon who chants the Ite, missa est, etc. etc.[122]

¶ Then bowing before the Altar, the Priest says:

Pláceat Tibi, sancta Trinitas, obséquium servitútis meae, et praesta: ut sacrifícium, quod óculis Tuae maiestatis indígnus óbtuli, Tibi sit acceptábile, mihíque, et ómnibus, pro quibus illud óbtuli, sit, Te mise-

May the performance of my homage be pleasing to Thee, O holy Trinity, and grant that the sacrifice which I, though unworthy, have offered up in the sight of Thy majesty, may be acceptable to Thee, and through

ránte, propitiábile. Per Christum Dóminum nostrum. Amen.

Thy mercy be a propitiation for me, and all those for whom it has been offered. Through Christ our Lord. Amen.

¶ *Then having kissed the Altar, he looks up towards Heaven and elevates his hands, which he afterwards joins, at the same time that he bows his head, saying in an audible voice:*

Benedícat vos omnípotens Deus, Pater, et Fílius, ✠ et Spíritus Sanctus.
R. Amen.

May almighty God bless you: the Father, and the Son, ✠ and the Holy Ghost.
R. Amen.

¶ *And having turned himself to the People, before he has entirely completed this prayer, he gives his blessing,*[123] *by making the sign of the Cross over them with his outstretched right hand just as he invokes the Persons of the Holy Trinity. (The Benediction is omitted at Masses for the Dead.) Then turning to the Gospel-side of the Altar, he says:*

P. Dóminus vobíscum.
R. Et cum spíritu tuo.

P. The Lord be with you.
R. And with thy spirit.

¶ *He then traces the sign of the Cross, first upon the Altar on the commencement of the Gospel;*

then upon his forehead, lips, and breast; and, afterwards, reads the particular Gospel appointed for the occasion; but more generally it happens that the Gospel of S. John is the proper one to be recited.

P. ✠ Inítium sancti Evangelii secúndum Ioannem.

R. Glória Tibi, Dómine.

In princípio erat Verbum, et Verbum erat apud Deum, et Deus erat Verbum. Hoc erat in princípio apud Deum. Omnia per Ipsum facta sunt: et sine Ipso factum est nihil, quod factum est; in Ipso vita erat, et vita erat lux hóminum: et lux in ténebris lucet, et ténebrae eam non comprehendérunt. Fuit homo missus a Deo, cui nomen erat Ioánnes. Hic venit in testimónium, ut testimónium perhibéret de lúmine, ut omnes créderent per illum. Non erat ille

P. ✠ The beginning of the holy Gospel according to John.

R. Glory be to Thee, O Lord.

In the beginning was the Word, and the Word was with God, and the Word was God: the same was in the beginning with God. All things were made by Him; and without Him was made nothing that was made. In Him was life, and the life was the light of men; and the light shineth in darkness, and the darkness did not comprehend it. There was a man sent from God, whose name was John. This man came for a witness, to give testimony of the

lux : sed ut testimónium perhibéret de lúmine. Erat lux vera, quae illúminat omnem hóminem veniéntem in hunc mundum. In mundo erat, et mundus per Ipsum factus est, et mundus Eum non cognóvit : in própria venit, et sui Eum non recepérunt. Quotquot autem recepérunt Eum, dedit eis potestátem filios Dei fíeri, his qui credunt in nómine Eius : qui non ex sanguínibus, neque ex voluntáte carnis, neque ex voluntáte viri, sed ex Deo nati sunt. ET VERBUM CARO FACTUM EST, et habitávit in nobis : et vídimus glóriam Eius, glóriam quasi Unigéniti à Patre, plenum grátiae et veritátis.

R. Deo grátias.

light, that all men might believe through him. He was not the light : but was to give testimony of the light. That was the true light which enlighteneth every man that cometh into this world. He was in the world, and the world was made by Him, and the world knew Him not. He came unto His own, and His own received Him not. But as many as received Him, He gave them power to be made the sons of God, to them that believe in His name, who are born, not of blood, nor of the will of the flesh, nor of the will of man, but of God. AND THE WORD WAS MADE FLESH,[124] and dwelt among us ; and we saw His glory, the glory as it were of the Onlybegotten of the Father ; full of grace and truth.

R. Thanks be to God.

¶ *The following V. R. and Prayer are in some places said every Sunday and Holiday after Mass:* [125]

V. Dómine, salvum fac regem nostrum N.

R. Et exaúdi nos in die qua invocavérimus Te.

V. Dómine, exaúdi oratiónem meam.

R. Et clamor meus ad Te veniat.

V. Dóminus vóbiscum.

R. Et cum spíritu tuo.

Oremus.

Quaesumus omnipotens Deus: ut famulus Tuus N. rex noster, qui Tua miseratione suscepit regni gubernacula, virtutum etiam omnium percipiat incrementa: quibus decenter ornatus, et vitiorum monstra devitare, et ad Te, qui via, veritas, et vita es, gratiosus valeat pervenire.

V. O Lord, save N. our king.

R. And hear us in the day on which we call upon Thee.

V. O Lord, hear my prayer.

R. And let my cry come unto Thee.

V. The Lord be with you.

R. And with thy spirit.

Let us pray.

We beseech Thee, O Almighty God, that Thy servant N. our king, who by Thy mercy hath undertaken the government of these realms, may also receive an increase of all virtues, wherewith being adorned, he may avoid every enormity of sin; and come at length to Thee,

Per Dóminum nostrum, etc.	who art the way, the truth, and the life. Through Christ our Lord, etc.
R. Amen.	R. Amen.

BENEDICTION WITH THE BLESSED SACRA-MENT [126] AFTER MASS.

¶ *The Priest having opened the Tabernacle* [127] *and drawn aside the little curtain, returns to the foot of the Altar-steps, puts incense into the thurible without blessing it, and kneeling, incenses the Blessed Sacrament. He intones the Hymn:* Tantum ergo Sacramentum, *which the Choir finishes. At the* Genitori Genitoque *he again incenses the Blessed Sacrament, and then recites the Collect:* Deus, qui nobis, *etc. He then puts on the Humeral Veil, and going up to the Altar, adores,* [128] *and muffling his hands in the extremities of the Veil, takes up the Pyx;* [129] *and turning round slowly, and with the most religious reverence, blesses with it the people, who are the while profoundly bending in silent worship. The bell is rung during this ceremony, to announce when the solemn act of blessing commences and finishes, that all may know how long to continue bowed down in adoration. The Priest having given the Benediction, deposits the Pyx on the Corporal, takes off the*

Humeral Veil, replaces the Pyx in the Tabernacle, genuflects, and closes the door.

Tantum ergo Sacraméntum
  venerémur cérnui :
et antíquum documéntum
  novo cedat rítui :
praestet fides suppleméntum
  sénsuum deféctui :

To this mysterious table now
  our knees, our hearts, and sense we bow.
let ancient rites resign their place
  to nobler elements of grace :
what our weak senses can't descry
  let stronger faith the want supply.

Genitóri, Genitóque
  laus et iubilátio :
salus, honor, virtus quoque,
  sit et benedíctio :
procedénti ab utróque
  compar sit laudátio.
      Amen.

To God the Father born of none,
  to Christ His co-eternal Son,
and Holy Ghost whose equal rays
  from both proceed, be equal praise :
one honour, jubilee, and fame,
  for ever bless His glorious name.
      Amen.

V. Panem de caelo praestitísti eis. [*T. P.* Allelúia.]

V. Thou hast given them bread from heaven. [*In Paschal time:* Alleluia.]

R. Omne delectaméntum in se habéntem. [*T. P.* Allelúia.]

R. Replenished with whatever is delicious. [*In Paschal time:* Alleluia.]

Oremus.

Let us pray.

Deus, qui nobis, sub sacraménto mirábili, passiónis Tuae memóriam reliquísti : tríbue quaesumus, ita nos Córporis et Sánguinis Tui sacra mystéria venerári, ut re-

O God, who in this wonderful sacrament, hast left us a perpetual memorial of Thy passion: grant us, we beseech Thee, so to reverence the sacred mysteries of Thy

E

demptiónis Tuae fructum in nobis iúgiter sentiámus. Qui vivis et regnas, etc.

Body and Blood, as in our souls to be always sensible of the redemption Thou hast purchased for us. Who livest and reignest, etc.

NOTES

ON THE

RUBRICS

NOTES ON THE RUBRICS, ETC.

(1)

A SPRIG of the hyssop-plant was used for sprinkling the water of purification on the people under the Mosaic dispensation;[1] and at the going out of the children of Israel, they were commanded to dip a bunch of hyssop in the blood of the paschal lamb, and sprinkle their door-posts with it.[2]

(2)

The English word Mass, in Latin *Missa*, is derived from the word *missio*, dismissal. It was the practice in the primitive Church, during the celebration of the mysteries of the Lord's Supper, to dismiss from the assembly, before the Creed, all those who had not been perfectly initiated into the truths of the Gospel and admitted to the communion of the faithful : this was denominated the *Missio* or Dismissal, whence is formed the Latin abbreviation *Missa*, and the English Mass.[3]

---

[1] *Numbers*, XIX, 18. [2] *Exodus*, XII, 22.

[3] The earliest instance of the use of the word *Missa* for the Liturgy occurs in the Letters of S. Ambrose ; see Epistle XX, 4.

The derivation of the term by which the principal afternoon service is designated is somewhat similar. Vespers, or Evening Song, constitute the sixth amongst the Seven Canonical Hours, as those forms of prayer are called which each ecclesiastic, from the Sub-deacon upwards, is bound to repeat every day, either in public or in private. The term Vespers is derived from Vesper, the star that appears towards sunset, the time appointed by ancient usage for the recital of Evening Song.[1]

The antiquity of this form of prayer may be traced back to the earlier ages of the Church, since it is not only especially noticed in the Apostolic Constitutions,[2] but mentioned by S. Basil, S. Ambrose, and S. Hierome, the last of whom denominates it the 'Hora Lucernaris,' or time of lighting lamps at the decline of day.

It may be proper to observe that the Vestment which, in most places, is worn by the officiating priest at Vespers is the Cope.

(3)

The use of Images in the house of God is authorised by Scripture. Moses was commanded

---

[1] Vespera fit quando Sol occidit. S. AUGUSTINI *in Psalmum* XXIX *Enarratio* 2. Vesperum autem nominatur a sidere, qui Vesper vocatur, et decidente sole exoritur. S. ISIDORI *de Ecclesiasticis Officiis* lib. I, cap. XX, § 2 ; *Etymologiarum* lib. VI, cap. XIX, § 2.

[2] Ἑσπέρας γενομένης, συναθροίσεις τὴν ἐκκλησίαν, ὦ ἐπίσκοπε· καὶ μετὰ τὸ ῥηθῆναι τὸν ἐπιλύχνιον ψαλμὸν. Lib. VIII, cap. 35, *apud* LABBEUM, *Concil. Gen.*, tom. I, col. 584.

to place the images of two Cherubim upon the Ark;[1] and Solomon 'carved all the walls of the Temple round about with divers figures and carvings.'[2] By making a reverence before the Crucifix, Catholics do not intend to worship the image of their Divine Redeemer, but the Redeemer Himself. All Christians bow the head when they hear the holy name of Jesus pronounced; Catholics bow also when they behold His figure. The sound and the figure are both images of Jesus.

(4)

There are two forms which the Church employs for offering up the Eucharistic Sacrifice—one called *High Mass;* the other, *Low Mass.* Both are the same in essence, and differ in the ceremonies only, which are more numerous and solemn in the celebration of High than in that of Low Mass. By Solemn High Mass it is intended to signify the Mass at which a Deacon and Sub-deacon minister.

The Roman Missal prescribes that we should kneel during the whole of Low Mass, except at the recital of the Gospel.[3] If, therefore, ill health or weakness do not compel us to sit down occasionally, we ought to comply with the Rubric, and

---

[1] *Exodus,* xxv and xxvi.   [2] *3 Kings,* vi, 29.
[3] 'Circumstantes in Missis privatis semper genuflectunt, praeterquam ad Evangelium.' *Ritus servandus in celebratione Missae.*

hear Mass in a kneeling posture, which is the one most becoming a sinner who is present at the commemoration of the death of his crucified Redeemer.

Through a devotional respect for the Blessed Eucharist, the priest who celebrates Mass, as also those who receive the Holy Communion, are fasting from the previous midnight. That this custom of receiving the Blessed Sacrament fasting was instituted by the Apostles may be gathered from a passage in the writings of Tertullian.[1]

(5)

Acolytes constitute the highest of the four minor orders in the Latin Church, in which they have been employed, from the remotest antiquity, to perform the inferior ministry at the Altar. S. Cornelius, who suffered martyrdom in 254, and his African contemporary, S. Cyprian,[2] in their epistles severally mention these subordinate clerks. The Roman Pontiff, in that part of his letter to Fabius,[3] Bishop of Antioch, where he enumerates the clergy of Rome, says that there were 'forty-six priests, seven deacons, seven sub-deacons, forty-two acolytes, together with fifty-two exorcists, lectors, and doorkeepers.' The Fourth Council of Carthage, celebrated in the year 398, takes especial

---

[1] *Ad Uxorem*, lib. II, cap. 5.   [2] Epist. LV.
[3] EUSEBII *Hist. Eccl.*, lib. VI, cap. 43.

notice of the form of their ordination, and directs that 'when an acolyte is ordained, let him be instructed by the bishop how he is to perform his office. But let him receive from the archdeacon the candlestick, with a wax taper, that he may know that to him has been consigned the duty of lighting the lights of the church. And let him receive an empty cruet, to supply wine for the Eucharist of the Blood of Christ.'[1] The same formula is recited in the Sacramentary of S. Gregory. The term is Greek, and derived from the word Ἀκόλουθος, which signifies a young servant or attendant. One amongst their most conspicuous offices within the sanctuary is, as S. Isidore informs us,[2] to bear about the wax tapers. It has been the custom for several centuries to allow lay persons, even youths, to discharge the ministry at the Holy Sacrifice and other functions, without having the ordination of acolytes.

(6)

This mark ✠, whenever it is found, expresses that the Priest, at those words to which it is affixed, makes the sign of the Cross.

---

[1] Acolythus cum ordinatur, ab episcopo quidem doceatur, qualiter in officio suo agere debeat. Sed ab archidiacono accipiat ceroferarium cum cereo, ut sciat se ad accendenda ecclesiae luminaria mancipari. Accipiat et urceolum vacuum, ad suggerendum vinum in eucharistiam Sanguinis Christi. LABBEI *Concil. Gen.*, tom. III, col. 951.

[2] See Note 35, p. 97.

(7)

Before commencing the Psalm, the Priest recites a versicle of it : ' I will go,' etc., called the
Antiphon, which, as its two Greek component
words indicate, signifies alternate utterance or
sound. He and his two assistants alternately
repeat the verses of this introductory Psalm.
Such an alternation in singing or reciting Psalms
and Hymns may be traced up to the earliest ages
of the Church. So ancient is it, that its introduction is attributed[1] to S. Ignatius, a disciple of the
Apostles.[2] In the Church service it is usual to
select, very often from the Psalm itself about to
be commenced, some verse which is repeated both
before and after saying it. Sometimes the same
verse or Antiphon is repeated by one side of the
choir, at the closing of each verse of the Psalm,
the whole of which is recited by the other. As
there is no portion of the Psalter more appropriate
for the ministers of God to recite when about to
offer up sacrifice than this verse : ' I will go
unto the Altar of God,' it has in consequence
been chosen as the Antiphon to the Psalm :
' Judge me,' etc., and directed to be said on every

---

[1] SOCRATIS *Hist. Eccl.*, lib. VI, cap. 8.

[2] S. Ignatius, who suffered martyrdom at Rome under Trajan,
was appointed by S. Peter to fill the episcopal chair of Antioch
on the death of Evodius, the immediate successor, in that see, of
the Prince of the Apostles.

occasion by the Priest at the commencement of Mass.

(8)

This Psalm, on account of the expressions of joy which it contains, is omitted at Masses for the Dead; and during Passion-time, that is, the fortnight before Easter.

(9)

This is denominated the minor Doxology, or short hymn of Glory. The first part of it: 'Glory be to the Father, and to the Son, and to the Holy Ghost,' is presumed to have been framed by the Apostles.[1] The second portion: 'As it was in the beginning, is now, and ever shall be, world without end. Amen,' is ascribed to the Council of Nice assembled in the year 325, and was appended by the Nicene Fathers as a contradiction to the doctrines of Arius, who maintained that the Son was not in the beginning, nor equal to the Father.[2]

The custom still observed by the people of standing up at Vespers, during the 'Glory be to

---

[1] That the first of the two versicles which compose the 'Glory be to the Father' was in use as a prayer amongst the faithful anterior to the Council of Nice is certain. S. Basil, who lived a little more than forty years after it was held, notices, in his letter to Amphilochius, this hymn as ancient; and the illustrious S. Athanasius, who flourished at the time the Council of Nice was celebrated, in referring to this Doxology, makes no mention of its being then but recently introduced.

[2] BENEDICTI XIV *de Sacrificio Missae* lib. II, cap. III, § 3.

the Father,' etc., and of the choir bursting out into
a louder chorus, no doubt owes its origin to the
same cause which introduced this Doxology at the
close of each Psalm. To express their belief in
the doctrine of the holy and undivided Trinity,
it appears that the people were instructed to stand
up, and mingle their voices with the swelling
strain of the choir, and thus proclaim their loud
and unanimous assent to that dogma, as it were
by acclamation. The antiquity of this rite is
attested by Cassian, who flourished about the year
424, when he incidentally mentions it, not as if
of recent introduction, but as a ceremony established throughout Gaul at the time when he was
writing. 'In this province' (Gaul), remarks that
author, 'at the conclusion of a Psalm, all standing
up, unite in singing together, in a loud strain:
"Glory be to the Father," etc.'[1]

At a later period, Theodemar, twelfth Abbot of
Monte Casino (778–797), notices the standing up,
and the inclination of the head during the recital
of the 'Glory be to the Father,' as a rite of
ancient institution.[2]

---

[1] Illud etiam quod in hac provincia (Narbonensi nempe) vidimus,
ut uno cantante in clausula psalmi, omnes astantes concinant cum
clamore: Gloria Patri, et Filio, et Spiritui Sancto, nusquam per
omnem Orientem audivimus. Io. CASSIANI *de Coenobiorum Insti-*
tutis lib. II, cap. 8.

[2] Sunt et alia quae a maioribus instituta servamus: nudato exceptis infirmis capite ad officium stamus: flectimus cervicem, quoties
Gloria canitur. *Epist. ad Theodoricum,* quoted by LE LORRAIN, *De*
l'ancienne coutume de prier et d'adorer debout, tom. I, p. 189.

(10)

While reciting the prayer : ' I confess,' etc., the Priest, with his hands joined, bends down his head profoundly, to express his confusion for his sinfulness, and to imitate the humble ' Publican, who would not so much as lift up his eyes towards heaven.' [1]

(11)

At these words he strikes his breast. This manner of expressing grief for sin is both ancient and scriptural. The Publican mentioned in the Gospel [2] struck his breast, saying, ' O God, be merciful to me a sinner ; ' and at the Crucifixion, ' the multitude that saw the things that were done, returned striking their breasts.' [3] The striking of the breast is meant to signify, not only that we are indignant against this bosom of ours, which has so often rebelled against heaven, but that we desire that it may be bruised and softened by compunction, and that the stony heart may be exchanged for one of flesh. [4] In the Old as well as in the New Law, the confession of sins has invariably preceded Sacrifice. The High Priest under the Mosaic dispensation, before

---

[1] *S. Luke*, XVIII, 13.
[2] *Ibid.*
[3] *Ibid.*, XXIII, 48.
[4] *Ezekiel*, XI, 19.

he offered the emissary goat, was directed 'to confess all the iniquities of the children of Israel, and
all their offences and sins.'[1]

Some Protestants have objected that in this
prayer Catholics make a confession of their sins,
not only to God, but also to the Saints. In
answer to this, it should be observed that we
here confess, not only to the Saints in heaven,
but also to our brethren upon earth; and, in both
instances, we employ the same expression: and
thus we comply with the injunction of S. James,
who says, 'Confess your sins one to another.'[2]
Now, as it is not the slightest derogation from
God's honour to confess to sinners on earth, it is
impossible to conceive how it can be unlawful to
confess our guilt and acknowledge our transgressions to the Saints in heaven, who are, at the
day of final retribution, to sit in judgement on
us; for it was thus that our Divine Redeemer
addressed His Apostles: 'Amen, I say to you,
when the Son of Man shall sit on the seat of
His Majesty, you also shall sit on twelve seats,
judging the twelve tribes of Israel;'[3] and
S. Paul exclaims: 'Know you not that the Saints
shall judge this world?'[4] The present form of
the Confiteor came into general use during the
thirteenth century.

---

[1] *Leviticus*, XVI, 21. [2] *S. James*, V, 16.
[3] *S. Matthew*, XIX, 28. [4] 1 *Corinthians*, VI, 2.

(12)

Not only did the Archangel Gabriel salute the Blessed Virgin Mary with this respectful language: 'Hail, full of grace, the Lord is with thee; blessed art thou amongst women;'[1] but she herself, under the inspiration of the Holy Spirit, declared that 'all generations should call her blessed.'[2] By this prayer Catholics partly realise this prophetic declaration uttered by 'the Mother of our Lord.'

(13)

Of the Archangel Michael it is said in the prophecy of Daniel: 'Michael shall rise up, the great prince, who standeth for the children of Thy people.'[3]

(14)

S. John Baptist was, as it were, the conclusion of the Old and the beginning of the New Testament. He was 'the Angel sent before the face' of the Redeemer; 'the voice of one crying in the wilderness, Prepare ye the way of the Lord, make straight His paths.' It was he who preached the Baptism of penance unto the remission of sins.[4]

(15)

It was to S. Peter that Jesus Christ made this splendid promise: ''Thou art Peter, and upon this

---

[1] *S. Luke*, I, 28.   [2] *Ibid.*, I, 48.
[3] *Daniel*, XII, I.   [4] *S. Mark*, I, 2, 3, 4.

rock I will build My Church, and the gates of hell shall not prevail against it. And I will give to thee the keys of the kingdom of heaven; and whatsoever thou shalt bind upon earth, it shall be bound also in heaven; and whatsoever thou shalt loose upon earth, it shall be loosed also in heaven.'[1] S. Paul was associated with S. Peter in preaching the Gospel at Rome, and in founding the Roman Church, of which the first Pope or Bishop was S. Peter.

(16)

The Saints in heaven are addressed in this prayer for three reasons: I. Because their perfect charity, or love of God, induces them to feel a concern about every offence perpetrated against their heavenly Sovereign. II. Because they take particular interest about everything which regards us here below, and participate in that 'joy which is in heaven upon one sinner doing penance.'[2] III. Because it not unfrequently happens that Almighty God grants, through the intercession of His favourites, the pardon which He denies to the sinner himself. The Lord thus spoke to Abimelech: 'Abraham shall pray for thee, and thou shalt live;'[3] and He likewise said to the friends of Job: 'Go to My servant Job; and My

---

[1] *S. Matthew*, XVI, 18, 19. [2] *S. Luke*, XV, 7.
[3] *Genesis*, XX, 7.

servant Job shall pray for you; his face I will accept, that folly be not imputed to you.'[1]

(17)

S. James bids us confess our sins 'one to another.'[2]

(18)

When we address ourselves to God, we say: 'Have mercy on us.' When we address ourselves to Saints, to Angels, or to men, we say: 'Pray for us.' 'Jesu mercy, Lady help.'

(19)

The words: 'Dominus vobiscum,' or 'the Lord be with you,' are found in several passages of the Old Testament. 'Booz said to the reapers: The Lord be with you. And they answered him: The Lord bless thee.'[3] Such, too, was the salutation of the Angel Gabriel to the Blessed Virgin Mary.[4] The response: 'And with thy spirit,' is furnished by those words of S. Paul to Timothy: 'The Lord Jesus Christ be with thy spirit.'[5] Anciently, when travellers met, they greeted one another thus in passing, a custom still kept up in some parts of Germany and Spain.

---

[1] *Job*, XLII, 8.   [2] *S. James*, V, 16.
[3] *Ruth*, II, 4.   [4] *S. Luke*, I, 28.
[5] *2 Timothy*, IV, 22.

(20)

The Priest kisses the Altar, out of respect and affection towards that spot on which Jesus Christ is daily immolated; for we may well exclaim with S. Optatus, Bishop of Milevis, who flourished towards the year 365 : 'What is the Altar but the seat of the Body and Blood of Christ?'[1] The use of Altars in the Church, and the respect which has been invariably manifested towards them from the earliest ages, will be noticed in a separate chapter.

The Priest is directed to kiss[2] that part of the Altar under which are deposited the Relics of some Martyr or other Saint. Thus there is furnished another testimonial of reverence to our Divine Redeemer, through the respect which is exhibited towards the earthly remains of those who have exemplified His precepts by their virtues, or sealed the profession of His doctrines with their blood. In the earliest ages of the Church, the holy Sacrifice of the Mass used to be offered on the tombs of the Martyrs; hence arose the custom of enclosing a portion of their Relics beneath the table of the Altar. It is but

[1] Quid est enim Altare, nisi sedes et Corporis et Sanguinis Christi. S. OPTATUS *de Schismate Donatistarum*, lib. VI.

[2] The meaning of kissing sacred things is well explained by Pope Nicolas I., *Responsio ad Bulgaros*, apud LABBEUM, *Concil. Gen.*, tom. XV, col. 405.

becoming that beneath our earthly Altars should repose the Relics of the Saints, since S. John remarks of them in his vision of the Heavenly Sacrifice: 'I saw under the Altar the souls of them that were slain for the word of God, and for the testimony which they held.'[1]

(21)

By the express command of God, the use of Incense was very frequent in the service of the Jewish Temple.[2]

(22)

This portion of the Service derives its name from its having originally been sung when the Priest entered the Church from the Sacristy, on his way to the Altar. According to present use, the Choir at High Mass chants it as the Priest is approaching the Altar, but the Priest reads it at the Altar immediately before the Kyrie.

The Introit as a rule consists of an Antiphon, a verse, or verses, of a Psalm—the version usually the old Latin, not the Vulgate—and the 'Gloria Patri.' Some Introits, called irregular, are taken from other parts of Scripture; this is the case with thirty-five out of the hundred and fifty-nine Introits in the Pian Missal, whilst seven others are by uninspired writers. The introduction of

---

[1] *Apocalypse*, VI, 9.   [2] *Exodus*, XI, 5; *S. Luke*, I, 10, 11.

Introits is attributed by some to S. Celestine, by others to S. Gregory the Great.

(23)

'Kyrie eleison' are two Greek words, which signify 'Lord have mercy.' Such a petition is most appropriately recited at the commencement of the tremendous mysteries. Then it is that we should supplicate the mercies of Heaven in cries like those of the blind men of Jericho,[1] with the perseverance of the Canaanean mother,[2] and as humbly as the ten lepers.[3] 'Kyrie eleison' is said thrice, in honour of God the Father; 'Christe eleison' thrice, in honour of God the Son; and 'Kyrie eleison' thrice, in honour of God the Holy Ghost.

(24)

This has been denominated the Angelic Hymn, because it commences with the words chanted by Angelic voices in the midnight air at the birth of our Divine Redeemer, which was announced to the shepherds by an Angel zoned in light, with whom 'there was a multitude of the heavenly army, praising God, and saying: Glory be to God in the highest, and on earth peace to men of good will.'[4] This Canticle, as the Fathers of the

---

[1] S. Matthew, xx, 30.   [2] Ibid., xv, 22-27.
[3] S. Luke, xvii, 13.   [4] Ibid., ii, 13, 14.

Fourth Council of Toledo, celebrated in the year 633, observed, consists of the strain sung by the multitude of the heavenly army, and of pious aspirations composed by the pastors of the Church. The Greeks call it the greater Doxology. Its author is unknown, but it is found nearly, though not quite, in its present form in the Apostolic Constitutions.[1] It was introduced into the Mass by the Roman Church, first of all on Christmas Day, when it was sung at the first Mass in Greek, at the second in Latin. Afterwards bishops said it on Sundays and festivals,[2] priests only on Easter Sunday; this restricted use was maintained until the end of the tenth century. The 'Gloria in excelsis' is now said in all Masses except those of the Sundays in Advent and from Septuagesima to Palm Sunday inclusive, and of all *ferias* outside the Paschal season. It is not said in votive Masses, except in those of the Angels, and of the Blessed Virgin on Saturday. Being a canticle of gladness, it is also omitted in Masses for the Dead.

In commencing this hymn, so beautiful for its devout sentiments, and venerable for its antiquity, the Priest outstretches and elevates his hands,

---

[1] *Constitutiones Apost.*, lib. VII, c. 48, *apud* LABBEUM, *Concil. Gen.*, tom. I, col. 530.

[2] The *Liber Pontificalis* attributes its introduction to Pope S. Telesphorus; its use on Sundays and feasts of Martyrs to S. Symmachus.

and turns his eyes towards heaven. A pious sensibility naturally dictates such gestures. They exhibit in a feeling manner those inward profound emotions, and that religious elevation of the soul, experienced by the fervent Christian; and testify, that whilst his lips are resounding with those angel-notes of praise, 'Glory be to God on high,' they echo but the accents of a heart that sighs to embrace and retain the joys of Heaven for all eternity. The inclination of the head at the name of God is to manifest our worship of God, made man for our redemption. At the conclusion, the Priest makes the sign of the Cross, according to the custom of the ancient Christians, who sanctified all their principal actions by calling to their minds the sacrifice of Christ's atonement by this holy symbol.

(25)

The Priest bows down before the Altar, because he who wishes to communicate a benediction to others must first of all, by his humility, incline Heaven to bestow the blessing he desires to impart. He kisses the Altar because it is the throne of Jesus. He turns round towards the congregation, because he speaks a holy greeting; and he holds his arms extended to signify, by such a natural expression of sincere and warm affection, that he is acting in the name of Jesus, the loving Father of the faithful.

(26)

Nothing can be more impressive than this scriptural and very ancient custom of extending the arms during the time of prayer in a way which represents the form of a cross. It was thus that Moses prayed upon the mountain, while the children of Israel were combating on the plain with the Amalekites.[1] The Psalmist makes frequent mention of it: 'Hear, O Lord,' he cries, 'the voice of my supplication when I lift my hands to Thy holy temple.'[2] 'Lift up your hands to the holy place.'[3] 'I stretched forth my hands to Thee.'[4] S. Paul refers to this ceremony when he says: 'I will that men pray . . . lifting up pure hands.'[5] That this was the ordinary attitude of Christians when praying is evident both from the testimony of the earliest writers of the Church,[6] and from those monuments of Christian antiquity which are extant. Tertullian, in his book on prayer,[7] and Prudentius, in his hymn on the Martyrdom of S. Fructuosus,[8] particularly mention it. S. Ambrose died praying with his arms

---

[1] *Exodus*, XVII, II.   [2] *Psalm*, XXVII, 2.   [3] *Ibid.*, CXXXIII, 2.
[4] *Ibid.*, CXLII, VI.   [5] *Timothy*, II, 8.
[6] Thus S. Cyprian: 'Hierarcha pius . . . elevatione manuum crucis mysterium representans, confidenter orat.' See PAMELIUS, *Liturgica Latinorum*, tom. I, p. 194. See also S. ATHANASIUS, *Epistola ad Castorem de canonicis coenobiorum constitutionibus.*
[7] *De Oratione*, cap. 14 : 'Nos non attollimus tantum, sed etiam expandimus, et de Dominica Passione modulamur et orantes confitemur.' See also *Apologeticus*, cap. 30.
[8] Περιστεφάνων liber, Hymnus VI, v. 107.

extended in the form of a cross.[1] In the fresco-paintings with which the Christians of the first ages adorned the chambers of their Catacombs at Rome are still visible many figures with out-stretched hands, in the act of praying.[2] The Sarcophagi which contained the bodies,[3] and the Cippi or marble slabs that covered the tombs of the Martyrs,[4] as well as articles of domestic furniture,[5] exhibit figures in similar positions. Anciently this gesture was common both to the Clergy and Laity during the time of prayer; but now, with the exception of some places in Belgium, Holland, and Germany, where the people still employ it in the Churches, especially during the prayers recited after the Way of the Cross, it is observed by the Priest only.

(27)

Amongst ancient ecclesiastical authors the word 'Collect' signifies a meeting of the faithful for the purposes of prayer.[6]

---

[1] Ab hora circiter undecima diei usque ad illam horam in qua emisit spiritum, expansis manibus in modum crucis oravit. PAULINUS. *Vita S. Ambrosii.*

[2] ARINGHI *Roma Subterranea*, tom. I, pp. 541, 565, 581, and 585. NORTHCOTE and BROWNLOW, *Roma Sotterranea*, vol. II, plates XII, XIII, XIV, and XVIII, and pp. 139, 156, 158, 162, 168, 196, and 209. See also Part 2 of this work, chap. XII, § 29.

[3] BOTTARI, *Roma Sotterranea*, plate CXXXVI.

[4] ARINGHI, tom. I, p. 606.

[5] F. BUONARRUOTI, *Osservazioni sopra alcuni frammenti di Vasi Antichi di vetro*, Firenze, 1716, plates XVIII and XXI; NORTHCOTE and BROWNLOW, vol. II, plate XXII.

[6] In the writings of the Fathers the following expressions : col-

In the early times of Christianity it was usual for the people to assemble in a particular Church on fast-days, but especially during seasons of public calamity, in order afterwards to proceed in regular procession to another Church previously determined upon, for the celebration of what was called, in the language of the period, a station.[1] When the Clergy and the people had assembled at the place appointed, the Bishop, or the Priest who was to officiate, recited over the collected multitude a short prayer, which, from the circumstance, was denominated the Collect, or the gathering prayer.[2]

As the Mass is the principal service of the Church, for the celebration of which the faithful are collected, we see the propriety of denominating by the term Collect that prayer which the Priest puts up to God in behalf of those amongst His servants who have come together to adore Him. In fact, the ancient mode of saying the

lectas agere—congregari ad collectam—which are of frequent occurrence, are to be understood in this sense.

[1] The ceremony was denominated 'Station,' because it was at the second Church that the procession stopped to hear Mass and listen to a sermon. It was on occasion of these stations that Pope S. Gregory the Great preached the greater number of his Homilies to the Roman people.

[2] In the Sacramentary of S. Gregory there are two prayers for the Feast of the Purification : the first is entitled, The Collect at S. Adrian's—the church at which the Clergy and people met, before proceeding to S. Mary Major's, where the second was recited as the Collect in the Mass of the Festival.

Collect furnishes another warrant for the propriety of such a designation. Before the Celebrant began the prayer itself, he exhorted, as he does now, the people to offer their petitions to Heaven by saying: 'Let us pray.' The Deacon then proclaimed aloud: 'Let us kneel down;' and after a pause, which was employed by all present in silent supplication, that minister a second time cried out: 'Stand up again.' The Priest then, rising from his knees, prayed aloud.[1] Though not the name, the form, however, of prayer which we have in the Collect may be traced up to Apostolic origin. Many of the occasional Collects now in use are proved, by referring to the Sacramentaries of Popes Gelasius and Gregory, to have been composed more than thirteen hundred years ago.

It may in conclusion be observed, that as it is the official duty of the Priest to stand between the Altar of God and the people, to collect the vows and the petitions of those around him, and offer them up all together to the throne of grace and mercy, hence the formula employed for such a purport has been very properly, from this

---

[1] An illustrious Father of the Greek Church, S. Basil, who died in the year 379, refers, in his book on the Holy Ghost, c. xxvii, to this ceremony, which is still observed throughout the Latin Church at the Quatuor Tempora or Ember days, on Good Friday and on Holy Saturday; with this only difference, that at High Mass the Sub-deacon, and at Low Mass the Acolyte, without allowing any time to transpire in silence, says : "Stand up again."

circumstance alone, denominated Collect,—from the collection which the pastor makes of the prayers of his flock, and from his afterwards compressing in one common summary the requests of each single individual.

(28)

By making a reverence before the Crucifix, by bowing his head as he pronounces the holy name of Jesus, and by kissing the text of the Gospel, the Priest intends to honour and worship, not an image, nor a book, nor a sound, but Jesus Christ Himself in Heaven, who is represented and called to his remembrance by these several sensible signs and figures. To these symbols of Jesus the Priest exhibits no more honour than the Jewish priesthood, by an express command of God, manifested to the Ark of the Testament, and to the Temple. Catholics neither worship nor pray to, nor repose any trust in images, as the heathens did in their idols; nor do they believe any power or virtue to reside in them. They are expressly taught by the Church, 'that images have neither life nor sense to help them.'[1]

(29)

Such an admonition is addressed by the Priest to his congregation for the purpose of warning

---

[1] *Concilium Tridentinum*, Sessio XXV.

them that his prayers are for the common benefit ; and of assuring them that it will be in vain for him to lift up his hands towards Heaven in their behalf unless they also elevate their hearts at the same moment.

(30)

The Acolyte in the name of the people answers 'Amen' at the end of the Collect, Secret and Post-Communion, and thus ratifies what the Priest has been saying, according to the custom of the Jews and primitive Christians. Amen is a Hebrew word, employed to confirm what has been announced, and, according to the tenor of the discourse to which it is appended, signifies either 'That is true,' or 'May it be so,' or 'I agree to that.' It is, in reality, a form of speech indicative of an assertion, a desire, or a consent. 1. When the *Amen* is uttered after a declaration of the truths of Faith, such as, for instance, the Creed, it is a simple assertion, and signifies 'That is true.' 2. When it follows a prayer for some blessing or spiritual good, such as the conversion of nations, health of soul and body, or rest to the spirits of departed brethren, the *Amen* expresses a wish. 3. After a prayer pledging us to the performance of anything, the *Amen* declares our determination to comply with the engagement.

(31)

The Jews commenced the public service of their Sabbath by reading Moses and the Prophets :[1] the first Christians followed their example, and during Divine worship on the Sunday read passages from the Old or New Testament.[2] But as these extracts were more generally made from the letters of S. Paul, the Doctor of the Gentiles, this scriptural lecture received the appellation of the Epistle.[3] The Epistle of each Sunday is taken from the letters of S. Paul, or of the other Apostles, and not without a spiritual meaning; for in causing the writings of God's envoys to be recited previous to the reading of the Gospel, the Church appears to imitate the example of Jesus Christ, who deputed some among His disciples to go before Him into those quarters which He was about to honour with a visit.[4] It is thought that the present distribution of Epistles and Gospels of the Sundays throughout the year was arranged by S. Hierome at the desire of Pope Damasus about the year 376.

---

[1] *Acts,* XIII, 15.

[2] TERTULLIANI *Apologeticus,* cap. 39. In the Ambrosian and Mozarabic Missals, two lessons—one from the Old, the other from the New Testament—are appointed to be read before the Gospel.

[3] RABANUS MAURUS *de Sacris Ordinibus,* cap. 19. He died in 856.

[4] See the Treatise, *De Divinis Officiis,* written in the eleventh century, cap. 40, § 11, in MIGNE, *Patrologiae Cursus,* tom. CI, col. 1250.

Portions of the sacred writings are read during the recital of all the other offices of the Church. At Vespers, for instance, is said the Little Chapter, which is a short lesson, containing a few sentences selected from some portion of the Old or New Testament. It is mentioned as early as the sixth century, by the Council of Agde, in Gaul, celebrated in the year 506. The Venerable Bede says, 'that in imitation of the children of Israel, who, in the time of Ezra, used to read four times during the day out of the Volume of the Law, a practice was introduced into the Church of reciting a lesson from the Sacred Scriptures, after each portion of the daily psalmody, known at present under the appellation of the Canonical Hours.' [1]

(32)

After the Epistle, in order to unite prayer with instruction, part of one of the Psalms is recited; this is called the Responsory, because it answers to the Epistle, or more commonly the GRADUAL, from the custom which anciently prevailed of chanting it whilst the Deacon ascended the steps (in Latin, *gradus*) of the Ambo,[2] in

---

[1] BEDAE *Allegorica Expositio in Esdram*, lib. III, cap. 28.

[2] These Ambones are still to be seen in some of the oldest churches at Rome, such as S. Clement's, S. Laurence's, and several others. In the church at Aachen the Epistle and Gospel are still sung in an Ambo on the south side of the choir. The custom of singing them in the Roodloft—which is nothing else but a double Ambo—is still kept up in some churches on the Continent.

which the Gospel used to be recited.[1] The versicles composing the Gradual were chanted alternately and by many voices, which responded one to another. The Gradual is always used at Mass except in Paschal time from Low Sunday to the Octave of Pentecost.

(33)

After the Responsory or Gradual is sung the ALLELUIA, which consists of a verse of a Psalm preceded by two Alleluias and followed by a third, to which, from Low Sunday to the Octave of Pentecost, is added a second verse of a Psalm and a fourth Alleluia. ALLELUIA is a Hebrew term which signifies 'Praise the Lord;' but as it expresses a transport of joy which cannot be adequately rendered by any term in Greek or Latin, it has been retained in its original form. Tobias, wishing to signify the joy which is to distinguish the flourishing periods of the Church of Christ, or of the New Jerusalem, proclaims that 'Alleluia shall be sung in all its streets;'[2] and S. John assures us that the inhabitants of heaven hymn their praises in Alleluias.[3]

In very early times the Alleluia was followed by a long series of jubilant notes sung to its last vowel without any words. This series of

---

[1] RABANUS MAURUS *de Sacris Ordinibus*, cap. 19.
[2] *Tobias*, XIII, 22. [3] *Apocalypse*, XIX, 1-6.

notes was called the Sequence, but owing to the
difficulty of remembering these vocalisations, experienced by even the most skilful cantors, a
custom arose in the North of Gaul of setting
words to these notes. About the year 860 a
monk of the Abbey of Jumièges, which had been
laid waste by the Normans, sought refuge at the
Monastery of S. Gall in the diocese of Constance. He brought with him the Antiphoner of
his monastery, which contained several of these
Sequences with words set to them. This volume
was a source of inspiration to a young monk
of S. Gall named Notker,[1] who at once set to
work to imitate and improve on them. Notker's
work found favour, and his compositions were
introduced into the use of most Churches and
Orders, and were called 'Prosae ad sequentia,'
and later on 'Prosae.' Of the many Proses composed during the Middle Ages four only were
retained in the Pian Missal. The first of these
is the 'Victimae Paschali,' sung at Easter, the
author of which was Wipo, chaplain of the
Emperors Conrad II. and Henry III. (d. 1050);
the second is the 'Veni, Sancte Spiritus,' for
Pentecost, which, according to Duranti,[2] is the
production of Robert, king of the Franks (d.
1031); the third is the 'Lauda Sion,' for the

---

[1] The B. Notker died abbot of the monastery in 912.
[2] *Rationale*, lib. IV, cap. 22.

feast of Corpus Christi, composed by S. Thomas of Aquin (d. 1274); the fourth is the 'Dies irae,' ascribed by some to Cardinal Latino Malabranca, a Dominican friar who died in 1294, but with better reason to Thomas of Celano, a Franciscan who lived in the middle of the thirteenth century. The 'Stabat mater dolorosa,' attributed by some to Pope Innocent III. (d. 1216), is more probably by the Franciscan Jacopone da Todi (d. 1306). It was restored to the Roman Missal by Benedict XIII. in 1727.

(34)

In all Masses from Septuagesima till Holy Saturday, on week-days in Advent, and on all vigils[1] observed as fasts, the ALLELUIA is omitted, and replaced by a portion of a Psalm called the Tract, from being sung by the Cantor alone *tractim*, that is, without break or interruption of other voices.

(35)

S. Jerome, in his able answer to Vigilantius, written about the year 406, thus refers to this ceremony : 'Throughout all the churches of the East, whenever the Gospel is recited, they bring forth lights, though it be at noonday; not certainly to drive away the darkness, but to

---

[1] Except on Holy Saturday and Whitsun-eve ; the reason being that these Masses were originally celebrated in the night, as may be gathered from the Collects and Preface.

manifest some sign of joy.'[1] Those attendants who answer and wait on the Priest, and at High Mass carry the lights, are thus noticed by S. Isidore, Bishop of Seville from 599 to 636:— 'Those who in the Greek tongue are denominated Acolytes, are, in Latin, called Taper-bearers, from their carrying wax-candles at the reading of the Gospel, or the offering of the Sacrifice. Then tapers are lighted and borne by them.'[2]

(36)

Amongst the nations of antiquity, an offering of perfumes was regarded as a token of the most profound respect and homage. Moses received particular instructions from God to erect an Altar of Incense in the Tabernacle. The early Christians imitated the example of the Jews, and used incense at the celebration of their Liturgy. The ceremony of burning incense at this part of the Holy Sacrifice should figure to us, that as a grateful perfume exhales from the glowing thurible, so a sweet odour is diffused throughout the soul by the Gospel of Jesus Christ, whose bosom glowed with love for man.

(37)

By standing up during the Gospel, we express our readiness to answer the call of the inspired volume, and to obey the precepts which it delivers to us.

---

[1] S. HIERONYMI *contra Vigilantium liber.*
[2] S. ISIDORI *de Ecclesiasticis Officiis* lib. II, cap. XIV.

(38)

This is the remnant of a very ancient ceremony practised in the Greek [1] and Latin Churches. At the General Councils, a copy of the sacred volume was placed upon an elevated and richly ornamented throne.[2] At other times, the holy book was laid on the Altar, as may be perceived in a mosaic executed about the year 451,[3] which still ornaments the cupola of S. John's Church at Ravenna. In his Annotations on the Greek Liturgies, Goar has the following note on this ceremony of depositing the volume of the Gospels on the middle part of the Altar, as on a royal throne : ' Evangelium altaris medio perpetuo accumbens, Christum Regem throno Suo insidentem manifestat : et Sacerdos primo ad altare appulsu, in Evangelio Christum veneratur : Diacono humilitatis et status sui conscio, thronum illum regium adorare contento.' [4]

(39)

It is thus that the Priest signifies that the Gospel he is about to read is the book of Jesus

---

[1] See the Liturgies which bear the names of S. James, of S. Basil, and of S. John Chrysostom. Precisely the same ceremonies as we observe immediately before and at the chanting of the Gospel are also prescribed by the Greek Church.

[2] CYRILLI *Apolog. ad Theodosium.*

[3] CIAMPINI *Vetera Monimenta*, tom. I, p. 236, tab. LXX.

[4] GOAR, Εὐχολόγιον, *sive Rituale Graecorum*, p. 122.

crucified; and by this action he imitates the piety of the early Christians, who never commenced any work without first making the sign of the Cross.

(40)

The Priest and people here, and at the last Gospel, sign, first, their foreheads with this emblem of Christianity, to manifest, as S. Augustine observes, that, so far from blushing at the Cross, they not only do not conceal this instrument of redemption in any secret place, but bear it on their foreheads,[1] and with S. Paul, glory in it;[2]—then, their mouths: 'For with the heart we believe unto justice; but with the mouth confession is made unto salvation;'[3]—and lastly, their bosoms, by way of admonition that the precepts of Christ should be imprinted in indelible characters on the heart of every true believer in the Cross.

(41)

This is done both out of reverence for the Word of God, and to signify that everything which emanates from such a hallowed source is sweet and venerable.

---

[1] Usque adeo de Cruce non erubesco, ut non in occulto loco habeam Crucem Christi, sed in fronte portem. S. AUGUSTINI *in Psalmum* CXLI *Enarratio,* v. 4.

[2] *Galatians,* VI, 14.   [3] *Romans,* X, 10.

(42)

This is in accordance with what we read of 'the great multitude of people who came to hear Jesus, and to be healed of their diseases.'[1]

(43)

Such a ceremony testifies our reverence, and expresses our joy in the Gospel, and affection towards Jesus, inspired by His divine words.

(44)

This tribute of respect is offered to the Priest, because he is the principal sacrificing minister who should 'manifest the odour of his knowledge in every place,' according to the language of S. Paul.[2]

(45)

The Creed is said every Sunday during the year, and on all those feasts the objects of which are in a manner comprehended in it; such as the different festivals instituted in honour of Christ, and of His Mother the Blessed Virgin Mary; of the Apostles and Doctors of the Church, by whose arduous labours and writings the doctrine included in this symbol of Christianity has been disseminated through the world. It is not known

---

[1] *S. Luke,* VI, 18.   [2] *2 Corinthians,* II, 14.

when the recitation of the Creed was first introduced into the Latin Mass, though certainly not later than the ninth century. The practice of singing it appears to have sprung up in the tenth.

There is a liturgical peculiarity which must be interesting to the reader. The custom of saying the 'Our Father' and the 'Creed' in silence at Compline, and at the other portions of the divine service, excepting at Mass when they are recited aloud, appears to be a remnant of that ancient law, denominated the 'Discipline of the Secret,' which was most religiously observed by the faithful throughout the world during the first five ages of the Church, and in countries where there was a mixed population of heathens and Christians, until the twelfth century.[1] According to this apostolical institution, neither the Lord's Prayer nor the Creed[2] was permitted to be recited aloud at those parts of the public service at which it was possible for any unbeliever or uninitiated person to be present.[3] It was only after the Catechumens had been diligently instructed, and were about to receive baptism, that they were

---

[1] EMANUELIS A SCHELSTRATE *Dissertatio de Disciplina Arcani*, Romae, 1685, c. VI.

[2] BENEDICTI XIV. *de Sacrificio Missae* lib. II, cap. XIX, § 4.

[3] Writing to his sister Marcellina in 385, S. Ambrose observes: 'Post lectiones atque tractatum, dimissis Catechumenis, Symbolum aliquibus competentibus in baptisteriis tradebam basilicae.' *Epist.* XX, *Marcellinae sorori.*

taught these prayers.   Hence may be readily perceived the original reason why the Lord's Prayer is recited, at Mass, in an elevated tone of voice, and at Vespers, and the Canonical Hours,[1] in perfect silence.   The presence of the unbeliever, the Jew, and the Catechumen was willingly tolerated during the recital of various parts of the public service, and of the commencement of the Liturgy or Mass.   But it was one of the official duties of the Deacon to see that all such persons had withdrawn from the assembly before the Creed was recited.[2]

(46)

Whenever we address ourselves to the Divinity, we ought to elevate our hearts towards Heaven. The exterior lifting up of the hands is a figure of the interior elevation of the mind towards God.

(47)

This inclination of the head is to exhibit our profound respect for the ineffable perfections of the Deity.

---

[1] That the Benedictines have always recited the Lord's Prayer at Lauds and Vespers aloud is simply owing to the fact that none but monks and inmates of the monastery were present at their offices.

[2] A canon of the Fourth Council of Carthage enacts that the Bishop shall not forbid anyone, whether he be heathen, heretic, or Jew, from coming into the church, and staying there to hear the Word of God until the dismissal of the Catechumens. 'Ut episcopus nullum prohibeat ingredi ecclesiam et audire verbum Dei, sive gentilem, sive haereticum, sive Iudaeum, usque ad Missam Catechumenorum.'

(48)

At these words, all kneel down to venerate the mystery of the Incarnation, and to adore God made man: 'Who, being in the form of God, thought it not robbery to be equal with God; but debased Himself, taking the form of a servant, being made in the likeness of a man, for which cause God also hath exalted Him, and hath given Him a name which is above all names: that in the name of Jesus every knee should bow, of those that are in heaven, on earth, and under the earth.'[1]

(49)

By making the sign of the Cross we express that our hopes of a joyful resurrection, and of the happiness of eternal life, are founded solely on the merits of Jesus crucified.

(50)

As long as the Discipline of the Secret[2] was enforced, the Catechumens were dismissed from the Assembly immediately after the recitation of the Creed. Not only were the Catechumens or persons who had not been purified by the re-generating waters of Baptism excluded from the

---

[1] *Philippians*, II, 6–10.
[2] See above, Nº 45, and Part 2, ch. I, Nº xxiii, p. 222.

Sacrifice of the Mass, but also the public penitents, or Christians who had defiled the robe of
baptismal innocence by the blacker stains of sin,
and were, in consequence, considered, in those
times of primitive fervour, unworthy to remain and
attend at the Eucharistic Sacrifice. When they
had left the church, what was called the Mass
of the Faithful commenced with the salutation,
'Dominus vobiscum.' The faithful must assist at
this portion of the Mass on all Sundays and days
of obligation under pain of mortal sin.

(51)

The Offertory is an Antiphon which the Priest
recites prior to the Oblation, and which is
chanted by the choir immediately after the
'Dominus vobiscum.' It owes its name to a
practice which was anciently observed in the
Church by the faithful, who, at this part of the
Mass, presented their offerings of bread and wine
to be consecrated at the Holy Sacrifice, a practice
which began to fall into disuse in the eleventh
century, but was still kept up in some churches
on the greater festivals until the end of the last
century. The choir, in singing this Antiphon
whilst the Priest is offering the bread and wine,
imitates the chant of the Jewish sanctuary at the
celebration of the Aaronic sacrifice: 'For when
the High Priest stretched forth his hand to make

a libation, and offered of the blood of the grape, he poured out at the foot of the Altar a divine odour to the most high Prince. Then the sons of Aaron shouted, they sounded with beaten trumpets, and made a great noise, to be heard for a remembrance before God. Then all the people together made haste and fell down to the earth upon their faces, to adore the Lord their God, and to pray to the Almighty the Most High. And the singers lifted up their voices, and in the great house the sound of sweet melody was increased.'[1]

It should be remembered that, although all the ancient Liturgies contain an oblation of the gifts before consecration, the five prayers with which this oblation is now made are of comparatively recent date. Hence the variety in the various diocesan uses which since the sixteenth century have gradually fallen out of use and been replaced by the Pian Missal.

(52)

The matter, as it is called, of the Sacrifice is composed of wheaten bread and wine of the grape. The Latin Church, in imitation of our Divine Redeemer,[2] employs unleavened bread in the celebration of the Blessed Eucharist; a

---

[1] *Ecclesiasticus*, L., 16–20.
[2] *S. Matthew*, XXVI, 17 ; *S. Mark*, XIV, 12 ; and *S. Luke*, XXII, 7.

practice which is mentioned by our countryman Alcuin, in a letter written in the year 798.[1]

(53)

The Corporal is a square piece of fine linen on which the Host is consecrated. It is so called because it touches the Body[2] of our Lord. It has been known by such an appellation for more than ten centuries.[3] In the Ambrosian rite, the Corporal is likened to the linen cloths in which the Body of our Saviour was shrouded in the sepulchre, and on unfolding it at the Offertory, the Priest recites what is termed the 'Oratio super sindonem.' Anciently the Chalice also was covered by the Corporal, a practice still retained by the Carthusians. The Greeks make use of a similar square piece of linen cloth, which they spread out as we do.[4] In their Liturgies it is called εἰλητόν, a word which implies precisely the same meaning as our Corporal.[5] In explaining what is to be understood by the εἰλητόν, or Corporal,

---

[1] Panis, qui in corpus Christi consecratur, absque fermento ullius alterius infectionis, debet esse mundissimus. *Epist. xc, Ad Fratres Lugdunenses.*

[2] In Latin *Corpus.*

[3] 'Sindon quam solemus Corporale nominare.' AMALARII, presb. Metensis, *De Ecclesiasticis Officiis* lib. III, cap. 19.

[4] GOAR, Εὐχολόγιον, pp. 70, 162. It should not escape the learned reader's notice, that, in the Greek Liturgies, the word by which the Priest is designated is ἱερεύς, an appellation which the classic writers anciently employed to signify, not merely a minister of religion, but more especially a sacrificing priest.

[5] *Ibid.*, p. 70.

Germanus, Patriarch of Constantinople (1222), says: 'It signifies the linen cloth in which was wrapped the Body of Christ when it was taken down from the Cross, and deposited in the monument.'[1] At a much earlier period Pope S. Silvester (314–336) attached the same meaning to the Corporal when he decreed that the Sacrifice of the Altar should be consecrated not on silk nor on dyed cloth, but only on pure linen.[2] An eminent saint of the Greek Church, S. Isidore (c. 412), who spent the greater part of his life at Pelusium on the Nile, and was at first the disciple, afterwards the bosom friend and strenuous vindicator of S. John Chrysostom, observes, in one of his epistles, when speaking of the Corporal: 'That this piece of linen cloth which is spread under the divine gifts, serves the same purpose as the one employed by Joseph of Arimathea. For as that holy man enveloped with a winding-sheet, and deposited in the sepulchre, the Body of the Lord, through which the universal race of mortals participated in the resurrection: in the same manner we, who consecrate bread of pro-

---

[1] Τὸ εἰλητὸν σημαίνει τὴν σινδόνα, ἐν ᾖ ἐνειλήθη τὸ σῶμα τοῦ Χριστοῦ, ἐκ τοῦ σταυροῦ καταβὰν καὶ ἐν μνήματι τεθέν. *Theoria mystica*, apud GALLANDIUM, *Bibl. vet. patr.*, tom. XIII, p. 209. The Theory is an exposition of the symbolism of the Greek Liturgy.

[2] 'Hic constituit ut Sacrificium altaris non in serico neque in panno tincto celebraretur, nisi tantum in linteo ex terreno lino procreato, sicut Corpus Domini nostri Iesu Christi in sindone lintea munda sepultum est, sic Missa celebraretur.' ANASTASII Bibliothecarii *Hist. de vitis Rom. Pont.*

position on the linen cloth (or Corporal), without doubt find the Body of Christ.'[1] This spiritual signification, which has been attributed from all antiquity to the piece of linen called the Corporal, as well as the very term itself, by which it is denominated in the Greek and Latin Churches, though an indirect, is a very convincing argument in demonstration of the belief of the real and corporeal presence of Jesus Christ in the Blessed Sacrament, which has been professed at every age, and by every nation of the Christian world.

The Corporal must be blessed by a bishop, or a priest having special faculties.

(54)

A circular plate of silver gilt, or gold, used from the earliest times to receive the Host consecrated at Mass. It is consecrated with chrism by the Bishop.

(55)

From the Latin *Hostia*, Victim.

(56)

Though merely bread, still, by anticipation, it is called an unspotted Host or Victim, as it is

---

[1] 'Pura illa sindon, quae sub divinorum donorum ministerio expansa est, Iosephi Arimathensis est ministerium. Ut enim ille Domini Corpus sindone involutum sepulturae mandavit, per quod universum mortalium genus resurrectionem percepit : eodem modo nos propositionis panem in sindone sanctificantes, Christi Corpus sine dubitatione reperimus.' Lib. I, *Epist.* 123.

about to be converted by Almighty God during the consecration into the Body of Jesus Christ the one—the only Victim without stain or imperfection.

(57)

The Sacrifice of the Mass is never offered to any Saint, but to God only.

(58)

'In many things we all offend.'[1]

(59)

'First for his own sins, and then for the people's.'[2]

(60)

Hence it is evident that prayer is made, at every Mass, for all the faithful departed, as well as for the particular individual whom the Priest may especially commemorate afterwards, and in suffrage of whose soul he is offering up the holy Sacrifice to God.

(61)

A small quantity of water is mixed with the wine, according to a tradition of the Church which teaches us that water was mingled with the wine in the eucharistic cup by our Divine Redeemer. Indeed the Paschal wine which He used at the institution of the Holy Eucharist was always so

---

[1] S. James, III, 2.   [2] Hebrews, VII, 27.

mixed. That such was the general practice of the ancient Church is evident from S. Justin (d. 168),[1] S. Irenaeus (d. 202),[2] S. Gregory Nyssen (d. 394),[3] and numerous other early writers. This practice has been maintained not only in every rite according to which Mass is celebrated throughout the Catholic Church, but, with the solitary exception of the Armenian Monophysites, by every heretical sect that has preserved the priesthood.

(62)

This Prayer is modelled upon the words of the Prophet Daniel, ch. III, 39, 40.

(63)

On this, as on most other occasions, the Priest lifts up his eyes in imitation of Christ, who thus invoked the omnipotent power of His Heavenly Father.

(64)

This act naturally expresses of itself a supplication of the Most High.

(65)

The sign of the Cross is so frequently made during the celebration of Mass, and in blessing anything dedicated to the service of Almighty

---

[1] *Apologia*, I, § 65, written about the year 150.
[2] *Contra haereses*, lib. v, cap. II, § 3.
[3] *Oratio catechetica*, cap. XXXVII.

God, to indicate that all our hopes for the blessings prayed for are founded solely on the merits of Christ's passion, which He endured on the Cross.

(66)

In all the Greek Liturgies the oblations are here incensed.[1]

(67)

Who standeth, etc. 'There appeared unto him (Zachary) an Angel of the Lord standing on the right side of the altar of incense. And the Angel said to him: Fear not, Zachary; for thy prayer is heard.'[2] S. John, in his book of the Apocalypse, mentions that 'another Angel came and stood before the altar which is before the throne of God.'[3] No wonder that the Church, with these texts of Scripture before her eyes, implores the intercession of the Angels at this part of her Liturgy.

(68)

Dirigatur, etc. This Prayer, recited by the Priest while incensing the Altar, is composed of the second, third, and fourth verses of Psalm CXL.

(69)

These several incensings are, in the first instance, intended as so many tokens of respect for

---

[1] See the Liturgy of S. Chrysostom in GOAR, Εὐχολόγιον, p. 73.
[2] S. Luke, I, 11, 13.   [3] Apocalypse, VIII, 3.

those objects towards which they are employed ; but, in the second, there may be derived from them much public instruction. The incense which is burnt in honour of the Deity, is a symbol of what our prayers should be, and of the oblation which we ought to make of ourselves to Heaven. The incense with which the bread and wine are perfumed, is meant to indicate that the assistants unite their vows and prayers with those of the Celebrant who offers this oblation. The Priest encircles the Altar with the fuming thurible, to signify that, as the Altar is the throne of Jesus Christ, an odour of sweetness is diffused around it. The ministers of the sanctuary are incensed : first, to admonish them to raise their hearts, and to make their prayers ascend like grateful incense in the sight of God ; and, secondly, to put them in mind that they are those members of the Church who should continually strive to be able to say with truth : ' We are the good odour of Christ unto God in them that are saved ; '[1] and of whom it may be truly observed by men : ' God always manifesteth the odour of His knowledge by them in every place.'[2]

(70)

In all the cathedrals and old churches erected when England was Catholic, may be still observed,

---

[1] 2 *Corinthians*, II, 15.　　[2] *Ibid.*, II, 14.

on the Epistle, or south side of the Altar, or
rather, of the spot where the Altar once stood in
the chancel, as well as in the side-chapels, a small
niche in the wall, with a shallow basin of stone,
with a hole at the bottom, through which was
poured the water used at the washing of the
Priest's fingers.   It is indifferently called Piscina,
or Lavacrum.

(71)

S. Cyril of Jerusalem, who flourished towards
the middle of the fourth century, assigns to this
ablution a spiritual meaning.   This holy catechist
observes: 'You have seen the deacon give to
the sacrificing priest, and to the presbyters standing round God's altar, water to wash. He gave
it, not at all because of bodily defilement; by no
means.   For we do not enter into the church with
defiled bodies.   But that washing of hands is a
symbol that you ought to be pure from every sin
and prevarication.   For since the hands are a
symbol of action, by washing them we represent
the purity and blamelessness of our conduct.'[1]
The Apostolic Constitutions,[2] and the author of

---

[1] Ἑωράκατε τοίνυν τὸν διάκονον τὸν νίψασθαι διδόντα τῷ ἱερεῖ καὶ τοῖς
κυκλοῦσι τὸ θυσιαστήριον τοῦ Θεοῦ πρεσβυτέροις. οὐ πάντως δὲ ἐδίδου διὰ
τὸν σωματικὸν ῥύπον. οὐκ ἔστι τοῦτο. οὐδὲ γὰρ ῥύπον σώματος ἔχοντες τὴν
ἀρχὴν εἰσῄειμεν εἰς τὴν ἐκκλησίαν. ἀλλὰ σύμβολόν ἐστι τοῦ δεῖν ὑμᾶς
καθαρεύειν πάντων ἁμαρτημάτων καὶ ἀνομημάτων τὸ νίψασθαι. ἐπειδὴ γὰρ
αἱ χεῖρες σύμβολον πράξεως, νίψασθαι ταύτας τὸ καθαρὸν δηλονότι καὶ ἄμωμον
τῶν πράξεων αἰνιττόμεθα. S. CYRILLI Catech. Myst., V, 2.

[2] Εἷς δὲ ὑποδιάκονος διδότω ἀπόνιψιν χειρῶν τοῖς ἱερεῦσι, σύμβολον καθαρότητος

the Ecclesiastical Hierarchy,[1] a work which bears upon it the name of S. Dionysius the Areopagite, but is thought by many to have been written in the fourth or fifth century, affix a similar mystic signification to this ceremony.

In the Ambrosian rite the Priest washed his hands in silence, but the Psalm now recited accompanied the washing in the liturgies of S. Chrysostom and S. Basil. In the various uses of Latin Christendom there is great variety, as indeed in all the prayers between the Offertory and the Secret. According to Sarum use, the washing was accompanied by a prayer, preceded both in the Hereford and York use by the *Veni Creator*, and, in the last, by the sixth verse of Psalm xxv.

(72)

As this is a hymn of joy, as was before re-marked, it is properly omitted in the service for the Dead; and at a time when the pains and sufferings of Christ are commemorated.

(73)

The Sacrifice of the Mass cannot be offered to any being except the Deity alone; it would be impious and blasphemous to offer up Mass to any

ψυχῶν Θεῷ ἀνακειμένων. *Constitutiones Apost.*, lib. VIII, c. 11, *apud* LABBEUM, *Concil. Gen.*, tom. I, col. 552.

[1] Cap. III, § 10.

Saint or Martyr, however illustrious for virtue. What S. Augustine asserted more than 1400 years ago on this same subject, we reiterate at this moment: 'What priest, at the tombs of the Saints assisting at the Altar, ever said, We offer to thee, Peter, or Paul, or Cyprian? but what is offered is offered to God who crowned the Martyrs, at the sepulchres of those whom He crowned.'[1]

(74)

By the devotion which we here manifest towards the Saints, we exhibit our reverence towards Jesus Christ, and His Eternal Father, and the Holy Ghost; for it is purely through the merits of our Redeemer, and by the grace afforded by God, that the Saints are what they are, the favourites of Heaven, and brethren of Jesus Christ. We do not honour them for anything they possess of themselves, but we honour in them God's gracious gifts, which wrought their holiness, and formed the sacred spring of all their virtue. We therefore make them one of the mediums through which we convey our homage to the Almighty.

(75)

This prayer calls to our remembrance an expression of apostolical antiquity. Such was the

---

[1] S. Augustini *contra Faustum*, lib. xx, cap. 21. See also *De Civitate Dei*, lib. viii, cap. 27.

appellative with which S. Peter addressed the people at Jerusalem;[1] and it is a favourite expression of S. Paul.

(76)

So called, because these prayers are recited by the Priest in an under voice, audible to himself, but not heard by the surrounding congregation.

(77)

These words form the conclusion of the SECRET. The Priest elevates his voice when reciting them at Low Mass, in order to fix the attention of the people, and to invite them to unite their prayers with his. At High Mass he chants them.

(78)

Here the Priest elevates his hands, to impress upon the people, by this outward sign, the exhortation which he then delivers for the interior elevation of the heart to God.

(79)

Whilst pronouncing these words, he joins his hands and bows his head, to express as significantly as possible, by this corporal homage, that it is the worship of the spirit which God insists upon.

---

[1] *Acts,* II, 29.

(80)

It is called the Preface, from its being the introduction to the Canon of the Mass. It is an invitation to elevate our hearts to God, and to offer Him our thanksgivings for the stupendous work which He is about to accomplish through the ministry of His priest, by the words of consecration. In this instance, the Church proposes to imitate her founder, Jesus Christ, who returned thanks to His Eternal Father before He called Lazarus back to life from the tomb in which he had been four days buried; and when He multiplied the loaves,[1] and converted bread and wine into His own Body and Blood.[2]

That the form of prayer called the Preface is very ancient is certain; that it owes its introduction into the Liturgy to the Apostles is more than probable. This may be gathered from a variety of sources. S. Cyprian (A.D. 252), in his book on the Lord's Prayer, particularises the antecedent Preface by which the Priest prepared the minds of the brethren for the more solemn portions of the Mass.[3] It is also noticed in the Liturgy of the Mass contained in the Apostolical Constitu-

---

[1] *S. John*, VI, 11.   [2] 1 *Corinthians*, XI, 24.

[3] Ideo et Sacerdos, ante Orationem Praefatione praemissa, parat fratrum mentes, dicendo: 'Sursum corda;' ut, dum respondet plebs: 'Habemus ad Dominum;' admoneatur, nihil aliud se, quam Dominum cogitare debere. Cap. XXXI.

tions, where we find it thus described: 'Then the High Priest standing at the Altar with the presbyters makes a private prayer by himself, having on his white or bright vestment, and signing himself with the sign of the Cross on his forehead. Having done this, he says: 'The grace of Almighty God, and the love of our Lord Jesus Christ, and the fellowship of the Holy Ghost, be with you all.' And the people answer with one voice: 'And with thy spirit!' Then the High Priest says: 'Lift up your hearts;' and they all answer: 'We lift them up to the Lord.' The High Priest says again: 'Let us give thanks to the Lord;' and the people answer: 'It is meet and right so to do.' Then the High Priest says: 'It is very meet and right above all things to praise Thee, the true God,' etc.[1]

The frequent allusions which S. Augustine makes to the Preface will recur to everyone who is at all familiar with his writings.

The Greek Church has but one Preface in its

---

[1] Εὐξάμενος οὖν καθ' ἑαυτὸν ὁ ἀρχιερεὺς ἅμα τοῖς ἱερεῦσι. καὶ λαμπρὰν ἐσθῆτα μετενδὺς καὶ στὰς πρὸς τῷ θυσιαστηρίῳ, τὸ τρόπαιον τοῦ σταυροῦ κατὰ τοῦ μετώπου τῇ χειρὶ ποιησάμενος (εἰς πάντας) εἰπάτω 'Ἡ χάρις τοῦ παντοκράτορος Θεοῦ καὶ ἡ ἀγάπη τοῦ Κυρίου ἡμῶν Ἰησοῦ Χριστοῦ καὶ ἡ κοινωνία τοῦ Ἁγίου Πνεύματος ἔστω μετὰ πάντων ὑμῶν' καὶ πάντες συμφώνως λεγέτωσαν ὅτι 'καὶ μετὰ τοῦ πνεύματός σου.' Καὶ ὁ ἀρχιερεὺς ''Ανω τὸν νοῦν' καὶ πάντες ''Εχομεν πρὸς τὸν Κύριον.' Καὶ ὁ ἀρχιερεὺς 'Εὐχαριστήσωμέν τῷ Κυρίῳ' καὶ πάντες· ''Αξιον καὶ δίκαιον.' Καὶ ὁ ἀρχιερεὺς εἰπάτω ''Αξιον ὡς ἀληθῶς καὶ δίκαιον πρὸ πάντων ἀνυμνεῖν σε τὸν ὄντως ὄντα Θεόν.' Constitutiones Apost., lib. VIII, c. 12, apud LABBEUM, Concil. Gen., tom. I, col. 553.

Liturgy. In the Gallican, Mozarabic, and older Roman Liturgies there are proper Prefaces for nearly every festival. The purport of this variety was, that in each particular Preface might be designated some amongst the chief characteristics of that especial mystery for which thanks were rendered to God by the Church on that annual festival. In the Roman Church the number of Prefaces was about the end of the eleventh century reduced to ten, namely: the Common Preface, probably the most ancient one we have, since it may be found in the Sacramentary of Pope S. Gelasius (492); and those of Easter, the Ascension, Pentecost, Christmas, the Epiphany, the Apostles, the Holy Trinity, the Cross, and Lent.[1] The Preface recited on feasts of the Blessed Virgin Mary is attributed to Pope Urban II. (A.D. 1095); if it be not the composition of that pontiff, it at least received his approbation.

(81)

Everyone will immediately appreciate the expressive propriety of this part of the ceremonial,

---

[1] These are enumerated in a letter to the Bishops of Germany and Gaul falsely attributed to Pelagius II. (d. 590), quoted in the *Micrologus de ecclesiasticis observationibus*, a work written at the end of the eleventh century, after 1085. In the Missal of Leofric, the first Bishop of Exeter (d. 1072), this letter is cited, but the Prefaces enumerated are those of Christmas, Lent, Easter, Ascension, Pentecost, the Holy Trinity, the Holy Cross, the Apostles, and the dead.

at the same time that he recognises in the prayer
which accompanies these actions various passages
adopted from the Scriptures. The prophet Isaias,
in the description of his vision, says: 'The
Seraphim cried one to another and said: Holy,
Holy, Holy, the Lord God of Hosts, all the earth
is full of His glory;'[1] and S. John heard the
same jubilations hymned by the four living
creatures 'who rested not day and night saying:
Holy, Holy, Holy, Lord God Almighty.'[2]

This seraphic hymn, denominated, in the Latin
Church, the SANCTUS, is to be found in all the
Oriental Liturgies;[3] it is distinguished in most of
the Greek Liturgies by the appellation of *Epini-
cion*,[4] or hymn of triumph. In the Liturgy which
we have in the Apostolic Constitutions, it is particularly specified that all the congregation shall
unite in reciting it at the end of the Preface.
That prayer which is there given is beautiful,
and concludes thus: 'The innumerable armies
of angels adore Thee; the archangels, thrones,

---

[1] *Isaias*, VI, 3.					[2] *Apocalypse*, IV, 8.

[3] In his observations on the Syriac Liturgies, Renaudot remarks,
when speaking of the Preface: 'Terminatur Oratio (Praefatio) per
hymnum triumphalem, *Sanctus*. Talis est Praefationum omnium
Graecarum et Orientalium dispositio, absque ullo, praeterquam ex
verborum copia, discrimine, et quod omnes gratiarum actionem
continent, et in hymnum triumphalem desinunt, Latinis ea in parte
similes sunt.' RENAUDOT, *Liturgiarum Orientalium Collectio*, tom.
II, p. 78.

[4] See the Liturgies of SS. Chrysostom and Basil in GOAR, Εὐχολόγιον
(pp. 76, 166), where what we call the Sanctus is denominated the
Ἐπινίκιος ὕμνος.

dominions, principalities, dignities, powers, hosts, and ages; the cherubim and seraphim also with six wings, with two of which they cover their feet, and with two their faces, and with two fly, saying, with thousand thousands of archangels, and ten thousand times ten thousand angels, all crying out without rest and intermission: *and let all the people say together with them:* Holy, Holy, Holy, Lord of Hosts: heaven and earth are full of Thy glory: blessed art Thou for ever. Amen.'[1]

S. Cyril of Jerusalem takes particular notice also of this triumphal hymn in his explanation of the Liturgy. The Catechist observes: 'We also mention the seraphim whom Isaias by the Holy Ghost saw standing round about the throne of God, and with two of their wings veiling their faces, and with two their feet, and with two flying, and crying: Holy, Holy, Holy, Lord God of Hosts.'[2] The celebrated hymn called the Trisagion,[3] chanted in the Latin Church on Good Friday only, during the adoration of the Cross, is inserted in several of the Oriental

---

[1] Καὶ πᾶς ὁ λαὸς ἅμα εἰπάτω· Ἅγιος, ἅγιος. ἅγιος Κύριος Σαβαώθ, πλήρης ὁ οὐρανὸς καὶ ἡ γῆ τῆς δόξης αὐτοῦ· εὐλογητὸς εἰς τοὺς αἰῶνας· ἀμήν. *Constitutiones Apost.*, lib. VIII, c. 12, *apud* LABBEUM, *Concil. Gen.*, tom. I, col. 560.

[2] Μνημονεύομεν καὶ τῶν σεραφίμ, ἃ ἐν πνεύματι ἁγίῳ ἐθεάσατο Ἡσαΐας παρεστηκότα κύκλῳ τοῦ θρόνου τοῦ Θεοῦ, καὶ ταῖς μὲν δυσὶ πτέρυξι κατακαλύπτοντα τὸ πρόσωπον, ταῖς δὲ δυσὶ τοὺς πόδας, καὶ ταῖς δυσὶ πετόμενα· καὶ λέγοντα, ΑΓΙΟΣ, ΑΓΙΟΣ, ΑΓΙΟΣ, ΚΥΡΙΟΣ ΣΑΒΑΩΘ. *Catech. Myst.*, v, 6.

[3] Ἅγιος ὁ Θεος, ἅγιος ἰσχυρὸς, ἅγιος ἀθάνατος, ἐλέησον ἡμας.

Liturgies, and is frequently recited by the Greek and Oriental Christians in their public offices and private devotions.[1] This hymn was first introduced, as a public prayer, at Constantinople in the reign of Theodosius the younger, during the supplications offered up by the whole city to avert the horrors of an earthquake.[2]

(82)

The bell is rung as an admonition to the people that the Priest is about to enter upon the most awful portion of the Mass, namely, the Canon, or Invocation, which immediately precedes the Consecration; and for this reason, they are invited, by this ceremony, to redouble their attention, their reverence, and their fervour, from the moment that the 'Sanctus,' or seraphic hymn, commences. Instead of distracting, the ringing of the bell fixes the religious attention of the people; and if we may, without presumption, reason on the will of the all-wise Deity, it would seem that the observance of a similar practice was enjoined in the service of the Jewish Sanctuary for the like intent; since we read that the Lord thus commanded Moses: 'Thou shalt make the Tunic of the ephod all of violet . . . and beneath, at the feet of the same tunic, thou shalt

[1] RENAUDOT, *Liturg. Orient. Coll.*, tom. II, p. 169.
[2] S. IOANNES DAMASCENUS, *Expositio Fidei orthodoxae*, lib. III, cap. 10, *De hymno trisagio*.

make as it were pomegranates, of violet, and purple, and scarlet twice dyed, with little bells set between : so that there shall be a golden bell and a pomegranate, and again another golden bell and a pomegranate ; and Aaron shall be vested with it in the office of his ministry, that the sound may be heard when he goeth in and cometh out of the Sanctuary.'[1] The author of the book of Ecclesiasticus also notices, ' the ephod with many little bells of gold all round about, that as Aaron went in there might be a sound and a noise made, that might be heard in the temple, for a memorial to the children of the people.'[2]

(83)

Sabaoth is one of those Hebrew words which were left untranslated in the earliest Latin version of the Holy Scriptures, called the *Vetus Itala*, and has been preserved in three places in the translation by S. Jerome. Sabaoth is a plural, and signifies ' Armies.' As the Roman Missal has always followed the ancient Italic version, it has consequently preserved the word Sabaoth, instead of adopting the Vulgate translation of it, *exercituum*, that is, ' of armies.'

(84)

These words are borrowed from the Gospels of S. Matthew and S. Mark, who inform us that

---

[1] *Exodus*, XXVIII, 31-35.   [2] *Ecclesiasticus*, XLV, 10, 11.

our Divine Redeemer triumphantly entered into Jerusalem amid the acclamations of the people, who applied to him the words of the Psalmist,[1] and shouted 'Hosanna to the Son of David: Blessed is He that cometh in the name of the Lord: Hosanna in the highest.' [2]

(85)

Hosanna is another of those Hebrew expressions[3] which have been inserted, without translation, in the Liturgies of all the Churches. It is, in fact, two Hebrew words contracted by the Greeks into one; and signifies 'save now,' or 'save, we pray thee.' It was one of those favourite exclamations of joy in use amongst the Jews at the celebration of the feast of Tabernacles, when they went about with green boughs in their hands.[4]

(86)

The propriety of such gestures will be recognised when it is remembered that at the same time the Priest invokes the celestial Father in these words, 'Most merciful Father,' with which the Canon commences.

---

[1] *Psalm* CXVII, 26.   [2] *Matthew*, XXI, 9.
[3] Amen, Alleluia, and Sabaoth have already been enumerated as such.
[4] Hebrew and Talmudical Exercitations on S. Matthew, XXI, 8, in LIGHTFOOT, *Horae Hebraicae.*

(87)

The Priest exhibits this sign of reverence and affection towards the Altar, under the persuasion that in a few seconds it is to be made the throne on which will repose the Body and Blood of Jesus, verily and indeed present, but veiled under the appearances of bread and wine.

(88)

The Priest makes the sign of the Cross over the Host and Chalice as he repeats these words: 'Bless these gifts, these present, these unspotted sacrifices,' because we neither demand, nor do we hope to obtain, the benedictions of Heaven, except through the merits of Jesus, who paid our ransom on the Cross.

The frequent use of the sign of the Cross during the celebration of the Sacrifice of the Mass is attested by the most authentic testimonies. The Apostolic Constitutions remark how the Priest, standing at the Altar, signed himself with the trophy of the Cross.[1] S. Chrysostom informs us that the sign of the Cross was not only in perpetual use amongst Christians every hour, but more especially employed at the holy table, and in the ordination of priests; and that its splendour beamed forth with the

---

[1] See p. 119, n. 1.

Body of Christ at the mystic supper.'[1] With regard to its use in the Latin Church, S. Augustine asserts that it was united with every pious and religious office. 'What,' demands the Saint, 'is the Sign of Christ if not the Cross of Christ? which sign, unless it be applied either to the brows of the believers, or to the water out of which they are regenerated, or to the oil by which they are anointed with Chrism, or to the Sacrifice with which they are nourished, none of these rites is properly performed.'[2]

(89)

To this part of the Mass, beginning with 'Te igitur,' and finishing with the 'Pater Noster,' the whole of which is recited in an inaudible tone of voice by the Celebrant, has been affixed the term Canon; because, as the native meaning of this Greek word imports, this prayer has been laid down as the Rule, or Canon, which is to be rigidly followed by the Priest who offers up the Holy Sacrifice. The minutest variation from it can never be tolerated. The Canon of the Mass

---

[1] Οὗτος ἐν τῇ ἱερᾷ τραπέζῃ, οὗτος ἐν ταῖς τῶν ἱερέων χειροτονίαις, οὗτος πάλιν μετὰ τοῦ σώματος τοῦ Χριστοῦ ἐπὶ τὸ μυστικὸν δεῖπνον διαλάμπει. S. CHRYSOSTOMI Demonstratio quod Christus sit Deus, § 9.

[2] Quid est Signum Christi nisi Crux Christi? Quod signum nisi adhibeatur sive frontibus credentium, sive ipsi aquae ex qua regenerantur, sive oleo quo chrismate unguntur, sive sacrificio quo aluntur, nihil eorum rite perficitur. S. AUGUSTINI in Ioannis Evangelium tract. CXVIII.

according to the use of Rome was certainly written before the middle of the fifth century, probably as early as 416; prior to which it had been handed down by oral tradition.

(90)

These gifts and these presents are by anticipation called unspotted sacrifices, because they are shortly to become the Body and Blood of Christ, the Lamb of God, the only victim without stain or spot.

(91)

S. Paul says of the Church, that 'Christ loved it, and delivered Himself up for it, that He might present it to Himself a glorious Church, not having spot, or wrinkle, or any such thing, but that it should be holy, and without blemish.'[1] As the God of Truth cannot violate His promises, the Church has ever been, is, and will be, holy.

(92)

In praying for the Unity of the Church, it is but just that we should, in the first place, remember its visible head and centre upon earth, the Bishop of Rome or Pope; since, as long ago as the year 177, S. Irenaeus, in noticing the successors of those Bishops who had been appointed

---

[1] *Ephesians*, v, 25.

by the Apostles, says: 'As it would be tedious to enumerate the whole list of successions, I shall confine myself to that of Rome; the greatest, and most ancient, and most illustrious Church, founded by the glorious apostles Peter and Paul; receiving from them her doctrine, which was announced to all men, and which, through the succession of her bishops, is come down to us. . . . For, to this Church, on account of its superior Headship,[1] every other must have recourse, that is, the faithful of all countries; in which Church has been preserved the doctrine delivered by the Apostles.'[2] One of the bonds which connect us with the Chair of Peter—the centre of Unity—is prayer for its actual occupant.

(93)

The Apostles' Creed teaches us to believe in the Communion of Saints.

(94)

The Lord announced to King Ezechias, by the mouth of the prophet Isaias, that He would protect and save Jerusalem against the Assyrians for His own sake, and for David His servant's sake.[3] The Israelites frequently entreated the Almighty to hear their prayers, for the sake of Abraham,

---

[1] Propter potiorem principalitatem.
[2] *Contra haereses*, lib. III, cap. III.
[3] 4 *Kings*, XIX, 34.

Isaac, and Jacob. The Church, in like manner, refers to the memory of the Blessed Virgin Mary, 'the Mother of our Lord,' and of the other Saints of the New Law, to render God more propitious to her supplications for their sakes.

In the very ancient liturgy, called of S. James, and which was used in the church of Jerusalem, we find the following commemoration of the Saints :—*Bowing down, the priest says :* O Lord, do Thou vouchsafe to make us worthy to celebrate the memory of the holy fathers and patriarchs ; of the prophets and apostles, of John the precursor and Baptist, of Stephen the first of deacons and first of martyrs, and of the holy Mother of God and ever Virgin, Blessed Mary, and of all the Saints. *Raising his voice:* Wherefore we celebrate their memory, that whilst they are standing before the throne they may be mindful of our poverty and weakness ; and may, together with us, offer to Thee this tremendous and unbloody sacrifice, for the protection of the living, for the consolation of the weak and unworthy, such as we are, etc.[1]

S. Cyril, c. A.D. 350, in his instructions on this very liturgy, observes : 'We make a commemoration of all those who have fallen asleep before us, first of the patriarchs, prophets, apostles, and martyrs—that God, by their prayers and inter-

---

[1] RENAUDOT, *Liturg. Orient. Coll.*, tom. II, p. 36.

cession, may receive our supplications. Afterwards also we pray for the holy fathers and bishops who have fallen asleep before us, and lastly for all who have in past years fallen asleep amongst us.'[1]

(95)

To the twelve Apostles are united twelve from amongst the most illustrious martyrs who watered the foundation of the Church with their blood. Linus, Cletus, and Clement were fellow-labourers with S. Peter in the preaching of the Gospel at Rome; and all three severally became his successors in the Pontifical Chair. Xystus and Cornelius were two other popes; the first was martyred in the reign of Trajan, the latter in the year 252. Cyprian was the celebrated martyr, and bishop of Carthage. Laurence was deacon to Pope Sixtus II. Chrysogonus was an illustrious Roman, martyred at Aquileia, under Diocletian. John and Paul were brothers, who, rather than worship marble gods and idols, underwent a cruel death, by order of Julian the Apostate. Cosmas and Damian were physicians, who, for the love of God and of their neighbour, exercised their profession gratis.

---

[1] Εἶτα μνημονεύομεν καὶ τῶν προκεκοιμημένων, πρῶτον, πατριαρχῶν, προφητῶν, ἀποστόλων, μαρτύρων, ὅπως ὁ Θεὸς ταῖς εὐχαῖς αὐτῶν καὶ πρεσβείαις προσδέξηται ἡμῶν τὴν δέησιν· εἶτα καὶ ὑπὲρ τῶν προκεκοιμημένων ἁγίων πατέρων καὶ ἐπισκόπων καὶ πάντων ἁπλῶς τῶν ἐν ἡμῖν προκεκοιμημένων. S. CYRILLI Catech. Myst., v, 9.

(96)

It was a very common ceremony in the Old Law for the priest to hold his hands over the victim which was about to be offered up as a sacrifice.[1]

(97)

The adoration of the Eucharist is attested by all antiquity. S. Cyril of Jerusalem, a father of the Greek Church, thus addresses the recently baptized who were about to make their first Communion: 'After having thus partaken of the Body of Christ, approach also to the Chalice of His Blood, not stretching out thine hands, but bowing down, and in the attitude of homage and *adoration*, saying, Amen.'[2] S. Ambrose (d. 397) says: 'The very flesh of Jesus Christ, which, to this day, we adore in our sacred mysteries.'[3] S. Augustine remarks that—'Christ received flesh from the flesh of Mary: And because He walked here in that very flesh, and gave that same flesh to us to eat, for our salvation; no one eateth this flesh unless he have first *adored* it. We have

---

[1] *Exodus*, XXIX, 10, and *Leviticus*, I, 4.

[2] Εἶτα μετὰ τὸ κοινωνῆσαί σε τοῦ σώματος Χριστοῦ προσέρχου καὶ τῷ ποτηρίῳ τοῦ αἵματος, μὴ ἀνατείνων τὰς χεῖρας, ἀλλὰ κύπτων, καὶ τρόπῳ προσκυνήσεως καὶ σεβάσματος λέγων τὸ Ἀμὴν. *Catech. Myst.*, V, 22.

[3] Caro Christi, quam hodieque in Mysteriis adoramus, et quam Apostoli in Domino Iesu adorarunt. *De Spiritu Sancto*, lib. III, cap. 11.

found out in what sense such a footstool of our Lord may be adored : and not only that we do not sin in adoring it, but that *we sin in not adoring it.*'[1]

The elevation and adoration of the Body and Blood of Jesus Christ in the holy Sacrifice of the Mass are to be found in all the Oriental liturgies, whether Greek, Syriac, Egyptian, or Ethiopic,[2] and are distinctly pointed out in the liturgies of S. James, S. Chrysostom, and S. Basil.[3]

The following is the rubric for the elevation, extracted from the liturgy of S. Chrysostom : '*Here the priest and deacon adore, both saying in secret :* God be merciful to me a sinner. *And all the people likewise adore. But when the deacon shall observe the priest extending his hands and covering the holy bread, that he may perform the sacred elevation, he exclaims :* Let us attend ; *and the priest says :* Holy things for holy people ; *and the choir answers :* One is holy, one Lord Jesus Christ in the glory of the Father. Amen.'[4] The elevation and adoration

---

[1] De carne Mariae carnem accepit. Et quia in ipsa carne hic am-bulavit, et ipsam carnem nobis manducandam ad salutem dedit : Nemo autem illam carnem manducat, nisi prius adoraverit : inventum est quemadmodum adoretur tale scabellum pedum Domini, et non solum non peccemus adorando, sed peccemus non adorando. S. AUGUSTINI *in Psalmum XCVIII Enarratio,* v, 9.

[2] RENAUDOT, *Liturg. Orient. Coll.,* tom. II p. 114.

[3] *Ibid.,* tom. I, pp. 23, 82, 122, 265, 342.

[4] Εἶτα προσκυνεῖ ὁ ἱερεύς καὶ ὁ διάκονος ἐν ᾧ ἐστι τύπῳ, λέγοντες μυστικῶς τρίς. Ὁ Θεὸς ἱλάσθητί μοι τῷ ἁμαρτωλῷ. Καὶ ὁ λαὸς ὁμοίως πάντες μετα

of the sacred Blood in the chalice is afterwards
made, if possible, in a more impressive manner,
when, at the bidding of the priest, the deacon
approaches to receive the Holy Communion,[1]
announcing aloud—'I come to the immortal King,
I believe, O Lord, I confess.'[2]   During the earlier
ages of the Church, the elevation was rendered
particularly solemn in the East.   The screen
which separates the sanctuary from the body of
the church, in those countries which follow the
Greek rite, is perforated with three doorways,
which are now partially, but in ancient times
were quite covered over with curtains.   Once it
was the custom to let fall these curtains at the
commencement of the Canon, and they were
only withdrawn at the elevation, that the sacred
mysteries might receive the adoration of the

εὐλαβείας προσκυνοῦσιν, ὅταν δὲ ἴδη ὁ διάκονος τὸν ἱερέα ἐκτείνοντα τὰς χεῖρας,
καὶ ἀπωμενον τοῦ ἁγίου ἄρτου πρὸς το ποιῆσαι τὴν ἁγίαν ὕψωσιν, Ἐκφωνεῖ
πρόσχωμεν. Καὶ ὁ ἱερεὺς. Τὰ ἅγια τοῖς ἁγίοις. Ὁ χορος. Εἶς ἅγιος, εἷς
Κύριος Ἰησοῦς Χριστὸς εἰς δόξαν Θεοῦ Πατρὸς. GOAR, Εὐχολόγιον, p. 81.

[1] In the Greek liturgy, the elevation does not take place until
just before the Communion. In the Latin liturgy, the elevation
did not take place anciently until the Pater Noster.

[2] *Ibid.*, pp. 83, 84. On this point we possess the admission of a
candid French Protestant, who says : 'Des docteurs si illustres, ont
avancé que les Grecs ne reçoivent point la Transsubstantiation, que
je me fais une peine de vous dire le contraire. Cependant, il le faut
bien, puisque c'est la vérité ; apparemment qu'ils ont eu de mauvais
mémoires, ou qu'on leur a voulu parler de quelque secte qui n'est
pas connue en ces quartiers ici, car je puis vous assurer que les Grecs
de Constantinople, et de Smyrne, la croient purement et simplement
comme les Latins, et s'ils ne se mettent pas à genoux, lors de
l'élevation de l'Hostie, c'est que leur façon d'adorer n'est pas telle.'
Voyage de M. DU MONT, tom. IV, lettre I, p. 16.

people. To this ceremony S. Chrysostom refers in a stream of beautiful language, worthy of the golden-mouthed fountain of eloquence from which it flowed. Discoursing on the Blessed Sacrament of the Altar, the Saint exclaims : 'Here when the Sacrifice is offered up, and Christ is immolated, the victim of the Lord ; as soon as thou shalt hear the words : Let us all pray in common ; as soon as thou shalt perceive that the veils before the altar are drawn aside, then figure to yourselves that the heavens are let down from above, and that the angels are descending.'[1] And in another homily : 'Before that awful moment, be moved ; nay, tremble to the very soul, before you behold, as the veils are drawn aside, the angelic choir advancing—yes, mount spontaneously to heaven itself.'[2]

(98)

Up to the eleventh century, the elevation did not take place until about the end of the Canon. Towards the year 1047, Berengarius began to broach his errors concerning the Holy Eucharist. Not only were the heterodox opinions of this innovator immediately anathematised by several councils ; but the whole Latin Church unani-

---

[1] Ἐνταῦθα ἐκφερομένης τῆς θυσίας, καὶ τοῦ Χριστοῦ τεθυμένου, καὶ τοῦ προβάτου τοῦ Δεσποτικοῦ, ὅταν ἀκούσῃς, Δεηθῶμεν πάντες κοινῇ, ὅταν ἴδῃς ἀνελκόμενα τὰ ἀμφίθυρα, τότε νόμισον διαστελλέσθαι τὸν οὐρανὸν ἄνωθεν, καὶ κατιέναι τοὺς ἀγγέλους. In Epist. ad Ephesios cap. I, Homil. III, § 5.

[2] In Epist. I ad Corinth. Homil. XXIV.

mously adopted a ceremonial at the celebration of Mass—the elevation—which should furnish a most significant condemnation of the new doctrine of Berengarius, and at the same time be an unequivocal and practical profession of faith concerning the real presence of Christ in the Sacrament, in which bread and wine are transubstantiated into the Body and Blood of Jesus, uplifted by the priest, and adored by the people at the elevation. In the Greek and Eastern Churches, the ceremony of the elevation, which has always been observed by them, does not take place until just before the Communion.[1]

(99)

The bell is rung to fix the attention of the people, and to give them warning to prostrate soul and body, and to adore their crucified Redeemer concealed under the appearances of bread and wine. All Catholics should study to manifest, by their outward demeanour, the inward belief and consequent reverence which they cherish towards the Eucharistic mysteries. They should kneel on both knees in silent adoration, and avoid either suspending their own, or interrupting the devotion of their neighbours, by coughing, etc. etc., which sometimes violates the silence which ought profoundly to reign at the moment of the elevation. To excite their own devotion, let them occupy

---

[1] GOAR, Εὐχολόγιον, p. 81.

their thoughts with the real though veiled presence of Jesus, now throned upon the altar around which Cherubim and Seraphim are bending down in worship: let them call to remembrance the description just now quoted[1] from S. John Chrysostom, who, in such splendid strains of eloquence, sketches what takes place, at this tremendous time, within the sanctuary. There is something indescribably impressive in the suspension of the music, as well as of the singing, and in the silent pause which is observed in some places at the consecration and elevation, during which not one sound is audible, save only the tinkling of the bell—and each one is prostrate in the most profound adoration.[2]

There is a sublimity of worship produced by such a silence, that cannot be too earnestly recommended where music accompanies the celebration of the Mass.

(100)

Not the Hell of the damned, but that Hell into which, as we are taught to believe by the apostles, Jesus Christ descended 'after He was dead and buried;'—a place between Heaven and the Hell of the damned, denominated by Catholics the Limbus Patrum. To this middle state S. Peter

---

[1] See Note 97, p. 135.
[2] According to the Roman Ceremonial: 'Silet chorus, et cum aliis adorat. Organum vero si habetur, cum omni tunc melodia et gravitate pulsandum est.' Lib. II, cap. VIII, § 70.

refers, when he says that 'Christ being put to death indeed in the flesh, but enlivened in the spirit. In which also coming, He preached to those spirits that were in prison; which were sometime incredulous.'[1]

(101)

The Church avails herself of every occasion to impress upon the minds of the priest and of the people this truth, that the sacrifice of the altar is the very same with that which was offered on the Cross. She is solicitous that the priest, especially after the consecration, should behold, with an eye of faith, Jesus Christ immolated on the Cross, as S. Paul observes to the Galatians, 'before whose eyes Jesus Christ hath been set forth, crucified among you.'[2]

To produce this effect, she has ordained in her liturgy that all these words which designate the Body or the Blood of Jesus Christ should be accompanied by the sign of the Cross, to signify that the consecrated Host and contents of the Chalice are the same Body which was crucified, and the same Blood which was shed upon the Cross. These words, 'Sanctum sacrificium, immaculatam Hostiam,' were added to the Canon by S. Leo the Great (440-461).

---

1 *Peter*, III, 18-20.   2 *Galatians*, III, 1.

(102)

In all the ancient Liturgies, of the Eastern as well as the Western Church, prayer is invariably made for the souls of the faithful departed.[1]

(103)

According to the language of Christian antiquity, to die in peace is to die with the sign of ecclesiastical communion, in union and society with Jesus Christ and His Church.

(104)

After having prayed for certain persons in particular, the Church instructs us to pray for the souls of all the faithful departed in general, in order, as S. Augustine observes: 'That such religious duty, whenever it becomes neglected by parents, children, relations, or friends, may be supplied by our pious and common mother, the Church.'[2]   In the primitive Church, the names of those for whom the priest was to pray more especially, were enrolled on ivory tablets, called diptychs.

---

[1] Extracts from these several liturgies are given in Ch. xv on the Diptychs.

[2] Non sunt praetermittendae supplicationes pro spiritibus mortuorum, quas faciendas pro omnibus in Christiana et Catholica societate defunctis etiam tacitis nominibus eorum sub generali commemoratione suscepit Ecclesia ; ut quibus ad ista desunt parentes, aut filii, aut quicumque cognati vel amici, ab una eis exhibeantur pia matre communi. S. AUGUSTINI *de cura pro mortuis gerenda*, cap. IV.

Prayer for the dead is made, at this part of the holy Sacrifice, in the liturgy which we have in the Apostolic Constitutions;[1] and S. Cyril of Jerusalem, in his catechetical instructions to the recently baptized concerning the Mass of the faithful, at which they were about to be, for the first time, present, tells them that—'first, commemoration of the Saints is made, that God, by their prayers and intercession, may receive our supplications; and that then we pray for our holy fathers and bishops, and all who are fallen asleep before us, believing it to be a considerable advantage to their souls to be prayed for, whilst the holy and tremendous Sacrifice lies upon the altar.'[2]

(105)

In imitation of the publican who is described by our Redeemer in the Gospel as striking his breast and saying: 'O God, be merciful to me a sinner.'[3]

(106)

Mention is here made of several martyrs and saints belonging to the several orders and states

---

[1] Lib. VIII., cap. 13, *apud* LABBEUM, *Concil. Gen.*, tom. I, col. 564.

[2] Εἶτα καὶ ὑπὲρ (μνημονεύομεν) τῶν προκεκοιμημένων ἁγίων πατέρων καὶ ἐπισκόπων καὶ πάντων ἁπλῶς τῶν ἐν ἡμῖν προκεκοιμημένων, μεγίστην ὄνησιν πιστεύοντες ἔσεσθαι ταῖς ψυχαῖς ὑπὲρ ὧν ἡ δέησις ἀναφέρεται τῆς ἁγίας καὶ φρικωδεστάτης προκειμένης θυσίας. S. CYRILLI *Catech. Myst.*, V, 9.

[3] *S. Luke*, XVIII, 13.

of holy personages in the Church. S. John Baptist is of the order of Prophets; S. Stephen, of the order of Deacons; S. Matthias, of the order of Apostles; S. Ignatius, who suffered martyrdom at Rome, in the year 107, is of the order of Bishops; S. Alexander, who was put to death for the faith, at Rome, in the year 117, is of the rank of Popes; S. Marcellinus, who was martyred in the reign of Diocletian, is of the order of Priests; S. Peter, the fellow martyr of S. Marcellinus, of the order of Clerks; SS. Perpetua and Felicitas are of the state of married persons; S. Agatha, S. Lucy, S. Agnes, S. Cecily, and S. Anastasia are of the state of Virgins.

(107)

Here the priest holds the sacred Host in his right hand over the Chalice, which he takes in his left, and then elevates a little both the Host and the Chalice. Up to the eleventh century the Body and Blood of Christ were here held up to receive the adoration of the people. But, as has been already observed, about the year 1047 a more solemn elevation was adopted by the Church, to furnish a public and daily profession of its ancient faith concerning the Real Presence, in contradiction to the impious novelties of Berengarius. This, in consequence, is now denominated the minor or second elevation, in contradistinction to the first, which precedes it, and takes place

immediately after the consecration. Le Brun des
Marettes remarks that at the cathedral of Rouen a
formal elevation was still observed at this part of
the Canon, at the beginning of the last century.[1]

(108)

In the Latin Church, the 'Our Father' is
recited at Low, and sung at High Mass; in the
Greek Church, it is repeated or chanted by all
the people.

In many parts of Asia, the Sacrifice of the
Mass is offered up in ancient Syriac; in Africa,
especially in Egypt, in ancient Coptic, once the
common, but both for many centuries past, dead
languages. Though the Asiatic and African Christians of the present day talk a dialect quite different from the ancient Syriac and Coptic, with
which they are utterly unacquainted, still, in joining in the public offices and liturgy of the Church,
they recite the 'Our Father,' etc., in the obsolete
language, although they possess vernacular trans-
lations of this prayer into modern Arabic, which
they use in their private devotions.[2]

(109)

The priest invokes the suffrage first of the
Blessed Virgin Mary, whom S. Elisabeth, filled

---

[1] *Voyages Liturgiques de France*. Paris, 1718, p. 368.
[2] RENAUDOT, *Liturg. Orient. Coll.*, tom. II, p. 113.

with the Holy Ghost, denominated the 'Mother of our Lord.'[1]

That the Blessed Virgin is the mother of Jesus Christ, is indubitable : but Jesus Christ is God ; consequently, she is properly styled the Mother of God (Θεοτόκος), a title which was approved of by a general council held at Ephesus in the year 431. S. Peter and S. Paul conjointly founded the Church of Rome by their labours and their preaching ; and both of them cemented the foundation with their blood. Rome has ever exhibited especial veneration towards S. Andrew, as he was the brother of S. Peter, the prince of the Apostles.

(110)

At these words the priest makes on himself the sign of the Cross with the paten, which he afterwards kisses as the instrument of peace, and the disc on which is about to be deposited the Blessed Eucharist, the peace of Christians. He employs it in making the sign of the Cross, because it was by the Cross that Christ became 'our peace . . . and hath reconciled us to God in one body by the Cross, killing the enmities in Himself, and coming, He preached peace.'[2]

(111)

The fraction of the Host is one of the principal

---

[1] *S. Luke*, I, 41–43.   [2] *Ephesians*, II, 14–17.

ceremonies in the Canon of the Mass, and is found in every ancient liturgy, either of the Western or Eastern Churches. The fraction or breaking of bread by Jesus Christ at the Last Supper is particularly mentioned by three of the Evangelists, and by S. Paul, who tells us that Jesus took bread, and broke it, and gave it to His disciples, saying: 'Take ye and eat, this is My Body.' That this rite was ordained by Christ, and was something more than ordinary breaking of bread, may be inferred from the stress which the Apostle of the Gentiles lays upon it, when he thus interrogates the Corinthians: 'The bread which we break, is it not the partaking of the Body of the Lord?' and from the circumstance, that not only was Christ recognised by the two disciples at Emmaus in the breaking of bread,[1] but in the book of the Acts of the Apostles, the breaking of bread is synonymous with consecrating the Blessed Eucharist; for S. Luke informs us that it was on the first day of the week they assembled to break bread.[2]

(112)

This ceremony is interesting from its connection with a practice once followed by the Church. It was anciently a custom for the Sovereign

---

[1] *S. Luke*, XXIV, 35.　　　　[2] *Acts*, XX, 7.

Pontiff at Rome, and for the bishops of the other cities in Italy, to send by acolytes,[1] deputed for that purpose, a small portion of the Holy Eucharist which they had consecrated, to the various titular churches of the city.[2] The priest who was celebrating the Holy Sacrifice used to put this particle into the chalice, at the same time that he recited the prayer, 'The peace of our Lord,' etc.

That the Roman Pontiffs, on the other hand, were accustomed to receive the Holy Eucharist which was sent to them by bishops of distant churches, is attested in a letter concerning the churches of Asia, addressed by S. Irenæus to Pope Victor. The object of such a practice was to signify that communion of the same sacrifice and sacrament by which the head and members of the Church were spiritually united; so that, in the words of S. Paul, they might address each other: 'for we, being many, are one bread, one body, all that partake of one bread.'[3]

---

[1] S. Tharsicius was one of those acolytes, who, rather than betray what he was carrying to the Pagans who had seized him, suffered himself to be beaten to death with clubs. See *Martyrologium Romanum*, August 15.

[2] This is said to have been introduced by Pope Melchiades, who died in the year 314. See the *Liber Pontificalis*, XXXIII. S. Siricius (d. 398) further ordered that no Priest should celebrate Mass unless he had received the fermentum from the Bishop. See also a letter of Innocent I. to Decentius, Bishop of Eugubio, in MIGNE, *Patrologiae Cursus*, tom. xx, col. 556.

[3] 1 *Corinthians*, X, 17.

(113)

Every time that these words are repeated, all strike their breasts to testify a sorrow for their sins, of which, by this ceremony, they implore forgiveness from a merciful Redeemer.

(114)

S. Peter[1] and S. Paul[2] instruct the faithful to whom they directed their epistles, to 'salute one another with a holy kiss.' This ceremony was, in consequence, especially observed at the celebration of the Holy Eucharist, as we gather from all the public liturgies, and most ancient Christian writers. Justin Martyr,[3] Tertullian,[4] S. Cyril of Jerusalem,[5] as well as several others, particularly notice it; and in the Apostolical Constitutions is contained the direction: 'After the bishop has said: May the peace of God be with you all, and the people have answered: And with thy spirit; let the deacon say to all: Salute ye one another with a holy kiss; and let the clergy salute the bishop, the laymen their fellow laymen, and the women likewise one another.'[6]

[1] 1 *Peter*, v, 14.

[2] *Romans*, XVI, 16; 1 *Corinthians*, XVI, 20; 2 *Corinthians*, XIII, 12; 1 *Thessalonians*, v, 26.

[3] *Apologia I*, § 65.   [4] *Ad Uxorem*, lib. II, cap. 4.

[5] *Catech. Myst.*, v, 3.

[6] *Constitutiones Apost.*, lib. VIII, c. 11, *apud* LABBEUM, *Concil. Gen.*, tom. I, col. 552.

Hence arose the custom, which is still kept up in many places upon the Continent, and in several country congregations in England, of men and women occupying separate sides of the church.

(115)

Here those who have complied with the instruction of the Apostle, and have proved themselves,[1] and who are not conscious to themselves of sin, or have obtained pardon of it by the sacrament of Penance, accompanied with a firm purpose of amendment, advance towards the rails to receive the Holy Communion. As the Postcommunion is the prayer of thanksgiving after Communion, and is common both to priest and people, it is greatly to be desired that such as receive the Blessed Sacrament would present themselves at the proper time, which is at the *Domine, non sum dignus.* It is to invite communicants to approach the altar that the acolyte or minister rings the bell at this part of the Mass. The Communion is given in the following manner. The acolyte, kneeling on the epistle side of the altar, repeats the *Confiteor* (see page 6), as a public declaration of sorrow for sin on the part of those who are about to receive the

---

[1] But let a man prove himself. . . . For he that eateth and drinketh unworthily, eateth and drinketh judgment (in the Protestant translation, damnation) to himself, not discerning the body of the Lord. 1 *Corinthians*, XI, 28, 29.

Blessed Eucharist. The priest then turns round to the people, and says: '*May Almighty God be merciful unto you, and, forgiving you your sins, bring you to life everlasting.*' *R.* '*Amen.*' '*May the Almighty and merciful Lord grant you pardon,* ✠ *absolution, and remission of your sins.*' *R.* '*Amen.*' Having adored on his knees, he then takes the sacred Host into his hands, and turning about says: '*Behold the Lamb of God, behold Him who taketh away the sins of the world. Lord, I am not worthy that Thou shouldest enter under my roof; but only say the word, and my soul shall be healed.*' This last sentence he repeats thrice, which is as oftentimes recited along with the priest by the communicants, who, at each repetition, strike their breasts, in attestation of their sorrow for having ever sinned, and of their unworthiness to receive the Body and Blood of their Redeemer. The priest then descends to the rails, bearing within a kind of vase, called the Pyx, or upon the Paten, the Blessed Eucharist. Holding the communion-cloth spread over their hands, with their eyes reverently closed, the head modestly raised, the mouth conveniently opened, and the tip of the tongue resting upon the lip, the communicants successively receive the Body of Christ, which is administered to them in the following manner: the priest, holding one of the consecrated particles in his right hand, makes with it the sign of the Cross over the communicant, to call to his remembrance that it is the very Body of Jesus Christ which hung upon the Cross; and afterwards imparts it to him with these words: ✠ '*The Body of our Lord Jesus Christ preserve thy soul unto life everlasting. Amen.*' The communicants, on receiving the Sacrament, bend down and adore in silent but most fervent worship. They then retire from the rails, not with a hasty, but decorous step, with downcast eyes, and a becoming gravity.

(116)

To express in a lively manner that the sacred Body which he is about to take, is the very same which was sacrificed upon the Cross.

(117)

In the Greek Church each Eucharistic particle is called μαργαρίτης, or 'a pearl,' to signify that the smallest part of the Blessed Sacrament is a jewel of the greatest price. In the rubric of S. John Chrysostom's liturgy, 'the deacon, or in his absence, the priest, is directed to wipe the sacred Chalice thrice, and to take most particular care lest the particle called the "pearl" remain.'[1] S. Cyril of Jerusalem, who lived about A.D. 350, in his instructions for receiving the Holy Eucharist, thus exhorts the recently initiated: 'Receive

---

[1] GOAR, Εὐχολόγιον, p. 86.

the holy Body with such care, that you do not
suffer any part of it to be unhappily lost; for
should you let any of it fall, regard it as much as
the loss of one of your own members. Let not
one single crumb of that which is much more
precious than gold or gems, escape you.[1] Such
anxious solicitude would not have been exhibited
by the author of the liturgy, nor would the
sainted catechist have insisted on such scrupulous
attention about an atom of common bread. Both,
consequently, believed each particle of the Blessed
Eucharist to be no longer a crumb of bread, but
the real Body of Christ Jesus.

(118)

The priest who celebrates Mass receives under
both kinds, because he must consume the sacrifice
offered up under two species. At the Last Supper,
when Christ commissioned His Apostles to do as
He had done, He said to them : 'Drink ye all
of this.' No one, however, was present but the
Apostles, all of whom were then ordained sacrificing priests. The priest or bishop, nay, even the
Pope himself, who partakes of the Blessed Eucharist without saying Mass, receives the Communion
like any layman, under one kind only.

---

[1] Προσέχων, μὴ παραπολέσῃς τι ἐκ τούτου αὐτοῦ. ὅπερ γὰρ ἐὰν ἀπολέσῃς,
τούτῳ ὡς ἀπὸ οἰκείου δηλονότι ἐζημιώθης μέλους. S. CYRILLI Catech. Myst.,
V, 21.

(119)

The antiphon called the Communion varies with each Sunday and festival, and is generally, though not always, a versicle extracted from the Psalms. It is thus denominated because anciently it used to be chanted whilst the people communicated.

In the Apostolic Constitutions[1] it is prescribed that the thirty-third Psalm should be employed for this purpose. In his exposition of the liturgy used at his time in the ancient Church of Jerusalem, S. Cyril thus notices the chanting of the Communion : 'After this you hear one singing with a sacred melody, inviting you to the Communion of the holy mysteries, and saying : "O taste, and see that the Lord is good."'[2]

(120)

This prayer received its name from being recited just after the Communion ; and because it is an act of thanksgiving to God for the ineffable favour of having participated in the sacred mysteries. The form used in the ancient Church may be seen in the Apostolic Constitutions.[3]

---

[1] Lib. VIII, c. 13, *apud* LABBEUM, *Concil. Gen.*, tom. I, col. 565.

[2] S. CYRILLI *Catech. Myst.*, v, 20.

[3] Lib. VIII, c. 14, where it is called 'The declaration after Communion,' Προσφώνησις μέτα τὴν μετάληψιν.

(121)

The same ceremony is observed in the Greek liturgy, which directs the deacon to proclaim to the people: 'Let us proceed in peace.'[1] Anciently the people were expected to remain for instruction on ferial days and on the Sundays in Lent, on which days the words of dismissal were replaced by the invitation: 'Let us bless the Lord.'

(122)

In the Old Testament we frequently read that the priest, stretching forth his hands to the people, blessed them. *Leviticus*, IX, 22.

(123)

All make a genuflexion at these words, to adore the second Person of the Blessed Trinity, who was pleased to take flesh for our redemption.

(124)

Not only do Catholics honour the King,[2] because, as S. Paul observes, 'he is God's minister to thee for good; but if thou do that which is evil, fear: for he beareth not the sword in vain,'[3] but how-

---

[1] Ἐν εἰρήνῃ προσέλθωμεν. GOAR, Εὐχολόγιον, p. 85. According to the Apostolic Constitutions, the deacon declared to the people that Mass was finished by announcing: 'Depart in peace'—ἀπολύεσθε ἐν εἰρήνῃ. Lib. VIII, c. 15, *apud* LABBEUM, *Concil. Gen.*, tom. I, col. 568.
[2] I *Peter*, II, 17.   [3] *Romans*, XIII, 4.

ever widely they may differ from him in religious
belief, and though he even be a persecutor of the
Church, they nevertheless pray for him. In this
they not only obey the voice of the Apostle, who
desires that supplications, prayers, and interces-
sions be made for kings;[1] but they imitate the
faithful of the Old Testament, since we learn that
the Jews who were captives in Babylon accompanied the collection of money which they sent
to Jerusalem to Joakim the priest, for the service
of the altar, with this particular request: 'Pray
ye for the life of Nabuchadonosor, the King of
Babylon, and for the life of Balthassar his son,
that their days may be upon the earth as the days
of heaven.'[2] Moreover, they follow the example
of the primitive Christians, who, as Tertullian
informs us in his first Apology,[3] prayed for the
Emperors though they were Pagans; and, as we
gather from the letters of S. Dionysius of Alexandria, continued to offer up fervent prayers for the
health of the Emperor Gallus, notwithstanding
that he was persecuting them.[4]

(125)

The Benediction over the people with the
Blessed Sacrament is a rite frequently practised.
Catholics in every part of the globe, by this act of

---

[1] *i Timothy*, II, I, 2.   [2] *Baruch*, I, 7–11.   [3] Cap. xxx.
[4] Eusebii *Hist. Eccl.*, lib. VII, cap. I.

public adoration to the Blessed Sacrament, profess
their belief in the Real Presence and Transubstantiation. They would deem it the foulest act of
idolatry to worship a piece of bread. Since, however, they are assured by the word of God that
the second Person of the Blessed Trinity, who
became incarnate for us, is really present, though
concealed under the appearance of bread—as the
Holy Ghost was really present, though concealed
under the appearance once of a dove, another
time of a flame of fire—they exhibit divine adoration to Him, well knowing that it cannot be
idolatry to worship the true and living God, Christ
Jesus.

(126)

Such is the appellation given to a species of
small tower erected on the central part of the
High Altar, and in which the Blessed Eucharist
is reserved, not only for the use of the sick, but
to be occasionally exposed to the adoration of
the people, and to be perpetually present to excite
their devotion, and draw the faithful to the house
of God.

(127)

Catholics believe that in the Blessed Eucharist
are the Body and the Blood, together with the Soul
and the Divinity of Jesus Christ. They believe
that after the words of consecration, what was

bread is then changed, or, as it is called, transubstantiated into the Body of Christ, so that, not the substance, but the appearance only of bread remains. By bending the knee, Catholics, therefore, intend to worship Christ, and not a piece of bread. To bow the knee in divine adoration of a piece of bread, or of anything else besides the Deity, would be idolatrous and blasphemous.

(128)

The pyx is a vase with a cover, in which the Blessed Sacrament is reserved within the Tabernacle. It should be of gold, or of silver, gilt inside, and covered with a veil of silk. In England it is commonly called a ciborium.

The monstrance is a species of vessel employed, as its name implies, for showing the Blessed Sacrament to the people, to receive their worship. It is composed of a stem, which supports a crystal case, in the form of a tower, or of a sun surrounded by rays of glory.

END OF NOTES ON THE RUBRICS.

PART II.

DISSERTATIONS

ON THE

DOCTRINE AND RITUAL

OF THE

HOLY EUCHARISTIC SACRIFICE.

PART II.

——•——

CHAPTER I.

ON THE

HOLY SACRIFICE OF THE MASS.

————

SECTION I.

ON SACRIFICE IN GENERAL.

I.—NECESSITY OF INTERIOR AND EXTERIOR WORSHIP.

RELIGION is that reverential homage of the heart and mind which connects us with God by a perfect submission of ourselves to His sovereign majesty, and the profound prostration of the soul before the throne of His omnipotence, which we exhibit by exterior worship.

It is true that the most grateful offering to the Lord is that inward adoration—the homage and the breathings of the heart: because God is a Spirit; and they that adore Him must adore Him in spirit and in truth.[1]

---

[1] *S. John*, IV, 24.

But man is a compound, not a simple being. He is gifted with a soul which assimilates him to the angelic spirits; and he possesses a body, which constitutes a part of the visible creation.

Composed, therefore, of a body and a soul, we must, through the very constitution of our nature, offer up this oblation outwardly, in order to furnish a visible and a public manifestation of the inward emotions of the spirit towards the Divinity; and hence we must necessarily associate along with interior worship the rites of some exterior ceremonial, which, in fact, is nothing more than an outward sign, and a sensible declaration, indicative of that interior oblation of ourselves, which each one of us is bound to make to God our Creator, and perpetual preserver.

It is, therefore, impossible that true religion can in any way subsist without interior and exterior adoration. This will be more evident when we consider that religion, as its very name implies, is, as it were, a bond—a ligature, connecting men with one another, by the profession of a common faith, and a similarity of public worship, in which they outwardly unite to acknowledge their dependence upon God, and to manifest their affection and devotion towards Him.

II.—SACRIFICE OFFERED FROM THE BEGINNING OF THE WORLD.

Nature herself invariably inspired man with the idea that *sacrifice* was the first—the most essential act of exterior religion. From the world's foundation to the present moment, its existence may be more or less discovered amongst men throughout the earth, however widely separated from each other by almost immeasurable distance, or the interposition of barriers erected by nature, and utterly impossible to be surmounted.

The earliest record of the human race represents Cain as offering to God the fruits of the earth, and Abel as making a similar acknowledgment of homage with the ' firstlings of his flock.'[1] After the waters of the Deluge had subsided, and Noah, with his family, had issued from the Ark, ' he built an altar unto the Lord ; and taking of all cattle, and fowls that were clean, offered holocausts upon the altar.'[2]

The Almighty condescended to attest the holiness of Job by imparting efficacy to the prayers and the sacrifice which that model of resignation to the will of Heaven presented in behalf of his less righteous neighbours. The oblation of Melchisedech is too well known to demand our observations ; while Abraham was so sedulous

---

[1] *Genesis*, IV, 3, 4.   [2] *Genesis*, VIII, 20.

in sacrificing, that he was even ready to make
a victim of his only and well-beloved son Isaac.
The dictates inspired by nature were ratified
in the law delivered by God Himself to Moses,
in which are described with much minuteness
the various sacrifices to be offered by the Hebrew
people, and in which it is declared, that to withhold men from sacrificing, or to offer up a sacrifice to any other being whatever, save God alone,
were crimes of the most serious enormity : 'Wherefore the sin of the young men (the sons of Heli)
was exceeding great before the Lord,' says the
sacred text—'because they withdrew men from
the sacrifice of the Lord.'[1]

III.—WHAT SACRIFICE IS.

Exterior sacrifice, according to the proper acceptation of the term, is an offering or oblation
of some sensible thing, by a lawfully appointed
minister, in order to acknowledge, by the de-
struction, or, at least, the change effected in
the offering, the majesty and sovereign power
of God ; to proclaim His absolute dominion over
everything created, and—while we make a contrite declaration of our sinfulness, and confess
our weakness—to deprecate His wrath, and seek
His favour.

---

[1] I *Kings*, II, 17.

IV.—THE FOUR ENDS OF SACRIFICE.

Exterior sacrifice consists, therefore, in making an oblation to God of something tangible to the senses—of some outward substance to be destroyed, or to undergo some change. The tribute of such a homage is rendered for those four reasons which constitute the various ends of sacrifice. 1. It is presented to Almighty God to recognise His paramount and absolute dominion over everything created. 2. To thank Him for all those benefits conferred by Him upon us. 3. To supplicate a pardon for our sins, and to profess ourselves debtors to His violated justice. 4. To entreat for those helps of grace so absolutely necessary to fortify our weakness.

From the particular intention for which this act of highest worship may be rendered unto God, sacrifice derives a peculiar appellation, or is distinguished by a corresponding epithet. It is severally denominated *Latreutical*, or of praise and supreme adoration; *Eucharistic*, or of thanksgiving; *Propitiatory* and *Impetratory*.

V.—THE LEGAL SACRIFICES WERE OF NO AVAIL WHEN UNCONNECTED WITH THE FUTURE DEATH OF THE REDEEMER.

Of the various sacrifices in use amongst the Jews, the most distinguished were the holocaust, the sin-offering, and the peace-offering. Though these sacrifices were commanded by the sacred law delivered unto Moses, still they were 'but a shadow of the good things to come,'[1] 'weak and needy elements,'[2] in themselves incapable of pleasing, or appeasing Heaven. They received their virtues from the future death of the Redeemer; and whenever they were possessed of any efficacy, they derived it from the faith of those who offered them, and who contemplated prospectively, and kept steadily in view, the sacred Victim, 'the Lamb unspotted and undefiled,'[3] 'that taketh away the sin of the world,'[4] and 'which was slain from the beginning of the world.'[5]

VI.—A NEW SACRIFICE WAS NECESSARY.

A new sacrifice, the substance of these shadows, was necessary; for the Lord of Hosts had proclaimed to the Jewish people that He had no pleasure in them,[6] and would not receive a gift from their hands; He announced to them that there should be another, and a more acceptable sacrifice offered to His name amongst the Gentiles. The time predicted with so much precision by the prophets, for the appearance of the Messiah, at length arrived; and the Saviour came to offer to His heavenly Father this clean oblation spoken

---

[1] *Hebrews*, X, 1. [2] *Galatians*, IV, 9. [3] 1 *Peter*, 1, 19.
[4] *S. John*, I, 29. [5] *Apocalypse*, XIII, 8. [6] *Malachias*, I, 10.

of by Malachias, saying : 'Sacrifice and oblation Thou wouldest not : but a body Thou hast fitted to me. Holocausts for sin did not please Thee. Then said I : Behold I come : in the head of the book it is written of me ; that I should do Thy will, O God. Sacrifices, and oblations, and holocausts for sin Thou wouldest not, neither are they pleasing to Thee.'[1]

VII.—THE SACRIFICE OF THE CROSS A TRUE SACRIFICE.

That Jesus Christ, the great high priest, presented to His Father a real sacrifice upon the Cross, upon which He Himself was the victim, is a truth upon which the whole of Christianity revolves as on a hinge, for 'Christ hath loved us, and hath delivered Himself for us, an oblation and a sacrifice to God :'[2] and 'we have a great high priest that hath passed into the heavens, Jesus, the Son of God.'[3]

VIII.—ALL THE ANCIENT SACRIFICES COMPRISED IN IT. THE HOLOCAUST.—THE PEACE-OFFERING.—THE SIN-OFFERING.

The sacrifice of the Cross was a holocaust ; for our Blessed Redeemer offered up Himself wholly

---

[1] *Hebrews*, x, 5-8.   [2] *Ephesians*, v, 2.
[3] *Hebrews*, IV, 14.

and entirely without reserve for our offences.
And what could possibly become a more acceptable
oblation for a sacrifice of peace than the Word
itself made flesh, of whom the Eternal Father
said aloud: 'This is My beloved Son, in whom
I am well pleased.'[1] What victim could be better
calculated to draw down Heaven's blessings on
mankind than Christ Jesus, 'who, being in the
form of God, thought it not robbery to be equal
with God: but, taking the form of a servant, He
humbled Himself, becoming obedient unto death,
even to the death of the Cross.'[2]

That it was, in fine, an offering for sin, is
evident. 'For God indeed was in Christ, reconcil-
ing the world to Himself, not imputing to them
their sins:'[3] and 'If the blood of goats and of
oxen, and the ashes of an heifer being sprinkled,
sanctify such as are defiled, to the cleansing of
the flesh: how much more shall the Blood of
Christ, who by the Holy Ghost offered Himself
unspotted unto God, cleanse our conscience from
dead works, to serve the living God? And therefore He is the mediator of the New Testament:
that, by means of His death, for the redemption
of those transgressions which were under the
former Testament, they that are called may receive
the promise of eternal inheritance.'[4]

---

[1] *S. Matthew*, XVII, 5.   [2] *Philippians*, II, 6–8.
[3] 2 *Corinthians*, V, 19.   [4] *Hebrews*, IX, 13–15.

IX.—THE UNBLOODY SACRIFICE OF THE NEW LAW.

Although, indeed, it is true that Christ, 'blotting out the handwriting of the decree that was against us, has taken the same out of the way, fastening it to the Cross;'[1] and by one oblation hath perfected for ever them that are sanctified;[2] still, it is no less positively certain that He does not regard it as in any manner deteriorating the inestimable value of that ransom which He had paid for us, or detracting from the all-sufficiency of the sacrifice upon the Cross, not only to have left us the sacraments for our sanctification, but to be our mediator in heaven, where 'He is now always living to make intercession for us.'[3] This office of mediator He more especially exercises by presenting to His Father that one, same oblation of Himself, which He made, in a bloody manner, on Mount Calvary, and now causes to be every day commemorated in an unbloody sacrifice by His delegated priests, throughout the earth; thus realising the declaration of the prophet Malachias, that, 'from the rising to the setting of the sun, there should be made, amongst the Gentiles, a clean oblation to the Lord of Hosts.' In this way, too, He discharges the functions of His priesthood: for Christ Jesus 'hath an everlasting

---

[1] *Colossians*, II, 14. [2] *Hebrews*, X, 14.
[3] *Hebrews*, VII, 25.

priesthood:'[1] He is 'a high priest for ever according to the order of Melchisedech.'[2] Now it is a
doctrine on which S. Paul emphatically insists,
that 'every high priest is appointed to offer gifts
and sacrifices : wherefore it is necessary that He
(Christ) also should have something to offer.'[3]

That anyone can really be a priest—that a
priest can possibly fulfil that office characteristic-
ally distinctive of the sacerdotal order—that a
priesthood can exist, and, for a single moment,
have its chief and essentially peculiar function
exercised, without a real sacrifice, are such glaring
contradictions, that the most artful ingenuity may
toil in vain to reconcile them : for priest, priesthood, and sacrifice are co-relative expressions,
which necessarily presuppose the existence of
each other. Christ, therefore, as a high priest,
must have a real sacrifice, in which a real victim
is offered up, according to the rites, and by the
ministers belonging to His order of priesthood ;
but since this priesthood is to be everlasting in
its duration, it must, therefore, continue perpetually employed about its functions, the most
conspicuous amongst which is sacrifice. That
the Christian priesthood, from the period of its
foundation to the present moment, has been
occupied unceasingly in such an office, is a fact
authenticated in every page of profane as well as

---

[1] *Hebrews*, VII, 24.   [2] *Hebrews*, VI, 20.   [3] *Hebrews*, VIII, 3.

ecclesiastical history. That this sacrifice called the Mass, which is, and has been, and will continue to be, daily celebrated in the Church, according to the injunctions of its sacred institutor, is that real sacrifice of the new law, we will now proceed to demonstrate by a variety of arguments and proofs derived from Holy Scripture, and furnished by the several monuments of ecclesiastical antiquity.

SECTION II.

THE MASS A SACRIFICE.

X.—THE MASS A TRUE SACRIFICE.

THAT in the Liturgy of the Mass there is offered this real sacrifice may be evidenced by the most clear and unexceptionable authorities deduced from Holy Scripture. Such are the figures and prophecies illustrative of the Messiah, contained in the Ancient Testament; and in the New, the testimonies of the Evangelists, together with the authority of S. Paul.

XI.—SACRIFICE OF MELCHISEDECH.

The sacrifice and priesthood of the King of Salem first demands, and shall receive, our notice. In the Book of Genesis we read that 'Melchisedech, the King of Salem,' brought forth bread and wine, 'for he was the priest of the Most High God.'[1] This incident the royal prophet,[2] and S. Paul in his Epistle to the Hebrews,[3] apply to Christ in such a manner, as not merely to intimate that Melchisedech was a figure only of our Divine Redeemer, since the very same might equally be said of Aaron; but that Christ was

---

[1] *Genesis*, XIV, 18.   [2] *Psalm* CIX, 4.   [3] *Hebrews*, VII.

a priest for ever according to the order of Melchisedech, and not according to the order of Aaron. This S. Paul notices more unequivocally than the royal Psalmist.

From the double kind of difference which so manifestly distinguished the priesthood of Melchisedech from that of Aaron, we may gather two arguments in support of our assertion. The first, and, at the same time, the most important difference which characterised them, is found in the matter of sacrifice. Although the sacrifices of the Hebrew sanctuary, and the sacrifice of Melchisedech, agreed with reference to the selfsame object which they severally typified, as they all were images of the same Christ Jesus, still they varied in their signs. The sacrifices of Aaron were bloody, and, under the species of slaughtered animals, prefigured the passion and the death of Christ. The sacrifice of Melchisedech was unbloody, and, under the form of bread and wine, represented the Body and the Blood of that same Christ. If, therefore, Christ be a priest, not according to the order of Aaron, but according to the order of Melchisedech, He must have instituted some kind or other of sacrifice, which is an unbloody one, under the species of bread and wine.

That, by virtue of His priesthood, Christ had to offer sacrifice, in the species of bread and wine, is immediately deducible from the very type in which it was prefigured. In his sacrifice of bread and wine, Melchisedech, the priest of the Most High God, bore the most illustrious figure of Christ. Hence it follows that Christ also, in the institution of the Blessed Eucharist in bread and wine, not only acted as a priest, but truly sacrificed; since, otherwise, He would not have accurately realised this figure of Himself. If the same offering or sacrifice be not continued till the consummation of ages, Christ could not be a priest for ever according to the order of Melchisedech.

Another difference will be discovered to exist between the priesthood of Aaron and that of Melchisedech. The priesthood with which the King of Salem was invested was exclusively of one man alone, who, while he had no predecessor, was not succeeded in his sacerdotal office by any individual. The Aaronic priesthood was communicated to many, not only at the same time, but was regularly kept up by a formal and long-protracted succession. This difference the Apostle of the Gentiles notices in the most particular manner, in his Epistle to the Hebrews, where he says that Melchisedech was ' without father, without mother, without genealogy, having neither beginning of days, nor end of life ; '[1] and through the remaining portion of the chapter, applying all those circum-

---

[1] *Hebrews*, VII, 3.

stances to Christ, he proclaims of Him, that He is a priest for ever, who, while He had no predecessor, will never have a successor; since, not only He Himself lives always, but the Lord has sworn that His priesthood shall neither be changed, nor transferred, as it happened to the Levitical priesthood. This, moreover, S. Paul corroborated by those words, extracted from the Psalmist: 'The Lord hath sworn, and He will not repent, thou art a priest for ever.'[1] Now if the priesthood of Christ is to endure until the end of time, most certainly the rites and ceremonies of sacrifice must also last as long; unless, indeed, we have the temerity to suppose the priesthood of Jesus to be an empty and a vacant thing, or some idle and imaginary office. The bloody sacrifice upon the Cross was offered up but once;[2] it never can be repeated in a bloody manner, since Christ can die no more; for He is now immortal and impassible. There must, therefore, exist some other mode of sacrifice, which is to be perpetually performed; for how can anyone be a priest who has no kind of sacrifice to offer? Priest and sacrifice are terms which mutually imply the existence of each other; a truth so evident that, as was before observed, S. Paul declares that 'every high priest is appointed to offer gifts and sacrifices.'[3] Hence it must be

---

[1] *Psalm* CIX.   [2] *Hebrews*, X, 10.
[3] *Hebrews*, VIII, 3.

admitted that, in the Church of Christ, there does exist some true form of real sacrifice, which is celebrated by sacerdotal ministers carefully delegated to be the vicegerents upon earth, in the place of Jesus Christ, the great high priest ; such a form of sacrifice is discoverable nowhere, except in the holy and tremendous sacrifice usually denominated the Mass.[1]

The only point of mutual but exclusive coincidence between the priesthood of Melchisedech and that of Christ is an identity of matter—bread and wine—employed in the sacrifice.

The King of Salem received tithes of Abraham,

---

[1] Here the reader must be admonished of a serious imposition which has been practised by the Protestant translators of the New Testament, not only on the members of the Anglican Establishment, but on everyone who may chance to read her version of the Holy Scriptures. In his Epistle to the Hebrews, the Apostle says : 'In the which will, we are sanctified by the oblation of the body of Jesus Christ once' (*Hebrews*, x, 10) ; which sentence is thus translated in the Protestant version : 'By the which will we are sanctified through the offering of the body of Jesus Christ once *for all*.' Here we have '*for all*' added to the genuine text, for these words are not found either in the Greek original or in the Latin vulgate. It is impossible to consider this ingraftment on the word of God as the result of accident or negligence ; on the contrary, we must refer it to deliberate design, for the following reasons : 1. The Greek adverb, ἐφάπαξ, 'once,' but very seldom occurs in the New Testament, and only in the writings of S. Paul. The only passages, besides the one at present under observation, in which it is to be found are the following : *Romans*, VI, 10 ; *Hebrews*, IX, 12 ; 1 *Corinthians*, XV, 6. In all these places, the Protestant translators have rendered it by '*once*,' or '*at once*;' they, therefore, knew its proper force, and could when they chose render it according to its native meaning. 2. The unwarrantable introduction of these two words, '*for all*,' essentially corrupts this text, and perverts its sense against the Catholic, in

and blessed him and his companions ; but the Levitical priesthood also collected tithes, and bestowed their benedictions ; if Melchisedech had not been anointed with oil, had succeeded no one in the priestly office, nor was followed by any successor, the same may be observed in Abel ; if his genealogy was unknown—an incident, however, quite extraneous to the priesthood—this was common to Job, and others who were priests. The only way in which the priesthood of Melchisedech differed from every other priesthood before the promulgation of the second law, was in the oblation of bread and wine. This, therefore, must constitute the agreement between the sacrifice of Mel-

---

favour of the Protestant doctrine on the Holy Eucharist. No doubt, therefore, but they were advisedly inserted, to procure a scriptural authority for one of the novelties introduced by what is miscalled the Reformation. In fact, this citation from the writings of S. Paul is invariably adduced in its *vitiated form*, as a warrant for that modern doctrine first promulgated in England by the framers of the thirty-first amongst those articles of religion recognised by the Establishment, which teaches that 'The Sacrifices of Masses, in the which it was commonly said, that the priest did offer Christ for the quick and the dead to have remission of pain and guilt, were blasphemous fables and dangerous deceits.'

When the intelligent and sensible Protestant reflects that there is not one single personage registered in that Calendar of Saints appended to his Book of Common Prayer who did not live and die, or win the palm of martyrdom, in the belief of the Catholic doctrine of the Mass ; and that many of them were in the habit of daily offering up that Eucharistic sacrifice—he will censure the temerity, at the same time that he blushes for the inconsistency of his sect, in designating the practice of those very men whom she herself has recognised for Saints as a blasphemous fable,—and pronouncing the most venerable and best authenticated tenet amongst the articles of genuine Christianity as a 'dangerous deceit.'

chisedech and the sacrifice of Christ, who selected wheaten bread and wine of the grape, as the matter which should be transubstantiated into His Body and His Blood by the words of consecration.

That the motive which induced Melchisedech to bring forth bread and wine was not to present refreshment to the soldiers of Abraham, but to offer sacrifice to God in celebration of that Patriarch's victory, is evident, both from the language and the context of this passage in the Book of Genesis.

If Abraham and his servants partook of Melchisedech's oblation of bread and wine, it was for them a sacred refection, similar to those observed amongst the Israelites in their sacrifices of thanksgiving. It could not have been by way of corporal refreshment, since the sacred text informs us that Abraham's soldiers had already feasted on the provisions which they found among the spoils that they captured from the vanquished kings.[1]

---

[1] *Genesis*, XIV, 24. Some Protestants quarrel with the reading of this passage in our Catholic Bibles, and contend that the Hebrew particle '*vau*' should be rendered as it is in the Protestant version, '*and* he was a priest,' instead of '*for* he was,' etc. In defence of the Catholic translation of the particle '*vau*,' as preferable to the one followed in this particular passage by the authorised Bible of the Church of England, we may observe : 1st, That S. Jerome, a most eminent Biblical scholar, and a thorough master of the Hebrew language, has thus given the passage in his vulgate : '*Erat enim sacerdos*,' '*for* he was a priest.' With consistent Protestants, S. Jerome's authority must possess great weight, as they refer to his opinion with so much deference in the sixth of the Thirty-

XII.—THE SACRIFICE OF MELCHISEDECH ELUCIDATED BY THE WRITINGS OF THE FATHERS.

That the Church has invariably considered this passage in the Book of Genesis as demonstrative, not only of Melchisedech's having sacrificed in bread and wine, but also that his oblation was beautifully typical of the Eucharistic Sacrifice peculiar to the Christian dispensation, is evident from the attestations of the holy Fathers. For a proof of this, the curious reader is referred to a learned and invaluable work containing extracts from the writings of those early and venerable witnesses of the Faith.[1] In that work are recited the observations on this subject delivered by S. Cyprian,[2] Eusebius of Cæsarea,[3] S. Epiphanius,[4] S. Jerome,[5] S. Augustine,[6] and Theodoret.[7]

nine Articles. 2nd, Grammarians inform us that this particle is not only copulative, but indicative of a cause, and that the manner of construing it must be collected from the context of the passage. Parker, in his Hebrew Lexicon, enumerates as many as seventeen different ways in which it is employed in Scripture. 3rd, The English Protestant, like the Catholic Bible, has the particle 'vau' translated by the word 'for,' instead of 'and,' in the very same Book of Genesis (Genesis, xx, 3); the Hebrew text is וְהִוא בְּעֻלַת בָּעַל —literally thus, 'and she is married to a husband,' but which is rendered in the Protestant version, 'for she is a man's wife.' No Protestant can therefore rationally object to a mode of translation which is approved by the Establishment in her authorised version of the Sacred Scriptures.

[1] J. BERINGTON and J. KIRK, The Faith of Catholics on certain Points of Controversy confirmed by Scripture and attested by the Fathers of the first five Centuries of the Church. 3rd edition, London, 1846.

[2] Ibid., vol. II, p. 418. [3] Ibid., p. 428. [4] Ibid., p. 451.
[5] Ibid., p. 456. [6] Ibid., pp. 483, 484. [7] Ibid., p. 498.

XIII.—ILLUSTRATED BY AN ANCIENT MOSAIC AT RAVENNA.

But there is another curious and highly interesting illustration of this text, which, as far as the writer is aware, has hitherto never been introduced to notice. This is furnished by one amongst those numerous pictorial monuments of early Christian piety which decorate the ancient church of S. Vitalis at Ravenna.[1] The wall about the apse or recess, which overhangs the sanctuary, is encrusted with mosaic-work in which are represented various subjects chosen from the Old and New Testaments. Amongst those Scripture histories, two are prominently discernible: they are, the sacrifice of Abel, and the sacrifice of Melchisedech.

The King of Salem is represented as standing by an altar covered with a cloth, on which are two small circular loaves or cakes, between which stands a small two-handled chalice; a nimbus, or glory, surrounds his head; his arms are outstretched as he holds up a third cake. His robes resemble our vestments; the under one descends to the ankles like an alb, and the mantle is fashioned precisely as the ancient cope. At the opposite side stands Abel holding up a lamb.

---

[1] The church of S. Vitalis was built in the year 547, and adorned with mosaics at the same epoch.

Another mosaic in the church of S. Apollinaris
in Classe represents Melchisedech similarly attired,
standing at the back of an altar facing the
spectator, holding a loaf with both hands slightly
raised above the table, on which stands a two-
handled chalice between two loaves. At the left
or north end of the altar stands Abel holding up
a lamb, and at the opposite end Abraham with
Isaac before him, whom he is presenting. There
can be no doubt that these three subjects, and
particularly the sacrifice of Melchisedech, were
selected to indicate that they were ancient types
of the sacrifice of the new Law, called the Mass.
S. Theophilus, patriarch of Antioch,[1] remarks that
Melchisedech was the first man who became a
priest; and S. Cyprian[2] notices that the bread
and little vessel are symbols of the Blessed Sacrament. Indeed, these observations on these three
sacrifices are all but asserted in that prayer which
almost immediately succeeds the consecration:
'Upon which (the holy bread of eternal life and
the chalice of our everlasting salvation) vouchsafe
to look down with a propitious and serene countenance, and accept them, as Thou wast pleased
to accept the gifts of Thy just servant Abel, and
the sacrifice of our patriarch Abraham, and that
which Thy high-priest Melchisedech offered to

---

[1] Lib. II, *Ad Autolycum.*
[2] Epist. LXIII, *Ad Caecilium de Sacramento Dominici calicis.*

Thee, a holy sacrifice and immaculate victim. This representation, therefore, of the offering of bread and wine by Melchisedech, affords another ancient warrant for regarding it as a prefiguration of the Sacrifice of the Mass.[1]

XIV.—THE PASCHAL LAMB A FIGURE OF THE SACRIFICE OF THE MASS.

A second argument to prove the Mass to be a real sacrifice, may be drawn from the ceremony of

---

[1] In those ages, when printing was unknown, the pastors of the Church availed themselves of the arts to represent to their people, by means of fresco-painting, mosaic-work, and sculpture, executed on the walls of the churches, the scripture-history, and the truths of our holy religion. The reason was obvious : to the faithful, these were instructive volumes, written in intelligible and self-speaking characters. But as their religious instructors justly conceived that the guardians of the faith were the best expounders of its mysteries, instead of permitting the artist to select and treat the subjects according to his own imagination, they rather employed his pencil to inscribe in colours what they dictated to him ; and it is a well-attested fact that, in the first twelve centuries of the Church, painters, and those who wrought in mosaic, and artists in general, were, in the execution of their works, permitted to exercise their own liberty and invention no further than in the drawing of their pieces. The bishop or pastor of the edifice which was to be ornamented, not merely fixed upon the subjects, but invariably prescribed the precise manner in which each one should be treated in all its several, and even its smallest parts. (ANASTASII Bibliothecarii *de vitis Romanorum Pontificum* tom. III, *curante F. Blanchino*, p. 124.) Nor did they permit themselves to be directed by their own caprice, while guiding the labours of the painter or the sculptor ; but most religiously adhered to the traditions which had been handed down to them. We may, therefore, rest assured, that these ancient monuments are faithful and authentic records, not of the opinion of laymen and private individuals, but of the public doctrine of the Church at the period when they were executed.

the Paschal Lamb.[1] That the oblation of this victim was a figure of the Eucharist is evident from the words of the Apostle, who tells us : ' Christ our Pasch is sacrificed ; therefore let us feast, not with the old leaven, but with the un-leavened bread of sincerity and truth.' [2] From the Evangelists we learn that, immediately after our Divine Redeemer had concluded the legal observ-ance of the Passover, He proceeded to celebrate the Eucharist. By the identity of place and time, He more unequivocally assured His followers that the substance had, at length, arrived to realise the shadow, and that the old law, with its ceremonies, was abrogated, and made to yield its place to a new and better Testament. If we consider the circumstances attending on both these solemn rites, we shall observe that there was no one single figure of the ancient law bearing reference to Jesus the Messiah, which was so accurately ful-filled by Him, in the institution of the Eucharistic Sacrifice, as the ceremonial of the Paschal Lamb.

1. It was directed that the Paschal Lamb should be sacrificed on the evening of the four-teenth day of the first month :[3] a circumstance of which particular notice was taken by the law, and, in consequence, the Jews most diligently observed it : now it was immediately after having

---

[1] *Exodus*, XII.   [2] 1 *Corinthians*, v, 7, 8.
[3] *Exodus*, XII, 6.

celebrated the Passover with legal exactness, that our Divine Redeemer instituted the Blessed Eucharist. 2. The Paschal Lamb was immolated in remembrance of the passage of the Lord, and the liberation of the Israelites from their Egyptian bondage: the Eucharist is offered to commemorate the passage of our Saviour, by His bloody passion, from this world to the kingdom of His Father, and to celebrate our redemption from the tyranny of Satan, over whom Christ Jesus triumphed by His glorious death upon the Cross. 3. The Paschal Lamb was offered that it might be eaten, and be, as it were, the sustenance to fortify the traveller for a lengthened journey on which he was about to enter; since it was in the guise of travellers that the Jews partook of it, with their loins girt up, holding staves in their hands, and having sandals on their feet: and what is the Eucharist but a strengthening food, a sacred refection for men while on their pilgrimage through this desert-world, and journeying towards the land of promise—Heaven, their real and celestial country? 4. The Paschal Lamb could not be eaten except by the clean and circumcised, and within the precincts of the holy city; so the Eucharist cannot be partaken of with profit, but by those who have been baptized, are clean of heart and purified from sin, and by being associated with the Catholic Church, are 'come to Mount Sion, and to the City of the living God, the heavenly Jerusalem, and to the company of many thousands of Angels, and to the Church of the first born, who are written in the heavens, and to God the judge of all, and to the spirits of the just made perfect.'[1]

The Paschal Lamb was at the same time a sacrifice and a sacrament; because, after it had been offered up, it was eaten by the Israelites; so likewise the Eucharistic oblation is a sacrifice and a sacrament—a sacrifice, because our Pasch, Christ Jesus, is presented to His Father on our altars; and a sacrament, because the faithful receive Him there, whose 'Flesh is meat indeed, and whose Blood is drink indeed.'

XV.—ACCOMPLISHMENT OF THE PROPHECY OF MALACHIAS, IN THE SACRIFICE OF THE MASS.

Another and most conclusive proof in favour of the Sacrifice of the Mass is furnished by the Prophet Malachias, who was commissioned to promulgate the following commination to the Jewish people. 'I have no pleasure in you, saith the Lord of Hosts. For, from the rising of the sun even to the going down, My name is great among the Gentiles, and in every place there is sacrifice, and there is offered to My name a clean oblation: for My name is great among the Gentiles, saith the Lord of Hosts.'[2]

This illustrious prediction cannot be applicable

---

[1] *Hebrews*, XII, 22, 25.   [2] *Malachias*, I, 10, 11.

to the Jewish sacrifices, because they are pointedly rejected, and so far from being offered up in every place, they were exclusively confined to the temple of Jerusalem; while the clean oblation which Malachias speaks of was to be made in every region of the earth, and not by Israelites, but by Gentiles. It cannot be referable to the unhallowed and impure rites of Paganism, which profaned, instead of glorifying, the name of the Almighty. It cannot be applied to designate that bloody sacrifice immolated on the altar of the Cross at Calvary, since that was offered once only, and in one place. It is, therefore, verified in no other way than by the unbloody sacrifice, by that clean oblation which is, and will be offered up by the Christian priesthood to the end of time, and in every nation that the sun can gaze upon, from his rising to his setting. This prophecy, therefore, refers to the Eucharistic sacrifice of our altars, called the Mass, which now supplies the place of all the ancient victims, and has been unceasingly celebrated from the death of Christ until the present moment, and continues to be everywhere duly celebrated.

Some amongst the innovators of the sixteenth century, to neutralise the force of this triumphant argument, endeavoured to affix a spiritual meaning to the prophet's declaration, and therefore interpreted it as expressive of a sacrifice, improperly so called, of praise and thanksgiving, of

prayer, good works, and patience. Nothing, however, could be more erroneous than this modern
gloss upon the inspired pages. 1. The word
מִנְחָה, which occurs in the original Hebrew text
of this prophecy, indicates a particular species of
sacrifice, in which fine flour, oil, and frankincense,
commingled together, were employed as the oblation :[1] and it should be remarked that the Holy
Scriptures, whenever the term 'sacrifice' is used in
a figurative sense, invariably attach some adjunct
to it, which immediately discriminates the meta-
phoric meaning; and hence, in various portions
of the sacred volume, we meet with the following
expressions: 'a sacrifice of praise,' 'a sacrifice
of righteousness,' 'a sacrifice of joy,' etc. The
Minchah[2] of the Hebrew scripture is translated
by the word θυσία, or sacrifice, in the Septuagint,
and is the term employed to signify the oblation
of Cain and of Abel.[3] 2. That it cannot be, with
accuracy, understood of a spiritual offering composed of prayer, devotion, or thanksgivings, will
immediately be evident, when we remember that
such a kind of sacrifice had, after the days of

---

[1] *Leviticus*, II, 1, and VI, 14, 15.

[2] GESENIUS, in his *Hebrew Lexicon* (as translated by Christopher
Leo, Cambridge, 1825), says of this word: 'In the Mosaic ritual,
it is applied especially to the unbloody sacrifices, as offerings of meat
and drink, which were offered with the animal sacrifices. Hence
Sacrifice and offering, *Psalm* XXXIX, 7 ; *Jeremiah*, XVII, 26 ; *Daniel*,
IX, 27.'

[3] *Genesis*, IV, 4, 5.

Malachias, who lived about four hundred years anterior to the coming of the Messiah, been rendered very frequently, by Jew as well as Gentile, and had indeed been made from the earliest period of the human race, by every sincere adorer of the Deity; whereas the prophet announces the future institution of a pure oblation—a sacrifice peculiar to a subsequent covenant, and which was not only to be exclusively offered up by Gentile believers, but should supersede all the various Levitical sacrifices which would then be abrogated.

XVI.—CHRIST ANNOUNCES A NEW SACRIFICE.

That a new sacrifice, which should be offered up 'in spirit and in truth,'[1] was requisite, our Divine Redeemer proclaimed to the Samaritan woman, who proposed to Him the question about the place on which it was necessary to adore. Now that the adoration indicated by our Blessed Redeemer is synonymous with sacrifice, may be inferred from a variety of circumstances: for the difference between the Jews and the Samaritans was about the place on which the exterior worship of sacrifice could legally be exhibited, since both were thoroughly persuaded that man could invoke the Lord by supplications and by prayers, —could observe the various forms of simple adoration, and present his heart to Heaven, in

---

[1] *S. John,* IV, 23.

every region of the earth. Our Divine Redeemer
entered into the idea of the Samaritan woman,
and answered her by saying: 'The hour cometh,
when you shall neither on this mountain, nor in
Jerusalem, adore the Father;'[1] or, in other words,
the time is fast approaching when sacrifice shall
be no longer offered, either on Mount Gerizim
or in the Jewish temple; but true adorers shall
adore the Father in spirit and in truth, without
being circumscribed within the limits of one
peculiar or favoured city, by a new and better
sacrifice; spiritual, not carnal; true, and not
typical or figurative; effected by the Holy Spirit,
and the mysterious words of consecration—not
by pouring out the blood of goats and of oxen,
nor by sprinkling the ashes of a heifer; illustrious, not from being a shadow of the good
things to come, but because it is that very thing
itself, the adorable reality.

XVII.—THE SACRIFICE OF THE MASS PROVED FROM S. PAUL.

'Fly,' exclaims the Apostle of the Gentiles,
'fly from the service of idols. I speak as to
wise men: judge ye yourselves what I say. The
chalice of benediction, which we bless, is it not
the communion of the Blood of Christ? and the
bread, which we break, is it not the partaking of

---

[1] *S. John*, IV, 21.

the Body of the Lord ? For we, being many, are one bread, one body, all that partake of one bread. Behold Israel according to the flesh : are not they, that eat of the sacrifices, partakers of the altar ? What then ! Do I say, that what is offered in sacrifice to idols is anything ? or, that the idol is anything ? But the things which the heathens sacrifice, they sacrifice to devils, and not to God. And I would not that you should be made partakers with devils. You cannot drink the chalice of the Lord, and the chalice of devils ; you cannot be partakers of the table of the Lord, and of the table of devils.'[1]

This passage from S. Paul proves, by a triple argument, the Mass to be a real sacrifice.

1. The Apostle institutes a comparison between the table of the Lord, where the believers in Jesus receive the Holy Eucharist, and the table of the Gentiles, who sacrifice to idols, and the table of the Jews, on which the people offered up their carnal victims to the true and living God. From this parallel it follows, that the table of the Lord is an altar, and consequently, the Eucharist a proper sacrifice ; for, without a most egregious anomaly in language, an altar can never be erected, unless for the purposes of real sacrifice. 2. The Apostle institutes a comparison between the Eucharist and the sacrifices of the Jews and

---

[1] 1 *Corinthians*, x, 14-21.

Gentiles. He declares, by the most unequivocal expressions, that, as the faithful receive at the table of the Lord, the Body and the Blood of Christ,—so the Jews and the Gentiles participate in those victims, in the immolation which they severally offer up in sacrifice upon their respective altars. S. Paul's comparison would, however, not only be quite imperfect, but utterly inapplicable, if the Eucharist were not as much a real sacrifice to the Almighty, as were the victims which the Hebrew nation sacrificed to Him, and the immolations and libations of the Gentiles, made in honour of their imaginary Deities. 3. The Apostle traces a resemblance between that society which the Christian has with the Godhead by a participation in the sacred Eucharist, and the society which the Gentile formed with his idols by eating those meats which had been offered in their honour. He teaches that the individual who partakes of the victim sacrificed to idols, becomes himself an idolater; and hence he exhorts the believers at Corinth to 'fly from the service of idols.' While urging such advice, he employs this train of argument: 'those who eat of the sacrifices partake of the altar,' and consequently unite with the heathens, as they sacrifice to devils, and, therefore, make themselves their worshippers.

If the form of argument adopted by S. Paul be just, we may pursue it in reasoning on the

Eucharist; and conclude, that those who eat of that venerable oblation, become partakers of 'the table of the Lord,' and, consequently, join in offering that victim immolated to God, and identify themselves with those who make it,—and, in this manner, honour the Almighty, by the most solemn, as well as the highest act of adoration; and thus verify the assertion of the Apostle of the Gentiles, who assures the Hebrews, in his Epistle to them, that we 'have an altar, whereof they have no power to eat who serve the tabernacle.'[1]

That in the Mass there is offered a real and propitiatory sacrifice to God is a truth not only declared in Scripture, but corroborated by the history and the institutions of the Church,[2] and unanimously attested by the writings of her Pastors, in characters as brilliant as the stars that light the firmament. Volumes might be filled with such testimonies, but for want of space I must reluctantly pass on, without gleaning and

---

[1] *Hebrews*, XIII, 10.

[2] For a triumphant illustration of those arguments in proof of the sacrifice of the Mass, deduced from the liturgies and ceremonials of the Church, the inquiring reader is referred to a work entitled *Christianity; or, The Evidences and Characters of the Christian Religion* (London, 1827), the masterly performance of the late Right Rev. Dr. Poynter, a prelate conspicuous for his piety, his enlightened zeal, and profound theological learning. He who pens this notice rejoices to possess the present opportunity of recording his tribute of reverence to the memory of that venerable bishop, some extracts from whose work are found in Appendix I.

offering to the reader the most conspicuous amongst them. There is, however, one in particular, so very appropriate and interesting, that it would be unpardonable not to bestow on it especial notice.

Who is ignorant of the tender but afflicting scene which took place at the separation of the aged and venerable Xystus, the second of that name who filled the throne of S. Peter, and the youthful and heroic S. Laurence, while the lictors of the emperor Valerian [1] dragged the holy Pope to martyrdom? As the pontiff was led away, his deacon S. Laurence followed weeping; and, at last, burst forth into this pathetic exclamation: ' Father, whither art thou going without thy son? whither art thou hastening, O holy priest, without thy deacon? Thou wert never wont to offer sacrifice without me thy minister: wherein have I now displeased thee? Hast thou found me wanting in my duty? Try me now, and see whether thou hast made choice of an unfit minister for dispensing the Blood of Christ!' [2]

---

[1] The emperor Valerian issued his cruel edicts against the Church in the year 257.

[2] Ambrosiaster *de Officiis Ministrorum*, lib. I, cap. XLII, § 204. A. BUTLER, *Lives of the Saints*, August 10.

SECTION III.

ON THE REAL PRESENCE.

XVIII.—THE REAL PRESENCE.

FROM reviewing the proofs which so clearly
establish the Mass to be a real sacrifice, we
naturally proceed to investigate another most
important tenet comprehended in that doctrine.

For eighteen centuries the Catholic Church has
been sedulous in teaching, as one amongst those
articles of faith delivered to her by the Apostles,
who received it from the lips of truth itself, the
Son of God, that in the sacrament of the altar
usually denominated the Eucharist,[1] are received
the real Body and the real Blood, together with
the Soul and the Divinity of Jesus Christ—the
very 'Word made flesh,' which, conceived by the
Holy Ghost, and born of the Blessed Virgin Mary,
was afterwards affixed to the Cross, and died for

---

[1] The primitive Fathers denominate the sacrament instituted by
our Saviour at the Last Supper by the term Eucharist, a Greek
word which signifies 'thanksgiving.' Such an appellation is most
appropriate, since it intimates that our Redeemer offered up thanksgivings to the Lord at its institution ; and also instructs us concerning
the necessity of presenting our grateful thanks to heaven, whenever
we receive this abridgment of all God's wonders ; this standing
memorial of our redemption through the Blood of Jesus ; and the
pledge of a bright eternity.

our redemption. The following are some amongst the numerous arguments she exhibits for her unvarying belief in this dogma.

XIX.—THE PROMISE MADE BY CHRIST THAT HE WOULD GIVE US HIS FLESH AND BLOOD TO EAT AND DRINK.

In the sixth chapter of S. John, we observe that Jesus, after having wrought the great miracle of feeding five thousand persons in the desert with five barley loaves and two small fishes, took occasion to unfold the doctrine of the Real Presence to the wondering multitude. The Evangelist informs us that the Saviour thus addressed them: 'I am the living bread which came down from heaven. If any man eat of this bread, he shall live for ever; and the bread that I will give is My flesh, for the life of the world. The Jews therefore strove among themselves, saying: How can this man give us his flesh to eat? Then Jesus said to them: Amen, amen, I say unto you: Except you eat the flesh of the Son of man, and drink His blood, you shall not have life in you. He that eateth My flesh, and drinketh My blood, hath everlasting life; and I will raise him up in the last day. For My flesh is meat indeed; and My blood is drink indeed. He that eateth My flesh, and drinketh My blood, abideth in Me, and I in him. As the living Father hath sent Me, and I live by the Father; so he that eateth Me, the same also shall live by Me. This is the bread that came down from heaven. Not as your fathers did eat manna, and are dead. He that eateth this bread shall live for ever. Many, therefore, of His disciples hearing it, said : This saying is hard, and who can hear it? After this many of His disciples went back, and walked no more with Him.'[1]

This passage of Scripture claims our particular attention. Here our Divine Redeemer promises to give His followers an especial kind of nourishment —a food which would surpass the manna of the desert—itself a wondrous bread—the bread of angels,[2] rained down from heaven, where it was miraculously produced, and which exhibited such wonders in all its several circumstances. 'When the dew fell in the night upon the camp, the manna also fell with it.'[3] It fell only round about the camp of the Israelites, and that too every day except the Sabbath.[4] In such quantities did this bread of heaven rain down upon the Jews for those forty years of their wandering through the wilderness, that it was sufficient to nourish the whole multitude of more than a million of people, each one of whom, though he might gather, could not secure, except on the Sabbath, more than sufficient for his daily maintenance, which was a gomor, or, according to our English measure, about three quarts.[5] Every sixth day it came down in double

---

[1] *S. John*, VI, 51–59, 61, 67.   [2] *Psalm* LXXVII, 25.
[3] *Numbers*, XI, 9.   [4] *Exodus*, XVI, 27.   [5] *Exodus*, XVI, 18.

quantities, and though it infallibly putrified when reserved beyond one single day, yet on the Sabbath it never suffered such an alteration.[1] This same manna which melted away before the beams of the morning sun when left in the fields, on being conveyed within the tent acquired such hardness and consistency that it could be ground in the mill or pounded in a mortar; and would even so far resist the action and the heat of fire, as to be boiled in a pot, and made up into cakes.[2] Any bread, therefore, which could possibly surpass it in excellence, must be wondrous indeed; hence that food alluded to by Christ, and signified to be superior to the manna of the ancient Israelites, must, like it, not only come from heaven, but comprehend still greater wonders; and that it did is evident from every expression of our Saviour.

1. His future gift was not to be common, inert, inanimate bread, but *living bread*,[3] consequently with life in it, quickened with a spirit; yes, it was to be—it is the very Flesh of Jesus, animated by His radiant, spotless soul, and sanctified by its union with His divinity. 2. But this is not all: if we interrogate the sacred text concerning the nature of that bread from heaven, with which the Redeemer pledged Himself to furnish all His faithful followers; He Himself, not merely once by accident, but oftentimes and formally repeated

---

[1] *Exodus*, XVI, 20-22.   [2] *Numbers*, XI, 8.   [3] *S. John*, VI, 51.

for answer, that the food He promised was to be His true, His very Flesh; 'His Flesh indeed, His Blood indeed.' The Jews were scandalised; they asserted that it was impossible, as they cried aloud : How can this man give us His flesh to eat? This is a hard saying and who can hear it?

Now, apart from that celestial charity, which instead of placing, would rather have removed the stone of scandal in the path of those who sought and trusted to its guidance; apart from a sacred love for truth, even common honesty would have imperatively demanded that Christ, the Author of all truth—Truth itself—should not allow a portion of His disciples to abandon Him, merely through a misrepresentation of one single sentence, which, according to their unanimous and public construction of it, uttered in His presence, insisted on a tenet which He never intended to promulgate, especially since it would have cost no further trouble than a word to disabuse them of their error, had it been one ; and to develope the real meaning of His doctrine, had they misconstrued it. While it is certain that the Jews literally understood our Saviour as having intimated that He would give them His very flesh and blood to be their nourishment, it is at the same time equally evident that He intended to define, in clear and intelligible language, how they were to understand His words. Instead, however, of correcting the notion that

possessed them, of His having said they were
to eat His real flesh and drink His real blood, by
attaching a figurative meaning to His words, He
not only reiterates the selfsame expressions, and
several times repeats the selfsame doctrine, but
employs a most solemn formula of speech in use
among the Jews, in order to affix still more deeply
in their minds the impression of a Real Presence,
and to satisfy them that they had rightly construed the import of His discourse, which was,
that they should have His real flesh and blood to
eat and drink. Nor does He once so much as
remotely insinuate that He was to be understood
as having spoken in a figurative manner.

As it was fitting that He, the very truth, should
not allow His chosen apostles, His numerous disciples, thousands among the Jews, and millions of
Christians in after ages, to mistake the meaning
of His expression on a subject of primary importance, we may legitimately conclude that, had the
multitude been wrong in interpreting His discourse to indicate a manducation of His real flesh
and blood, far from declining to resolve a difficulty, and remove the scandal which alienated
from His preaching so many ' who walked with
Him no more,' the Saviour would not have hesi-
tated to rectify the error, especially in reference
to His Apostles, whom He had selected to receive,
and afterwards disseminate, the knowledge of
His doctrines ; but would have pursued the same

course on this occasion which He invariably followed in other less important instances. It was His custom to explain, at least to His disciples, whatever might have been at first unintelligible in His public preaching to the multitude, or in His private conferences with themselves. Nicodemus could not comprehend the words of our Divine Redeemer on the necessity of Baptism; and this ruler of the Jews, in consequence, observed : 'How can a man be born when he is old?' But Jesus removed the difficulty by unveiling the import of His words, as He answered : 'Unless a man be born again of water and the Holy Ghost, he cannot enter into the kingdom of God.'[1] The disciples did not comprehend Him when he bade them beware of the leaven of the Pharisees; but, while He chided their inaccurate interpretation of this expression, he informed them that He animadverted on the pernicious doctrines of those Hebrew teachers. On another occasion, Jesus remarked to His apostles : 'I have meat to eat, which you know not.' They misconstrued the observation, and demanded if any man had brought Him anything to eat? But in explanation of what He had said, He answered them : 'My meat is to do the will of Him that sent Me.'[2] Towards the conclusion of His discourse, our Saviour referred to His future Ascension. He

---

[1] *S. John*, III, 5.   [2] *S. John*, IV, 32-34.

noticed it as a circumstance which would offer still greater difficulties to be surmounted by those amongst His auditors whose present incredulity refused to believe, that, although He was actually present, He could possibly give them His Flesh and Blood. Had, then, our Divine Redeemer promised to bequeath nothing more than a bit of common bread, which should represent His Body, it is impossible to imagine how the Jews would have had to experience greater difficulty in believing such a doctrine after than before Christ's Ascension. This is evident; for a sign to which a specific meaning is once unequivocally affixed is, at all times, equally intelligible to the parties initiated in its import. If, on the other hand, Christ intended, as He really did, to assure His followers that He would bestow His very Flesh and Blood to be their sacramental nourishment; then, indeed, we immediately perceive the force of our Saviour's reference to His future Ascension; we understand how the doctrine which appeared so 'hard' to the intelligence of His followers, at the very moment while they viewed Him standing in the body visible and palpable amongst them, would necessarily become ten thousand times more difficult to their stubborn belief, at a subsequent period, when they should behold His Body taken up, and wafted in radiance to the throne of God. Unless our Saviour had been anxious to persuade the Jews that the bread from

heaven about to be given to the world was not
a symbolic piece of bread, but His real Body,
He never would have studied, by predicting the
miraculous event of His elevation into heaven,
to induce them, when it should be realised, 'to
submit their reason to the obedience of faith.'
When, therefore, we learn that Jesus, knowing in
Himself that His disciples murmured at this, said
to them : 'Doth this scandalise you? If then you
shall see the Son of man ascend up where He
was before?'[1] We are certain that He insisted
still more pointedly in requiring belief in the
Eucharist : we hear Him teaching His disciples
that after the removal of His Body from among
them, and in the absence of the natural appearances of flesh and blood, they were, however, to
have no hesitation in acquiescing in this mysterious
dogma. Hence we may collect that our Lord, in
promulgating this tenet of the Real Presence,
noticed in its favour the very argument which
its adversaries at the present hour wield in combating against it, whilst they assert that the Body
and Blood of Christ must be as far from our altars
as heaven is from earth : though they teach that
'the Body and Blood of Christ are verily and
indeed taken and received by the faithful in the
Lord's Supper.'[2]

---

[1] *S. John*, VI, 62.
[2] The last answer but three in the Protestant Catechism in the
Book of Common Prayer. How the inconsistencies—to say nothing

XX.—OBJECTION ANSWERED.

Against these arguments are advanced by the impugners of this tenet those words of Christ: 'It is the spirit that quickeneth: the flesh profiteth nothing.'[1] Such an expression, however, instead of invalidating, fortifies the doctrine of the Real Presence.

It was not until Christ had no less than six several times asserted, with much solemnity and in the most explicit language, that His Flesh and Blood should be really present and given in the sacrament, that He observed, 'It is the spirit that quickeneth,' etc. Had it, therefore, been His purport, in this latter sentence, to correct the interpretation that the multitude affixed to His former asseverations, which they construed as signifying the manducation of His very Body—had He really insinuated in the faintest manner that the Eucharist did not contain, but was a figure only of His Flesh and Blood; is it not self-evident that not only those Jews who 'strove amongst themselves,' and so loudly vociferated 'how can this man give us His flesh to eat,' but such among

---

of the irreligion—of the innovators of the sixteenth century, are exhibited when those men abridge the omnipotence of God, by denying the possibility of Christ's being present in the Holy Eucharist; and at the selfsame moment maintain that His Body and His Blood are verily and indeed taken and received, but that it is not possible for them to be verily and indeed given.

[1] *S. John*, VI, 64.

the disciples also who experienced the belief in
a real eating of His Body to be a thing so 'hard'
to recognise, would have encountered no difficulty
either in comprehending such a doctrine, or in
yielding their assent to it; and, instead of walk-
ing no more with their Teacher, would have been
more anxious to follow Him and to listen to His
precepts; and yet, what happened? They took
scandal at His words, and abandoned Him. The
retiring disciples, therefore, openly assure us by
their desertion of Jesus Christ the very moment
after He had uttered this expression, that they
did not understand Him to indicate by it that
the former parts of His discourse about the eating
of His Flesh and Blood were to be explained in
a figurative manner, but, on the contrary, conceived Him to reiterate, if possible with greater
earnestness than ever, the doctrine of the Real
Presence.

The words of Christ on which this objection
against the Real Presence has been attempted, but
without success, to be erected, bear a twofold
interpretation. It is not unusual with the writers
of the sacred volumes to designate the carnal and
human reason of man by the word 'flesh,' whilst
they employ the term 'spirit' to signify the grace
of God and the inspirations of the Holy Ghost.
Such a form of language is more particularly discernible when their object is to oppose the one
in contrast with the other. Jesus declared to

S. Peter : 'Flesh and blood hath not revealed it to thee, but My Father who is in heaven.'[1] S. Paul admonishes the Romans that the faithful 'walk not according to the flesh, but according to the spirit.'[2] Our Saviour, while insisting on the manducation of His real Body, in answer to the argument which the Jews, like the modern sceptics, deduced from human reason and their senses against its possibility, observed that at the same time it was incompetent for flesh or carnal reason to decide on such a dogma ; it was only by the grace of God—the light of heaven—' the quickening spirit,' that it could be believed in, or discerned, and hence He immediately remarked : ' There are some of you that believe not . . . therefore did I say to you, that no man can come to Me, unless it be given him by My Father.'[3] How remarkably this expression of the Saviour coincides with that which He uttered when S. Peter acknowledged His divinity : ' Flesh and blood hath not revealed it to thee, but My Father who is in heaven.'[4]

An extract from the commentaries of S. Augustine will not only furnish a second illustration of this passage, but will likewise testify what was the general belief of the Church upon the Eucharist so far back as fourteen hundred years

[1] S. Matthew, XVI, 17. [2] Romans, VIII, 4.
[3] S. John, VI, 65, 66. [4] S. Matthew, XVI, 17.

ago, when that zealous and learned Father, far from perceiving that any argument could be extracted against that sacrament from the words of our Redeemer, actually adduced these very words in his public instructions to the people on the Real Presence, in order to assure them that, though the Body of Christ, as mere simple flesh and blood, and separated from His Soul and Divinity, might not profit anything, yet, when animated by that Blessed Spirit and His Divine Nature, they profited a great deal. Hence it is that he exclaims: 'What means, *The flesh profiteth nothing?* Yea, it profiteth nothing as the Jews understood it: for they understood the flesh, so as it is divided into pieces in a dead body, or as sold in the shambles, not so as it is quickened by the Spirit. If the flesh profiteth nothing, the Word would not have been made flesh, that He might dwell in us.'[1]

XXI.—PROOF FROM THE INSTITUTION.— OBJECTIONS EXPLAINED.

What our Divine Redeemer promised at Capharnaum, He realised about a year afterwards at Jerusalem, where He went to celebrate the Passover.

The institution of the Blessed Eucharist is recorded with particular precision by four among the inspired writers of the New Testament, whose

---

[1] S. AUGUSTINI *in Ioannis Evangelium tract. XXVII.*

several recitals of this occurrence we shall carefully notice.

S. Matthew says: 'And whilst they were at supper, Jesus took bread, and blessed, and broke; and gave to His disciples, and said: Take ye, and eat: This is My Body. And taking the chalice, He gave thanks; and gave to them, saying: Drink ye all of this. For this is My Blood of the New Testament which shall be shed for many unto remission of sins.'[1] S. Mark relates that, 'Whilst they were eating, Jesus took bread; and blessing broke, and gave to them, and said: Take ye, this is My Body. And having taken the chalice, giving thanks He gave it to them. And they all drank of it. And He said to them: This is My Blood of the New Testament which shall be shed for many.'[2] S. Luke observes that, 'Taking bread, He gave thanks, and brake; and gave to them, saying: This is My Body, which is given for you. Do this for a commemoration of Me. In like manner the chalice also, after He had supped, saying: This is the chalice of the New Testament in My Blood which shall be shed for you.'[3] The words of the Apostle of the Gentiles are no less explicit and declaratory of the Real Presence than the words of these three Evangelists. It was thus S. Paul addressed the Corinthians: 'For I have

---

[1] *S. Matthew*, XXVI, 26–28.   [2] *S. Mark*, XIV, 22–24.
[3] *S. Luke*, XXII, 19, 20.

received of the Lord that which also I delivered
unto you, that the Lord Jesus, the same night in
which He was betrayed, took bread, and giving
thanks, broke, and said : Take ye and eat : this is
My Body which shall be delivered for you : this
do for the commemoration of Me.   In like manner
also the chalice, after He had supped, saying :
This chalice is the new testament in My Blood ;
this do ye, as often as you shall drink, for the
commemoration of Me.'[1]

It would have been practically impossible for
these inspired writers to have selected clearer or
more appropriate language to assure the world
that Christ bestows His real Flesh and Blood to
man in the Blessed Sacrament.   For that these
passages are to be interpreted not in a figurative,
but in their obvious literal sense, is evident from
the following reasons :—

1. Though S. Matthew, S. Mark, S. Luke, and
S. Paul wrote with different objects in view—at
different times, in different places, and to different people—they are unanimous in describing the
institution of the Sacrament, not only in the self-
same manner, but almost in precisely identical
expressions ; and so remote are they from letting
fall one syllable, however trivial, which could
in any way suggest to their readers that the
Saviour's words might be figuratively understood,

---

[1] 1 *Corinthians*, XI, 23-25.

that their narratives, on the contrary, preclude any such interpretations. According to them our Blessed Redeemer did not say: This piece of bread is nothing but a figure of My Body; but He positively assured His apostles that what He held in His hand was His very, His real Flesh: 'This is My Body'; and that what was contained in the chalice was His very, His real Blood: 'This is My Blood'; that very Body, too, which was given for us, was nailed to the cross, and died for our redemption—that very Blood which was shed for many. Since these passages from Scripture assure us that we precisely receive in the Sacrament neither more nor less than what was made to suffer for us on the cross, they compel us, therefore, to arrive at one of these conclusions: either that the true and real Body and Blood of our Saviour Jesus Christ are substantially present and given in the Sacrament; or that it was not His true and real Body which was given—not His true and real Blood that was shed for us, but the figure and the shadow only of His human nature.

The pious Christian who would shudder at the notion of believing that His Saviour deceived him by a pretended and a figurative death, should not defraud himself of the invaluable treasure of the Body and the Blood of Christ, nor continue to withhold his assent to a dogma delivered to him by the lips of that same Saviour; nor emulate the incredulous disciples, by crying out: 'How can this man give us his flesh to eat?' But further investigation into the nature of the Eucharist, and a close review of all the circumstances attendant on its institution, will reveal the error of the Protestant, and establish the truth of the Catholic belief, concerning this stupendous mystery.

2. As the Eucharist is not only a sacrament, but the principal and most wondrous of the Sacraments, it will be difficult to conceive why Almighty God should have chosen to depart from His usual method of employing language to be literally taken whenever He has been pleased to ordain these sacred rites, both in the new and ancient law, in order to make exception with reference to the Holy Eucharist, and adopt a figurative mode of speaking in its institution.

Circumcision,[1] and the eating of the Paschal Lamb,[2] together with the many sacrifices and expiations which we read of in Leviticus, which graced the Jewish covenant, and those sacraments which adorn the Christian dispensation, were ordained, or promulgated, in clear and simple language; and after collating the last chapter of the Gospel of S. Matthew, and the last chapter of S. Mark, we shall discover that this observation is particularly applicable in regard to Baptism. In S. John,[3] indeed, we see that our Divine Redeemer,

---

[1] *Genesis*, XVII.   [2] *Exodus*, XII.   [3] *S. John*, III.

referring to this sacrament of regeneration, makes use of a figurative expression ; but He hastens to explain it by assuring Nicodemus that the regeneration of which He had spoken was not carnal, but spiritual ; since, to enter heaven, man must be born again of water and the Holy Spirit.

3. That the Holy Eucharist should be considered as a covenant, likewise, is demonstrable from the form of its institution. Those words, 'This is My Blood of the new testament,' employed by our Divine Redeemer when He consecrated the wine in the chalice, bear such a manifest relation to those almost identical expressions which Moses used in establishing the ancient alliance,[1] that the Apostles must have actually referred to them for an explanation of what the Saviour said, and consequently concluded that, as Moses spoke of real blood when he thus addressed the Israelites : 'This is the blood of the covenant which the Lord hath made with you,' so Christ indicated and gave His real Flesh and Blood when He proclaimed of that covenant which He then contracted with His chosen people : 'This is My Blood of the new testament.'

4. We should particularly bear in mind that the Apostles only were present at the Last Supper ; and before them alone were pronounced

---

[1] *Exodus*, XXIV, 8.

the words at its institution. If the Saviour spoke
to the Scribes and Pharisees in parables, He
furnished an explanation of these enigmas afterwards to His Apostles, to whom He declared His
mysteries in intelligible language, and instantane-
ously removed the erroneous interpretation which
they at first attached to anything that He might
have mentioned. These, too, were the persons
whom He assured : 'To you it is given to know
the mystery of the kingdom of God ; but to them
that are without, all things are done in parables.' [1]
It was, moreover, after participating in the Pasch,
which with desire He had desired to eat with
them ; [2] and on that evening, when, having loved
His own who were in the world, He loved them
to the end ; [3] and, consequently, resolved to con-
fer upon mankind, through them, a mark of
singular affection. He was also making His last
will, and instituting the most awful and august
amongst His sacraments. He was realising the
figurative sacrifices of the ancient law, and giving
a substance to its shadows. A father, however,
who takes but an ordinary interest in his children's welfare, far from expressing the most important portion of his will in obscure or figurative
expressions, studies, on the contrary, to explain
himself in clear and intelligible terms. He who
loves his friends, will, at the hour of death,

---

[1] *S. Mark*, IV, 11.   [2] *S. Luke*, XXII, 15.   [3] *S. John*, XIII, 1.

address them with unequivocal sincerity, and do nothing to practise a deception on them. He who delegates a chosen few to be the messengers of genuine truth to others, will not, in the very last instructions to them, solemnly deliver an erroneous doctrine.

As a proof that by these words: 'This is My Body,' 'This is My Blood,' Christ intended nothing more than that the sacramental species were to be considered as a figure only of His Flesh and Blood, the followers of the Church of England instance some metaphorical expressions used by our Redeemer as He preached to the multitude, when He said to them: 'I am the door,'[1] 'I am the vine,'[2] etc. But these and similar expressions do not prove, in any way, that those words, 'This is My Body,' etc., should also be interpreted in a figurative manner.

1. Because, upon the words of institution, 'This is My Body,' 'This is My Blood,' our Divine Redeemer impressed their literal and natural meaning, not merely by the emphatic way in which we may presume He pronounced them, but by circumstances which accompanied their utterance, by the time and place in which they were delivered, and by their announcing the accomplishment of a former solemn promise. Corre-

---

[1] *S. John,* x.   [2] *S. John,* xv.

sponding circumstances are severally wanting in those expressions noticed by the opponents of the Real Presence. When Christ observed of Himself, 'I am the door,' He did not lay His hand on any individual door, and, after blessing it, declare: 'I am this door,' or, 'This door is My Body.' He never took hold of any particular vine and said: 'I am this vine,' or, 'This is My Blood.'

2. Neither a door nor a vine was ever known to be employed in the solemnisation of a ceremony which was the type of, and bore the clearest reference to, the coming of the Messiah, and for which a separate festival was annually celebrated within the walls of one distinguished city. But when Christ instituted the Holy Eucharist, He took one particular portion of bread in His hand, He blessed that particular portion, He brake it, and gave to His disciples, saying, while he held it in His hand: 'This is My Body.' This scene, moreover, took place immediately after He and His disciples had solemnised the Paschal supper, in a house within the precincts of the holy city of Jerusalem.

3. Those who refuse to recognise the doctrine of a Real Presence as included in those words of Jesus: 'This is My Body,' 'This is My Blood,' and plead, in their defence, that Christ should be figuratively understood on this occasion, as He is on those others, when He said: 'I am the door,'

'I am the vine,' must either have taken up such an argument without examination, or employed it with a knowledge of its sophistry. First of all, Christ expressly manifests His wish to be understood as employing those expressions of the door and the vine in a figurative manner, and supplies upon the spot a key to their interpretation, by remarking: 'I am the door. By Me, if any man enter in, he shall be saved; and he shall go in, and go out, and shall find pastures.'[1] And again: 'I am the true vine; and My Father is the husbandman. Every branch in Me, that beareth not fruit, He will take away: and every one that beareth fruit He will purge it, that it may bring forth more fruit. . . . As the branch cannot bear fruit of itself, unless it abide in the vine, so neither can you, unless you abide in Me.'[2] When Christ at the Last Supper uttered those words, 'This is My Body,' etc., He expressly manifested, as was just now proved in the observations on the words of Institution,[3] that He wished to be understood as employing such expressions in a literal sense; neither did He then, nor on any occasion, either before or afterwards, supply a figurative interpretation of them. It is, therefore, self-evident that no comparison can be legitimately instituted between them; nor can it be argued that, because those first expres-

---

[1] *S. John*, x, 9. [2] *S. John*, xv, 1–4. [3] See p. 216.

sions should be figuratively explained, the latter also must receive a similar interpretation. In the second place, there does not exist the slightest parallel between the metaphors of the door and the vine, and the words of Institution, 'This is My Body,' etc., though we measure the latter by Protestant principles, which refuse to recognise in them an authority for the Real Presence.

In order that there should be such a resemblance between these forms of speech, as to warrant the conclusion that because one was to be understood figuratively the other should properly be interpreted in a like manner, it would be necessary to take for granted that our Saviour, when He said: 'I am the door,' 'I am the vine,' intended to express that He was the sign or figure of a door or vine. Such a supposition is obviously absurd. When He calls Himself a vine or a door, it is to indicate that He possesses qualities of which a door or a vine present imperfect but sensible ideas. It was far from His intention to signify, either that He was an emblem of such things, or that they were figurative of Him. With similar facility, solutions may be severally furnished to those other difficulties which separatists have pretended to extract from Scripture, and have raised against this essential article of Christianity.

Against the argument which Catholics borrow from the words of the Institution, there is another objection which the opponents of the Real Presence have, with visible complacency, invariably repeated, from the time of Calvin to the present day; and as Horne has been one of the latest to exhibit this objection to public notice, it shall be recited in the words of that author. 'If the words of Institution had been spoken in *English* or *Latin* at first, there might perhaps have been some reason for supposing that our Saviour meant to be literally understood. But they were spoken in Syriac; in which, as well as in the Hebrew and Chaldee languages, there is no word which expresses to *signify, represent,* or *denote.* Hence it is that we find the expression *it is,* so frequently used in the sacred writings, for *it represents* or *signifies.* . . . It is further worthy of remark, that we have a complete version of the Gospels in the Syriac language, which was executed at the commencement of the second, if not at the close of the first century, and in them it is probable that we have the precise words spoken by our Lord on this occasion. Of the passage, *Matt.,* XXVI, 26, 28, the Greek is a verbal translation: nor would any man even at the present day, speaking in the same language, use, among the people to whom it was vernacular, other terms to express, " this represents my body," and " this represents my blood." ' [1]

[1] T. H. HORNE, *Introduction to the Critical Study and Knowledge of the Sacred Scriptures.* Fifth edition, vol. II, p. 590.

This passage involves, in reality, two difficulties; for while it asserts that in the Syrian or Aramæan language there are no words which mean 'to signify,' etc., it maintains that the auxiliary verb 'to be' was, in consequence, employed in that dialect to supply the deficiency, and to indicate a symbol.

Even if the observations of Horne, on which he pretends to construct an argument against the Real Presence, were in reality correct, still his argument could not be made available to overturn that doctrine the truth of which we are contending for, inasmuch as a host of venerable witnesses determined the meaning of this passage to be precisely what the Catholic Church has affixed to it for more than eighteen centuries. But the assertion of Horne is perfectly erroneous. So far is the Syro-Chaldaic or Aramæan dialect from not possessing any word to express a figure, that there is not one language known to be enriched with such a multitude of synonyms to signify the very idea. The learned and laborious scrutiny of an able master of the oriental languages has succeeded in detecting and enumerating no less than forty different words in Syriac, all expressive of our English substantive 'figure.' [1]

---

[1] See the dissertations illustrative of Syriac literature, by the late Cardinal Wiseman, entitled : *Horae Syriacae, seu commentationes et anecdota, res vel litteras Syriacas spectantia.* Romae, 1828.

We now approach the second difficulty. It was surmised by Horne that the use of the auxiliary verb 'to be,' in the sense of 'to signify,' prevailed so much amongst the Syrians as to persuade the belief that the words of Christ, at the institution of the Blessed Eucharist, were understood in a figurative manner by the Apostles. Now, it is lucidly demonstrated that the Syrians not only had more synonymous terms to indicate the word 'figure' than any other people, but were accustomed to employ such expressions much more frequently. That with the Syrians it was not a practice to use the verb 'it is,' instead of 'it represents,' 'it signifies,' may be easily substantiated by collating the Syriac with the Latin version of the Scriptures; when it will be ascertained, that in those passages in which the verb 'est' is inserted in the Vulgate, and where the perspicuous nature of the context entirely excludes all mistake with regard to its meaning, still the corresponding words which occur in the Syriac text are type and symbol.

The assumption, therefore, of Horne and all his predecessors is quite erroneous. Instead of the Syriac being such a barren language as not to possess one word which would express 'figure,' it is most remarkably abundant in terms indicative of this very meaning, and can enumerate no less than forty in its vocabulary.

Respecting the custom gratuitously presumed

to have prevailed amongst the Syrians, of employing the auxiliary verb 'to be' under the same acceptation as the verbs 'to represent,' 'to typify,' 'to signify,' it has been authenticated that it is of much more frequent occurrence in Latin, and used in Syriac less frequently than in any other language. Far, therefore, from weakening the argument which the Catholic deduces from the words of Institution in favour of the Real Presence, it is fortified by this attempted objection, since it is demonstrated that Christ had more than forty words at His command to express a figure, type, or symbol; and that He passed them over to select one which, of all others, was the best adapted to declare the Real Presence, while it precluded every excuse for assigning to His words a figurative signification.

XXII.—THE REAL PRESENCE PROVED FROM S. PAUL.

That the words of the Redeemer were intended to affix the belief in a real presence of His Body in the Sacrament, and that the minds of the Apostles received such an impress from them, may be ascertained from various testimonies; but, first of all, from the authoritative declaration of S. Paul, who unequivocally asserts such a doctrine in several portions of the first Epistle which he addressed to the Corinthians. In the tenth chapter he exclaims: 'The chalice of benediction, which we bless, is it not the communion of the Blood of Christ? And the bread, which we break, is it not the partaking of the Body of the Lord?'[1] It was the object of S. Paul to impress as forcibly as possible upon the Corinthians, that as the Israelites, according to the flesh, partook of the altar by eating of the immolated victim—so the Christian, by receiving the Eucharist, was made a partaker of the Body of Jesus Christ, which was sacrificed upon the altar of the Cross. The old was but a shadow of the new Law; hence, what was prefigured by the one, the other realised. As, therefore, the faithful under the Mosaic dispensation, by a real eating of the victim, partook of the sacrifice that had been offered; so, for the accomplishing of this type in the Christian covenant, we are given to participate in the sacrifice upon the Cross by a real manducation of that precious Victim, immolated there for man's redemption. Moreover, that this teacher of the Gentiles wished to signify, not a figurative, but the true and real presence of Jesus in the Sacrament, is corroborated by a casual remark which he makes when he says: 'We, being many, are one bread, one body, all that partake of one bread.'[2] Now, it is only in the Eucharist that, strictly speaking, we partake of one bread. There it is, indeed, that we all receive the very same,

---

[1] 1 *Corinthians*, x, 16. [2] 1 *Corinthians*, x, 17.

identical, and heavenly nourishment—the flesh of
Christ, which is perfectly and entirely the same
and one, though distributed to millions; for that
which the Christian feeds upon in this mysterious
banquet does not, as in other repasts, differ from
the bread which is given to another.   We all of
us become 'one bread and one body' by receiving
this great Sacrament; since, according to the
promises of Christ, all 'that eat His Flesh and
drink His Blood, abide in Him, and He in them.'[1]
The same Apostle remarks: 'For I have received
of the Lord that which also I delivered unto you,
that the Lord Jesus, the same night in which He
was betrayed, took bread, and giving thanks,
broke, and said: Take ye, and eat: this is My
Body, which shall be delivered for you: this do
for the commemoration of Me.   In like manner
also the chalice, after He had supped, saying:
This chalice is the new testament in My Blood;
this do ye, as often as you shall drink, for the
commemoration of Me.   For as often as you shall
eat this bread, and drink the chalice, you shall
show the death of the Lord, until He come.
Therefore whosoever shall eat this bread, or drink
the chalice of the Lord unworthily, shall be guilty
of the Body and of the Blood of the Lord.   But let
a man prove himself: and so let him eat of that
bread, and drink of the chalice.   For he that eateth

---

[1] *S. John*, vi, 57.

and drinketh unworthily, eateth and drinketh judgement to himself, not discerning the Body of the Lord.'[1] Here S. Paul, in the most explicit terms imaginable, asserts that the sacramental species, though they have the appearances of bread and wine, are, in reality, the very Body which was delivered, and the very Blood which flowed for us. He warns the Corinthians, that unto the unworthy, as well as to the worthy communicant, are given the Flesh and Blood of Jesus. He does not introduce one single word about 'Faith only;' nor does he intimate that the worthy Christian only can receive the Body of the Lord : on the contrary, he maintains that the true and real Body of Christ is given in the Sacrament to all men, whether infidels or true believers, whether saintly or sinful. Common sense persuades us that this is the doctrine of S. Paul : for if the unworthy, or such as had not proper or sufficient faith, do not receive the true Body and Blood of Christ in this Sacrament, how is it possible for them to be guilty of the Body and Blood of Christ ? How, too, can they, with justice, be accused of not discerning the Body of the Lord, if it be not present ? At most, they have received nothing but a simple piece of bread and drop of wine, in the place of that life-giving nourishment—the real Flesh and Blood of Christ,

---

[1] 1 *Corinthians,* XI, 23–29.

of which they would have, verily and indeed, partaken, had they prepared themselves by the necessary dispositions. But to insist that a man may be guilty of profaning, and of not noticing the Body of Christ, when it is not only not present, but as far from danger of profanation and neglectful slight as heaven is from earth, is about as rational as to maintain that the servant of a king may be actually guilty of murdering his royal master with his own hand, or of exhibiting an insulting levity and contemptuous disdain, even in the regal presence, though at the very time that contumelious subject be ten thousand miles from the person of his sovereign.

XXIII.—TAUGHT BY THE REST OF THE APOSTLES.

The belief in the Real Presence, insisted on with so much energy by S. Paul, the rest of the Apostles also delivered, along with the other doctrines of the Gospel, to all those nations which they converted by their preaching. This is evidenced by those Liturgies [1] that they drew up

---

[1] The term Liturgy is a compound of two Greek words—λέϊτος, *public*, and ἔργον, *work*, or *action*—and was employed to designate the service of the altar.

To veil the sacred mysteries from the gaze of vulgar ignorance and Gentile profanations, or, in Scripture language, not to cast 'pearls before swine,' the Discipline of the Secret, which is of Apostolic origin,[a] enacted that the faithful in general should conceal the Creed,[b] the Sacraments,[c] and the holy Sacrifice of the Mass,[d] from all knowledge of the uninitiated; and the members of the priesthood in particular were directed to convey the substance and formu-

for the Churches which they severally founded, as well as by the writings of those holy Pastors who imbibed their Christianity during a personal acquaintance with the Apostles, or who more immediately succeeded them in the office of public instruction. As each Liturgy contains the common form of prayer, and ceremonial order of public worship of that individual Church in which it was observed, it must exhibit a clear and well-

---

laries of the Liturgy by word of mouth to one another ; and though required to learn and retain them by memory with the most scrupulous precision, were prohibited from committing them to writing. During the early portion of the fifth age, Nestorius [e] attempted to engraft upon the Liturgy his errors concerning the Incarnation. To counteract this artifice, and to preclude the possibility of any future heresiarch propagating his novelties by disseminating them through the prayers and invocations of the public ritual, and for other weighty reasons, the Church resolved to vary from her ancient discipline, and ordained that all the Liturgies should be committed to writing. It was thus that S. Basil and S. Chrysostom, Popes Gelasius and S. Gregory the Great, S. Ambrose, and other learned and pious prelates of the Greek and Latin Churches, to adapt the public service to the discipline of the period, and the wants of such portions of the fold of Christ as were more immediately entrusted to their spiritual solicitude, in some passages retrenched, in others augmented, the prayers and ceremonies of the Liturgies ; and without adulterating in the slightest manner the substance or the doctrine of those apostolic monuments, gave them a new, and in many instances a more appropriate form. Hence it was that those Liturgies, which, up to the period of their renovation, had been denominated by the names of those Apostles who originally framed them, exchanged their ancient for a modern appellation, and were called after those venerable prelates by whom they had been remodelled.

---

[a] For the proofs of this, see EMANUEL A SCHELSTRATE, *Dissertatio de Disciplina Arcani*, Romae, 1685, the first, as well as the most able treatise which has hitherto been published on the subject.

[b] *Ibid.*, p. 15.　　　[c] *Ibid.*, pp. 18, 106.　　　[d] *Ibid.*, p. 20, *et passim.*
[e] LEONT. BYSANT. *contra Nest. et Eutych.*

authenticated profession of the faith delivered by the clergy, and believed by the people constituting that particular portion of the flock of Christ, from the earliest period in which such a form of ritual was introduced.

XXIV.—ALL THE ANCIENT LITURGIES ATTEST THE REAL PRESENCE.

Now, it is a most luminous fact, which should be incessantly kept in view throughout the progress of this investigation, that, on collecting all the several Liturgies, which had for so many hundred years a separate existence in those various parts of Christendom, kept so far asunder by natural as well as adventitious impediments; and on comparing these forms of prayer together, not only a great resemblance of parts, and a similarity in ceremonies, but a perfect and unvarying accordance with regard to doctrine, especially on the Real Presence, is discoverable through all of them without one solitary exception. This will be evidenced by a reference to those venerable documents.[1]

---

[1] The Abbé Renaudot made public, in the year 1716, a numerous collection of Oriental Liturgies, accompanied with notes, and a useful introduction—the whole comprised in 2 vols. 4to. Anterior to the learned Frenchman's labours in studying the antiquities of the Eastern Church, that pious and highly-accomplished scholar, Cardinal Thomasius, had bestowed a similar attention on the several Liturgies belonging to the West; and printed, in 1680, the ancient Sacramentaries of the Church of Rome, in that metropolis of Christianity. It was from this work of the Roman Cardinal that Dom Mabillon

From the fact of this perfect accordance between all the Liturgies which have existed in the Christian world, from the promulgation of the Gospel to the sixteenth century, must result one of these two consequences; either the Catholic dogma is a genuine and essential article of the

---

extracted in 1685 the Gallican Liturgy, which he had attentively collated with a manuscript of the sixth century, and with two other very ancient manuscripts. In 1640, Dom Menard, well known by his pursuits in ecclesiastical antiquities, published the Sacramentary of S. Gregory,[a] to which he attached some luminous annotations. The Mozarabic[b] Missal had already been printed, through the pious care of Cardinal Ximenes, in 1500. Père le Brun collected all those Liturgies, to which he added some others, which his precursors in this curious investigation had not been able to procure; he compared them all with one another, and with those modern ones drawn up by Protestants; so that at present nothing is wanting to assist the scholar to decide upon these venerable and most ancient monuments of genuine Christianity.

In proof of the Catholic doctrine of the Real Presence, Transubstantiation, and the holy Sacrifice of the Mass, copious extracts have been made from these liturgies, and translated into English by the Right Rev. Dr. Poynter, in his invaluable work entitled 'Christianity,' for some passages of which the reader is referred to Appendix I.

---

[a] S. Gregory the Great, whose charitable zeal, through the ministry of S. Augustine and his associates, converted England from Saxon Paganism to Christianity, was elected Pope in the year 590. A Sacramentary was anciently the volume which contained the prayers and ceremonies of the Liturgy or Mass, and of the administration of the Sacraments. It was, at the same time, a Missal, a Pontifical, and a Ritual, but contained very few rubrics. In the Greek Church it is called the Euchology.

[b] Such was the denomination given to those Christians in Spain who, though they lived intermingled with their Moorish conquerors, preserved their faith from contamination, and, by an annual donative, purchased the free exercise of it from their masters, who came from Arabia,—in the language of which country, such as were not descendants of Arabians, but had adopted their mode of life, and become incorporated with them, were designated Most-Arabs, a term that by Spanish enunciation has been converted into Mozarabics.

faith of Jesus Christ, since it has been handed down as such by the Apostles—universally believed by the nations and the people whom they taught, guarded and venerated on that account with the most religious jealousy by their more immediate successors, as well as by all their legitimate descendants in the sacred ministry to the present period—or the Scriptures have deceived us, the Church, the pillar and the ground of truth, has been shaken by error, and Christ has violated His last, most solemn promise; for, instead of being with the teachers of His Gospel 'all days, even to the consummation of the world,'[1] instead of sending the 'Spirit of truth to abide with them[2] and teach them all truth,'[3] He has, for more than eighteen hundred years, permitted them to preach erroneous doctrine, and to maintain unceasingly and everywhere that the true, the very Flesh and Blood of Christ are present, and received in the Blessed Eucharist.[4] But every sincere believer will acknowledge it to be impossible that the Scriptures could be wrong —that Truth itself could speak a falsehood, or

[1] *Matthew*, XXVIII, 20.   [2] *S. John*, XIV, 17.   [3] *S. John*, XVI, 13.
[4] So forcibly did this argument strike upon the learned Protestant Grotius, that he observes: 'I find in all the Liturgies—Greek, Latin, Arabic, Syriac, and others—prayers to God that He would consecrate, by His Holy Spirit, the gifts offered, and make them the Body and the Blood of His Son. I was right, therefore, in saying that a custom so ancient and universal, that it must be considered to have come down from the primitive times, ought not to have been changed.'—*Votum pro Pace.*

that Christ should break His promise; and therefore His Church has invariably taught those doctrines only which were dictated to her by the
Holy Ghost, and has, consequently, preserved
the genuine truth of Christ Himself, by teaching
His real presence in the Eucharist. Hence, as
each true follower of Jesus is commanded to hear
the Church, if we be such, we shall unhesitatingly declare an unreserved assent to this doctrine,
or otherwise incur the punishment denounced
against the contumacious, and be likened to the
heathen, and to the publican [1]—and be guilty, not
only of despising the Church, but also of despising
God, who sent down from heaven His well-beloved
Son, not merely to preach the truth, but to establish an infallible tribunal for its perpetual preservation—to build a sacred ark, which the Holy
Spirit should guard and overshadow with His
wings that beam with heavenly effulgence and
shed unerring light upon the sacred record, when
the body of the ministers of the Church approach
to read it.

---

[1] *Matthew*, XVIII, 17.

SECTION IV.

TRANSUBSTANTIATION.

FROM briefly noticing these proofs of the Real
Presence, we naturally pass on to another essential
dogma included in the Eucharist, namely, Transubstantiation.

XXV.—WHAT IS MEANT BY THE TERM.

This term the Church employs to express
that by the words of consecration the whole
substance of the bread is changed into the Body,
and the whole substance of the wine into the
Blood of Jesus Christ.

The truth of this doctrine is firmly established
—first, by Scripture, and, secondly, by tradition.

XXVI.—TRANSUBSTANTIATION PROVED FROM
SCRIPTURE.

In the sixth chapter of S. John, as we before
remarked, our Divine Redeemer promises to give
His followers, not an image, nor a figure of His
Body, but that very Body itself—'His Flesh to be
their meat indeed, and His Blood to be their
drink indeed.'[1] We are perfectly unable to dis-

---

[1] *S. John*, VI, 56.

cover how Jesus ever realised a promise tendered
in such a solemn manner, unless we admit that,
at the institution of the Eucharist, He Himself
converted, or, to use the language of the Church,
transubstantiated bread and wine into His Body
and Blood, and transmitted the exercise of this
stupendous power to His Apostles and their consecrated successors. A reference to the Last
Supper establishes the doctrine of Transubstantiation on an immovable basis. 'Jesus took bread;
and blessing, broke, and gave to them, and said:
Take ye, This is My Body,'[1] etc. Our Blessed
Redeemer neither said: 'This is a figure of My
Body—this chalice represents My Blood;' nor
did He observe: 'Here is My Body—here is My
Blood;' nor: 'Along with this bread is My Body—
along with this wine is My Blood.' No; but He
positively asserted, in the clearest way imaginable:
'This is My Body—this is My Blood;' or, in
other language: 'This which you now perceive
Me holding in My hands, and which was lately
bread, is now My very Body; not My figurative,
but My real Body; that very same—that true,
identical, substantial Flesh of Mine, to be ere
long nailed to a cross for your redemption; this
is My true, My real Blood, which shall be shed
for many.' That which is the Body of Christ
cannot possibly be bread; that which is the Blood

---

[1] *S. Mark*, XIV, 22.

of Christ cannot possibly be wine; therefore, since we are taught by Christ Himself, in terms most positive, that in the Sacrament we receive His Body and His Blood; since we are cautioned by S. Paul to approach the holy table in a worthy manner, lest we 'eat and drink judgement[1] to ourselves not discerning the Body of the Lord;' since, in fine, the immediate successors of the Apostles and the universal Church have been unanimous and urgent now for more than eighteen centuries in reiterating such an admonition; we are certain that bread and wine no longer exist there after consecration, and although we may perceive the appearances, yet the substance of the sacramental elements is changed, and what was bread and wine is transubstantiated into the Body and Blood of Jesus.

XXVII.—PROOF FROM S. CYRIL.

The language held by S. Cyril of Jerusalem, fifteen centuries ago,[2] while unfolding to the

---

[1] 1 *Corinthians*, XI, 29.

[2] In his work entitled *A Concise View of the Succession of Sacred Literature*, London, 1830, Dr. Adam Clarke, in the analysis of the first Apology for the Christians, addressed by Justin Martyr to the Roman Emperors, Titus, Ælius, Hadrian, etc., passes at page 97, vol. I, the following remark: 'He (Justin Martyr, A.D. 140) thus speaks of the Eucharist, p. 98: οὐ γὰρ ὡς κοινὸν ἄρτον οὐδὲ κοινὸν πόμα ταῦτα λαμβάνομεν; ἀλλ' ὃν τρόπον διὰ λόγου Θεοῦ σαρκοποιηθεὶς Ἰησοῦς, *in some measure* asserting the transformation of the elements.' Here we have a Protestant divine, whose hostility to the Catholic Faith is discernible in several parts of his writings, reluctantly acknowledging that the doctrine of Transubstantiation was, in the year 140,

Catechumens who were about to receive, for the first time, the Blessed Eucharist, explains the nature of the Sacrament so well, and furnishes such a splendid example of the uniformity between the present and ancient belief of Catholics upon this tenet, that it would be culpable to pass it by without notice. 'As then,' observes this Father, 'Jesus Christ, speaking of the bread, declared and said, "This is My Body," who shall ever dare to call His word into question? And, as speaking of the wine, He positively assured us and said, "This is My Blood," who shall doubt it and say, that is not His Blood? Once, in Cana of Galilee, He changed water into wine by His will alone; and shall we think it less worthy of credit that He changed wine into His Blood? Invited to an earthly marriage, He wrought this miracle; and shall we hesitate to confess that He has given to His children His Body to eat, and His Blood to drink? Wherefore with all confidence let us take the Body and Blood of Christ, for under the type or figure of bread His Body is given to thee, and under the figure of wine His Blood is given; that so being made partakers of the Body and Blood of Christ, you may become one body and

---

an article of Christianity. After this, the sensible Protestant must admit that his modern Church is wrong in rejecting, while the Catholic Church, so venerable for her antiquity, is right in retaining, the doctrine of Transubstantiation, which, by the admission of even Protestant divines, was industriously taught and pertinaciously adhered to by those primitive believers who sealed their faith with martyrdom.

one blood with Him. . . . Wherefore I conjure
you, my brethren, not to consider them any more
as common bread and wine, since they are the
Body and Blood of Jesus Christ, according to His
words; and although your sense might suggest
that to you, let faith confirm you. Judge not of
the thing by your taste, but by faith assure your-
self without the least doubt, that you are honoured
with the Body and Blood of Christ. This knowing, and of this being assured, that what appears
to you bread is not bread, but the Body of Christ,
although the taste judge it to be bread; and that
the wine which you see, and which has the taste
of wine, is not wine, but the Blood of Christ.'[1]
An innumerable host of Greek Fathers belonging to the earliest ages, and of writers who have
flourished at more remote periods, might, if it
were requisite, be drawn out in long array to combat for the dogma of Transubstantiation, which
is, and has at all times been, most strenuously
maintained throughout the eastern as well as
western parts of Christendom.[2]

---

[1] *Catech. Myst.*, IV, 320, 321.

[2] That our Anglo-Saxon ancestors believed in the doctrines of the
Real Presence and Transubstantiation, precisely as they are taught
at this moment by the whole Catholic Church, has been lucidly
demonstrated by the learned historian of England, Dr. Lingard, in
his work, *The Antiquities of the Anglo-Saxon Church*, in which that
writer observes: 'To them (the Anglo-Saxons) the modern doctrine, that the Eucharist is the mere manducation of the material
elements, in commemoration of the Passion of the Messiah, was
entirely unknown. They had been taught to despise the doubtful

XXVIII.—ILLUSTRATED BY A PRACTICE OF THE MODERN GREEK CHURCH.

That the modern Greeks do not differ from their more orthodox and ancient countrymen in the belief of this doctrine, is attested by a practice which everywhere prevails amongst them at this day, of representing by a picture or mosaic, on

The painting which usually ornaments the ceiling over the altar in Greek churches.

the ceiling of the apse or recess which canopies their altar, the Eucharistic species, indicated not by a figure of a piece of bread, but of a little infant cradled, as it were, within the paten or

testimony of the senses, and to listen to the more certain assurance of the inspired writings : according to their belief, the bread and wine, after the consecration, had ceased to be what their external appearance suggested ; they were become, by an invisible operation, the Victim of redemption, the true Body and Blood of Christ.' (P. 196.) Dr. Lingard, in a note, assembles a host of Anglo-Saxon witnesses, who bear testimony to his assertion.

sacramental plate, by the side of which is placed a chalice, which contains the blood,[1] as may be observed in the accompanying engraving on wood.

OBJECTIONS ANSWERED.

No arguments, whether erroneously imagined to be deducible from Scripture, or alleged by human, consequently fallacious reason, however specious they may at first appear, if leisurely and dispassionately examined, will be found available to neutralise the words of Christ, to invalidate the testimony of the Apostle of the Gentiles, or to annul the doctrinal and authoritative decision of the universal Church.

XXIX.—FROM S. PAUL.

Some passages have been noticed in the Epistles of S. Paul, in which that inspired writer is un-

---

[1] Dionysius, patriarch of Constantinople, caused a similar device to be painted at the beginning of the attestation which he sent, in the year 1672, to the King of France ; and Dositheus, in the Synod of Jerusalem, alluding to this national custom, makes use of the following unequivocal expressions : 'It is astonishing that the heretics have not remarked that Jesus Christ is represented on the hemicycle of the sanctuary under the likeness of an infant in the sacred disk ; whence they might have recognised that as the Orientals represent within the disk neither an emblem, nor grace, nor anything but Jesus Christ Himself, they consequently believe that the Eucharistic bread is nothing else, but that it is made to be substantially the Body itself of Jesus Christ.'[a]

---

[a] See P. Le Brun, *Explication des Prières et des Cérémonies de la Messe*, tome I, p. 463, where a sketch is given of the painting, similar to ours.

warrantably presumed to contradict the dogma of Transubstantiation, merely because he happens to have asked this question : 'The bread which we break, is it not the partaking of the Body of the Lord?'[1] and to have said a little later in the same Epistle : 'For as often as you shall eat this bread, and drink the chalice, you shall show the death of the Lord, until He come.'[2] It is true that S. Paul denominates the Eucharistic species by the term bread ; but what does he intend to indicate by such an appellation? Is it ordinary bread? No, he makes a particular distinction between common bread and that of which he is speaking. For he does not say : 'The bread which anyone breaks,' etc., or : 'As often as ye shall eat bread;' but he lays a heavy stress upon his words; he carefully observes a marked distinction by saying : 'The bread which *we* break,' etc., 'As often as you shall eat *this* bread,' etc. And at the closing of each sentence, he lets us know what constitutes the difference between the Eucharistic and unblessed ordinary bread. He teaches us that the chalice which he blesses is the 'communion of the Blood of Christ'—not a figure, but the Blood, the very Blood itself of Christ; and the bread which he breaks is the 'partaking of the Body of the Lord'—not an eating of the emblem, but of the very substance of the real Flesh of Jesus. As a

---

[1] 1 *Corinthians,* X, 16.　　　[2] 1 *Corinthians,* XI, 26.

warning of those serious consequences that will
follow from a profanation of this tremendous but
celestial banquet, the Apostle thus impressively
exhorts us: 'Therefore whosoever[1] shall eat this
bread,[2] or drink the chalice of the Lord unworthily,
shall be guilty of the Body and of the Blood of
the Lord. But let a man prove himself: and so
let him eat of that bread, and drink of the chalice.
For he that eateth and drinketh unworthily, eateth
and drinketh judgement to himself, not discerning
the Body of the Lord.'[3]   In all these passages, S.
Paul most positively says that the real Body and
Blood of Christ are present in the Eucharist, and
the unworthy and the worthy, and indeed everyone without exception, eat and drink of them,
whenever they receive the Sacrament. But real
blood cannot be at the same time real wine;
real flesh cannot be at the same time real bread;
therefore, not to make S. Paul contradict his own
words, we must understand him to say, that what
was bread and what was wine are, by the blessing

---

[1] Not only the man with faith—the guiltless, true believer—but
any man who has not faith—everyone in general, 'whosoever.'

[2] The Protestant translators of the Church of England version of
the Testament have been guilty of corrupting the original Greek
text in this passage of S. Paul, who does not say, 'and drink,' but
'or drink'—ἢ πίνῃ. This mistranslation was, no doubt, designedly
made, to favour the erroneous doctrine that communion under both
kinds is requisite. Christ, however, expressly taught the very contrary, when He declared that those who worthily received under one
kind only should have eternal happiness. 'He that eateth this bread
shall live for ever' (S. John, VI, 59).

[3] 1 Corinthians, XI, 27, 28.

uttered over them, changed, that is, transubstantiated into the Body and the Blood of Christ: and while indeed the accidents of bread and wine still remain even after the consecration, so they outwardly seem to be unchanged, and therefore may without any impropriety be called bread and wine, because they appear to the senses to be such; yet since their substances are changed, they are properly called what they inwardly and really are converted into, the Body and the Blood of Jesus Christ.

In Scripture language it not unfrequently happens that things which have been changed, or transubstantiated, even after transformation, still retain the name of that material which originally constituted them. 'Aaron took the rod before Pharao, and his servants, and it was turned into a serpent, . . . but Aaron's rod devoured their (the magicians') rods.'[1] Though Aaron's rod was transubstantiated into a serpent, still it was called a rod. 'Moses and Aaron did as the Lord had commanded: and lifting up the rod, he struck the water of the river before Pharao and his servants: and it was turned into blood . . . and the Egyptians could not drink the water.'[2] Here again, although the water had been converted into blood, its stream is however denominated water. After Christ had wrought the change of

---

[1] *Exodus*, VII, 10–12.   [2] *Exodus*, VII, 20, 21.

water into wine, still the Evangelist does not drop the first appellation of the liquor while noticing the observations of the chief steward, 'who had tasted the water made wine,[1] and knew not whence it was, but the waiters knew who had drawn the water.' When John sent his disciples to Christ, saying: 'Art thou He that art to come?' Jesus making answer, said to them: 'Go and relate to John what you have heard and seen. The blind see, the lame walk, the lepers are cleansed, the deaf hear, the dead rise again.'[2] It is self-evident that the man who sees is assuredly not blind; he ceases to be deaf who has the faculty of hearing; what therefore does our Saviour wish to signify? That those who had been blind now see; that those who had been lame now walk; that those who had been lepers are now cleansed; that those who formerly were deaf now hear; that those who had been dead now live again. These examples, scattered through the Holy Scriptures, would have warranted S. Paul to have severally observed of them: this rod is a serpent; this water is blood; this water is wine; the dumb man speaks; the deaf one hears; the dead Lazarus lives. Had then the Apostle of the Gentiles made use of similar expressions in reference to those miraculous events, his auditors would not have argued that his

[1] S. John, II, 9. [2] S. Matthew, XI, 2-5.

authority might thence be collected to deny such wonders; on the contrary, they would have recognised in these words his recorded declaration in their favour. While therefore we maintain that, with the greatest propriety of Scripture language, S. Paul might, and did indeed observe, that the bread which he broke was the Body of Christ; we at the same time contend that such a form of speech, instead of weakening, confirms, in the most conspicuous manner, the tenet of transubstantiation: since at the same time we are assured that Christ's real Body is in the Sacrament, the material is noticed from which it is transformed; and the term bread is employed to notify, not that it is real bread, but that it is formed originally from such a substance.

XXX.—OBJECTION OF THE TERM TRANSUBSTANTIATION.

To the person who objects that the word Transubstantiation is not to be discovered in any part of Scripture, it may be replied, that the terms Trinity and Incarnation cannot be found there either: and consequently, if a doctrine must of necessity be looked upon as anti-scriptural because the titles which ecclesiastical writers have appropriated to its designation cannot be traced back to the sacred pages, then the Protestant of the Church of England must yield to the reasoning of the Socinian and the Anti-Trinitarian, and reject, along with them, the doctrine of the Trinity and Incarnation : for neither of these words is read in any passage of the Testament or Bible. The intelligent and thinking Protestant would immediately reply to those who assailed these stupendous doctrines by such an argument, that if the names be not discernible, at least the doctrines designated by those expressions, 'Trinity' and 'Incarnation,' are expressly taught in Scripture, and are, therefore, to be most tenaciously maintained. Let him henceforth take his own solution for a similar difficulty which he raises against the Catholic dogma of Transubstantiation.[1]

To a dogma established from Scripture it is folly, not to say presumption, to oppose arguments deduced from the senses. That the doctrine of the Eucharist is founded on the Word of God has been demonstrated. To him, therefore, who

---

[1] That terms of identical meaning have been invariably employed throughout the East and West is attested by an author whose authority, as he was not a Catholic, will meet with more respect from our opponents. Samuel Parker, the Protestant Bishop of Oxford, thus observes : 'In the first place then it is evident to all men, that are but ordinarily conversant in ecclesiastical learning, that the ancient Fathers, from age to age asserted the *real* and *substantial* presence, in very high and expressive terms. The Greeks styled it Μεταβολὴ, μεταρρύθμισις, μετασκευασμὸς, μεταποίησις, μεταστοιχείωσις. And the Latins agreeable with the Greeks, *Conversion, Transmutation, Transformation, Transfiguration, Transelementation,* and at length, *Transubstantiation.* By all which they expressed nothing more nor less than the *real* and *substantial Presence* in the Eucharist.'—*Reasons for abrogating the Test imposed upon all Members of Parliament,* anno 1678, Octob. 30. London, 1688, p. 13.

refuses to yield acquiescence because his human
reason cannot grasp the mystery, we answer in
the words of a minister of the Established Church.
'While arguing upon this subject, some persons,
I regret to say, have been far too copious in the
use of these unseemly terms, *absurdity* and *impossibility*. To such language the least objection
is its reprehensible want of good manners: a
much more serious objection is the tone of pre-
sumptuous loftiness which pervades it, and which
is wholly unbefitting a creature of very narrow
faculties. Certainly God *will* do nothing absurd,
and *can* do nothing impossible; but it does not,
therefore, exactly follow that *our* view of things
should be always perfectly correct and wholly free
from misapprehension. Contradictions we may
easily *fancy* where, in truth, there *are* none.
Hence, before we venture to pronounce any particular doctrine a contradiction, we must be sure
that we perfectly understand the nature of the
matter propounded in that doctrine; for otherwise the contradiction may not be in *the matter
itself*, but in *our mode of conceiving it*. In regard
to myself, as my consciously finite intellect claims
not to be an universal measure of congruities and
possibilities, I deem it both more wise and more
decorous to refrain from assailing the doctrine of
Transubstantiation on the ground of its alleged
absurdity or impossibility. By such a mode of
attack we in reality quit the true field of rational

and satisfactory argument. The doctrine of Transubstantiation, like the doctrine of the Trinity, is a question, not of abstract reasoning, but of pure evidence. We believe the revelation of God to be essential and unerring truth. Our business, therefore, most plainly is, not to discuss the abstract absurdity and the imagined contradictoriness of Transubstantiation, but to inquire, according to the best means which we possess, whether it be indeed a doctrine of Holy Scripture. If sufficient evidence shall determine such to be the case, we may be sure that the doctrine is neither absurd nor contradictory. Receiving the Scripture as the infallible Word of God, and prepared with entire prostration of mind to admit *His* declarations, I shall ever contend that the doctrine of Transubstantiation, like the doctrine of the Trinity, is a question of pure evidence.'[1]

XXXI.—RECAPITULATION.

From the creation of the human race up to the present moment, sacrifice has always constituted the essential, as well as the most conspicuous part of man's external homage to the Godhead. The first society of religionists who ventured to mutilate the worship of the Deity, by the abstrac-

---

[1] G. S. FABER, *The Difficulties of Romanism*, London, 1826, p. 55. This passage is omitted in the 2nd edition.

tion of sacrifice, the most ancient and the most essential of its rites, were the Protestants.

In the law of nature, and under the Mosaic dispensation, existed a variety of sacrifices. In the Gospel-covenant there is but a single sacrifice. This sacrifice is of a twofold nature: the bloody one is that by which Christ was offered up to His Eternal Father, once, upon the altar of the Cross: the unbloody one, that by which the self-same Jesus is offered up daily upon our altars, but under the appearances of bread and wine—partly to commemorate His bloody sacrifice, partly for other purposes.

The unbloody sacrifice, denominated the Mass, is the same in essence as that bloody sacrifice of Calvary, and while in many respects it coincides with, in some it differs from it. It agrees with it in three different ways: 1. In the object im-molated; for in both it is Jesus Christ, the Lamb of God, that is presented by way of victim. 2. In the chief offerer; for Christ, in both instances, stands the victim, is in both the principal, or great high priest. 3. In the end; for as once upon the Cross, so now daily on our altars, Christ is offered for the sins of men.

The ways in which the unbloody sacrifice, called the Mass, differs from the bloody sacrifice at Jerusalem, are not many. On the Cross our Saviour was offered up in His human form, which was discernible to the senses of the multitude around Him : upon the altar He is offered with His Body veiled under the appearances of bread and wine, and in the manner of a sacrament. Two things distinct in themselves, though intimately connected with one another, are discernible in this stupendous mystery. The first is the consecration, by the efficacy of which the bread and wine are transubstantiated into the Body and Blood of Jesus ; the second is the manducation, by which we are made partakers in this great sacrifice. In the consecration the Body and the Blood are mystically separated, because Jesus Christ has separately pronounced : 'This is My Body'—'This is My Blood.' These words exhibit a forcible and efficacious representation of the violent death which our Saviour underwent for our redemption.

Thus the Word made flesh reposes on our altars ; and no one will refuse to acknowledge that the presence of Jesus Christ is a species of intercession all-powerful with God in favour of the human race, since the Apostle assures us that Jesus Christ appears in the presence of God for us ;[1] and as Bossuet appropriately remarks : 'We believe that Jesus Christ, present upon the altar, in this figure of His death intercedes for us, and represents continually to His Father the death which He suffered for the Church.' In this

---

[1] *Hebrews*, IX, 24.

same sense we answer that Christ offers Himself
for us in the Eucharist.

Such is the Christians' sacrifice, which so widely
differs from all those peculiar to the law of nature,
or celebrated in the Jewish Temple. It is a
spiritual sacrifice, where the victim, though identically present, still is not observable, excepting
to the eye of faith only; where the sword of the
sacrificer is the word of Christ, pronounced by
His ministering priest, and which works the mystic separation of the body from the blood; where
this blood is not poured out nor spilled, except in
mystery—and where there is no death, except by
representation. Still, it is a sacrifice, in which
Jesus Christ is verily contained, and immolated
to God, under this figure of death—a sacrifice
continually commemorating that once offered on
the Cross. The Eucharistic sacrifice abstracts
nothing from the sacrifice at Calvary: on the
contrary, it exists only by its connection with that
bloody sacrifice, and receives all its virtue and
all its efficacy from it. Such is the Catholic
doctrine on the Sacrifice of the Mass.

CHAPTER II.

HISTORY OF THE MASS

AND

LAY COMMUNION.

SECTION I.

HISTORY OF THE MASS.

I.—CHRIST SAID THE FIRST MASS.

OUR Divine Redeemer was the first to offer up that holy sacrifice, since called the Mass. This He did when, after having celebrated the Jewish Passover, He instituted the Holy Eucharist. Then it was that our Lord took bread and wine, and blessed them, and made them His Body and His Blood.[1] He deposited the holy Victim, which expiates the sins of man, upon the sacred table; and He placed it there in the form of a victim, because He produced a mystic separation of it by rendering His Body present under the species of bread, and His Blood under the species of wine. Thus was the table hallowed, and thence became

---

[1] *S. Matthew*, XXVI, 26.

an altar, upon which our Lord exhibited to His
Father's view the Victim of our reconciliation.
Afterwards He took it up from the altar, and
gave it to His disciples to partake of, accompanying the precious treasure with an imperative
injunction, which, at the same time that it commanded them to do as He had done, conferred
upon them the sacerdotal dignity required for
the due discharge of such an ordinance. At the
closing of this stupendous ceremony they chanted
their thanksgivings in a holy canticle.[1] Such are
the facts we find registered in the Gospel-record
of the institution of the Blessed Eucharist.[2]

II.—CHRIST DIRECTED THE APOSTLES TO CELEBRATE MASS.

The words of Jesus were too distinct and explicit not to be intelligible; hence the Apostles
knew that by this expression: 'Do this for a
commemoration of Me,' our Saviour meant to be
thus understood: 'As I took bread, and brake,
and gave to you, saying, This is My Body; and
really and substantially made it, by My heavenly
power, what I said it was—My Body, which is
given for you;[3] and as I, having taken the
chalice, giving thanks, gave to you, saying, This

---

[1] *S. Matthew*, XXVI, 20-30.
[2] *S. Mark*, XIV, 17–26 ; *S. Luke*, XXII, 14–20.
[3] *S. Luke*, XXII, 19.

is My Blood:—and really substantially made it what I then declared it was—My Blood, which shall be shed for many;[1]—and thus offered to My heavenly Father, in a mystic and unbloody manner, that same victim, My own same Body and Blood, which is to be immolated on the Cross in a visible and bloody manner—so do you take bread, and blessing it, make it My Body; and taking wine, bless it, and make it My Blood; and thus continually present to heaven, in an unbloody manner, not a different, but the self-same sacrifice which shall be offered up in a bloody manner once upon the Cross: 'Do this for a commemoration of Me,[2] for as often as you shall eat this bread, and drink the chalice, you shall show the death of the Lord, until He come.'[3]

III.—THE APOSTLES SAID MASS.

In order to obey the precept, and commemorate the death of their omnipotent and heavenly Teacher, we observe the Apostles most exact in exercising that marvellous prerogative with which He had invested them, of doing what He had Himself accomplished after supper in their presence, and which He bestowed upon them when He said: 'Do this for a commemoration of Me.'[4] In proof

---

[1] *S. Mark*, XIV, 24. [2] *S. Luke*, XXII, 19.
[3] 1 *Corinthians*, XI, 26. [4] *S. Luke*, XXII, 19.

of this we have only to consult the Scripture and interrogate antiquity. S. Luke informs us, in his Acts of the Apostles, that as they were ministering, or, to use the word employed by Erasmus in his version of this passage : 'as they were sacrificing to the Lord, and fasting, the Holy Ghost said to them : Separate me Saul and Barnabas.'[1] The same sacrifice which the Evangelist distinguishes by the term 'ministration,' we Catholics at the present day call the 'Mass.' S. Luke also informs us how the earliest converts to the Gospel 'were persevering in the doctrine of the Apostles, and in the commemoration of the breaking of bread, and in prayers,'[2] or, according to the language of that period, the first believers were most careful to attend at the Eucharistic Sacrifice or Mass : for the Mass is the celebration of the sacred mysteries, accompanied by a series of sublime instructions and solemn prayers, which precede, accompany, and follow its performance, indicated by this passage of the Acts. A remarkable accordance may be discerned between the practice of Catholics at the Apostolic period and that observed by Catholics at the present time. They were, like ourselves, not only most careful to hear Mass upon the Lord's Day, but were accustomed to make use of lights to afford more solemnity to its celebration ; and studied to pro-

---

[1] *Acts*, XIII, 2. [2] *Acts*, II, 42.

cure the benefit of verbal instruction in a sermon delivered by their pastors; since we read that 'On the first day of the week, when they were assembled to break bread, Paul discoursed with them . . . and there were a great number of lamps in the upper chamber, where they were assembled.'[1]

IV.—A CEREMONIAL INSTITUTED BY THE APOSTLES FOR OFFERING UP MASS.

In the absence of history, both religion and decorum would prohibit us from supposing, even for an instant, that the Apostles did not observe any certain rites in offering up the Eucharistic sacrifice : undoubtedly they were unanimous in agreeing with S. Paul, who thus admonishes the Corinthians: 'Let all things be done decently, and according to order.'[2]   It is not at all surprising, therefore, that we find an animated picture sketched by one of the Apostles, and which, we may presume, either represents the Liturgy as it was then celebrated, or became the model according to which it was afterwards arranged.

V.—ATTESTED BY S. JOHN.

'I was in spirit,' says S. John, in his book of the Apocalypse, 'on the Lord's day, . . . and I

---

[1] *Acts*, xx, 7, 8. The numerous lamps, particularly noticed here, were no doubt employed to give splendour to the sacred institution.

[2] 1 *Corinthians*, xiv, 40.

saw seven golden candlesticks: and in the midst
of the seven golden candlesticks one like to the
Son of Man, clothed with a garment down to the
feet, and girt about the paps with a golden girdle,[1]
. . . and behold, there was a throne set in
heaven, and upon the throne one sitting . . . and
round about the throne were four and twenty
ancients sitting, clothed in white garments:[2] and
I saw, on the right hand of Him that sat on the
throne, a book written within and without . . .
and in the midst of the throne . . . a Lamb standing as it were slain . . . and the four and twenty
ancients fell down before the Lamb, having every
one of them harps, and they sang a new canticle,
. . . and I heard the voice of many angels round
about the throne, . . . saying with a loud voice:
The Lamb that was slain is worthy to receive
power, and divinity, and wisdom, and strength,
and honour, and glory, and benediction.[3] I saw
under the altar the souls of them that were slain
for the word of God . . . and they cried with a
loud voice, saying: How long, O Lord, holy and
true, dost thou not judge and revenge our blood
on them that dwell on the earth?[4] And another
angel came, and stood before the altar, having a
golden censer; and there was given to him much
incense, that he should offer of the prayers of all

---

[1] *Apocalypse*, I, 10, 12, 13.   [2] *Ibid.*, IV, 2, 4.
[3] *Ibid.*, V, 1, 6, 8, 9, 11, 12.   [4] *Ibid.*, VI, 9, 10.

saints upon the golden altar, which is before the throne of God ; and the smoke of the incense of the prayers of the saints ascended up before God.'[1] Such is the recital furnished to us by S. John of the vision with which he had been favoured precisely on the Lord's Day, or first day of the week, on which it was the practice of the faithful to meet together for the celebration of the holy mysteries, or Mass.[2] The Apostle gives us the description of an assembly, over which presides a venerable pontiff, seated on a throne, and encircled by four and twenty ancients, or priests. The white robe, the garment reaching to the feet, together with the golden girdle, are enumerated amongst the sacerdotal vestments ; the harps, the canticles, and all the music of the angels' choir are noticed ; and of the instruments employed in sacrifice are specifically mentioned an altar, golden candlesticks, a golden censer, with its fire and smoking incense, and the sealed book. There is present a Lamb, standing as it were slain, and by consequence a victim, to whom Divine honours and supreme adoration are exhibited by every creature 'which is in heaven and on the earth.'[3] It is, therefore, a sacrifice at which Christ is present ; being at the same time both high priest and immolated victim. Under the altar are the

---

[1] *Apocalypse*, VIII, 3, 4.   [2] *Acts*, XX, 7.
[3] *Apocalypse*, V, 13.

sainted martyrs, who thence address their supplications to God; and before it stands an angel offering up the prayers of the saints, that is, of the faithful upon earth.

The observation of S. Irenæus[1] on these passages extracted from the Apocalypse is most apposite. That ancient Father very properly remarks: 'Either S. John, in order to shadow forth the glory and the splendour of the adoration which all the choirs of angels and the saints are continually exhibiting to God within His sanctuary of heaven, must have used an imagery and language descriptive of the ceremonial practised by the Christians of his time in their assemblies on the Lord's Day; or else the Liturgy of the Holy Sacrifice, or the Mass, must have been modelled according to the vision of that favourite disciple of our Lord.' In either case, the Liturgy or Mass bears deeply impressed upon it the type of Apostolical institution: a consequence we shall more readily acknowledge, when we remember that it is suggested by a writer who was taught his Christianity by the immediate scholars of the Apostles themselves, and who penned this observation about the year 167 of the Christian era, that is, more than seventeen centuries ago.

---

[1] *Contra haereses* lib. IV, cap. XVII, § 5, and cap. XVIII, § 6.

VI.—THE REMARKS OF SOME PROTESTANTS
NOTICED.

It is a familiar, but unwarrantable observation with separatists from the Catholic Church, that during the first four centuries neither adoration was paid to the Eucharist, nor any religious veneration manifested towards angels and saints, or to the relics of martyrs. Conscious of the overwhelming weight possessed by several arguments which could be drawn from those portions of the book of the Apocalypse we have just referred to, as demonstrative of a regular form of ceremonial for the Holy Sacrifice and public worship already established during the lifetime of S. John, and which by demolishing their favourite hypothesis would detect the very modern novelty of that mode of public service which they have framed upon its basis, in substitution for the olden one; they assert, in order to escape from the pressure of such arguments, that the Apocalypse is only the record of a vision, and not a history of facts; that the throne, the altar, and the sacrifice upon it, seen by S. John, were in heaven, and not upon the earth. Such a remarkable resemblance, however, exists between the more conspicuous outlines of this mysterious representation, drawn in so graphic a manner by the luminous pencil of the Evangelist, and those sketches of the celebration of the

Eucharistic mysteries, incidentally pictured by the earlier Fathers in their letters and other writings, and even by Pagans in their remarks upon the Christians around them, or traced with studious and minute accuracy in the Liturgies of each particular Church, that we are compelled to refer them to one original, from which they have all been copied with but very little and unimportant variation.

Bingham, notwithstanding all his prejudices in favour of his own sect, and his antipathy to Catholic doctrines, has been more liberal than many of his Protestant brethren, for he candidly acknowledges, in his notice of these very passages in the Apocalypse, that 'we have here seen the model of the worship of Christ, as begun and settled in the practice of the Church in the first ages; and we shall find it continued in the same manner in those that followed immediately after.'[1]

VII.—THE LITURGY INDICATED BY S. IGNATIUS.

The seven letters addressed by S. Ignatius to the Christians of Ephesus, and of Magnesia, of Trallia, and of Philadelphia, and of Smyrna, to S. Polycarp, and to the faithful at Rome, just before his martyrdom in that imperial city, about the year 107, furnish several passages more or less descriptive of the manner in which the Eucharistic

---

[1] Bingham, *Origines Ecclesiasticae*, book XIII, ch. II, sect. 2.

Sacrifice or Mass was offered, by each bishop encircled by a crowd of priests and deacons, at that epoch, throughout Asia Minor. A peculiar respect is due to the testimony of a personage who was second in succession from S. Peter in the chair of Antioch, had listened to the preaching of that prince of the Apostles and of S. Paul, and was the intimate disciple of S. John the Evangelist.

VIII.—NOTICED BY PLINY.

Pliny the younger, who was appointed to the government of Bithynia a few years after the death of the illustrious Bishop of Antioch, in a memorial he presented to Trajan notices, concerning the Christians in his province, that some of them who had been brought before his tribunal had declared to him that they were accustomed to assemble on a particular day before it was light, and amongst other parts of their worship chanted a hymn to Christ, as to their God.[1]

IX.—DESCRIBED BY S. JUSTIN.

Of the Liturgy observed at Rome about the year 150, S. Justin Martyr has left us an interesting description in the first of those two apologies he severally addressed to Antoninus Pius and Marcus Aurelius. 'To him who presides over the brethren, is presented bread and

---

[1] PLINII *Epistolarum* lib. x, 97.

a cup of water and wine, which he taking, gives praise and glory to the Father, through the name of the Son and the Holy Ghost, and returns thanks in many prayers that such gifts have been vouchsafed to us. These offices being duly performed, the whole assembly in acclamation answers 'Amen;' then the ministers, whom we call deacons, give to each one present to partake of the blessed bread and the wine and water, and take away some to the sick. This food we call the Eucharist, of which they alone are allowed to partake who believe the doctrines taught by us to be true, and have been washed by Baptism for the remission of sin, and unto regeneration. Nor do we take these gifts as common bread and common drink; but in the same manner as our Saviour Jesus Christ, incarnate by the word of God for our salvation, took flesh and blood, so we have been taught that the food with which, by change, our blood and flesh are nourished, being blessed by the prayer of His word, becomes the flesh and blood of that very incarnate Jesus.[1]

The same substantive form of sacrifice which we here observe described by S. Justin Martyr as practised by the Roman Christians in the second century, was carefully preserved in after ages. A prayer or ceremony, it is true, was occasionally added to the ritual; but always

---

[1] *Apologia* I, § 65.

through a wise economy, either to satisfy the devotion, or to express, with stronger emphasis against some newly broached heresy, the orthodox faith of the members of that Apostolic Church which stands this day a glorious monument to testify the truth of the promise made by Christ to Peter, when He said to that Apostle : 'Simon, Simon, behold, Satan hath desired to have you, that he may sift you as wheat : but I have prayed for thee, that thy faith fail not ; and thou, being once converted, confirm thy brethren ; '[1] and amongst whom are, and always could be found such saintly men, that the same encomiums which S. Paul pronounced upon their ancestors might with justice be passed upon some now living, and on individuals who have ornamented Christian Rome in every century—'Your faith is spoken of in the whole world.'[2]

The Liturgy of the Mass, as celebrated at Rome in the fifth and sixth centuries, is preserved in the Sacramentaries of Gelasius[3] and S. Gregory the Great. From the Roman monk S. Augustine, whom the latter pontiff, S. Gregory, sent to convert our Saxon forefathers, we received, along with the other doctrines of genuine Christianity, the Sacrifice of the Mass ; and the Liturgy we practise in celebrating it at the present day is

---

[1] *S. Luke*, XXII, 31, 32.　　　　[2] *Romans*, I, 8.
[3] Pope Gelasius died in the year 496. S. Gregory flourished a century later.

identically the same in substance, and varies but very little in some few unimportant ceremonies from the ritual sent by S. Gregory to England thirteen centuries ago. Thus, not only the doctrine of the Mass, but the form of solemnising it at the present hour, can be traced up through a well-connected chain of evidence to the time of the Apostles; and, though centuries intervene between us, still an identity of belief and practice links us together, and morally renders us one religious body with the primitive Christians.

SECTION II.

LAY COMMUNION.

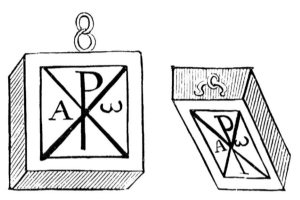

Arculae, small boxes of gold or other precious metal, used in the first ages of the Church by the faithful for carrying home the Blessed Eucharist after Mass.[1]

X.—BELIEF OF THE CHURCH ON LAY COMMUNION.

It is the belief of the Catholic Church that in the most holy Sacrament of the Eucharist the Body of Christ is not separated from His Blood, nor His Blood from His Body; nor is either of them disjoined from His Soul and His

---

[1] These boxes were found in the Vatican Catacombs, within different sarcophagi, each lying on the breast of the entombed deceased. They open in front, and have, fastened to the top, a ring through which might be passed a cord or string; and, thus suspended, they were no doubt carried round the neck. There is every reason to esteem these boxes as monuments of antiquity mounting up to the second or third century.—A. A. Pelliccia, *De Christianae Ecclesiae Politia*, tom. iii, Diss. i. They have engraved on them the monogram of Christ, ☧, and Alpha and Omega. Behind there is a dove, another symbol of our Redeemer.

Divinity; but all and the whole living Christ is entirely contained under each species; so that whoever receives under one kind becomes truly partaker of the whole Sacrament: nor is he deprived either of the Body or of the Blood of Christ.[1] The receiving of the Holy Communion under one or both kinds is an article of discipline which the Sovereign Pontiff can vary as he may deem expedient.[2] It is true, indeed, that the reception of the Blessed Eucharist under both kinds is an article of discipline which is still observed by the orthodox as well as the schismatical followers of the Greek ritual. So far, however, is the Greek Church from considering Communion under the two species as essential to the integrity of the sacrament, that during the whole of Lent, except on Saturdays and Sundays, and the feast of the Annunciation, the Mass, as it is called, of the Presanctified[3] is

---

[1] See J. BERINGTON and J. KIRK, *The Faith of Catholics*, p. 259.

[2] *Concilium Tridentinum*, Sessio XXII, *De Reformatione et de petitione concessionis calicis*, cap. XI.

[3] It is so denominated because it is a Mass in which the priest does not perform the consecration, but receives the Blessed Eucharist under one kind alone—that of bread, which was consecrated at a preceding Mass, and reserved for the occasion. By the Greeks the Mass of the Presanctified is called λειτουργία τῶν προηγιασμένων, οἱ προηγιασμένοι, or simply ἡ προηγιασμένη. This Mass is not peculiar to them, but is said throughout the Latin Church on Good Friday. Allacci assigns as a reason for the observance of this rite in the East, that the consecration being proper for festivals only, and all the days in Lent except Saturday and Sunday being fasting-days, they do not consecrate on the other days of the week, but receive the Holy Eucharist which had been reserved from the preceding

alone permitted by its rubrics to be celebrated ;[1] consequently the Greek priest who offers up Mass, as well as those amongst the laity who may choose to receive the Blessed Eucharist on any other day but Saturday or Sunday or the feast of the Blessed Virgin Mary, during the whole penitential season, take the Holy Communion under one kind only—that of bread.[2] In the Church of Constantinople, which is followed as their guide by most of the other

---

Sunday. For it should be observed that, when primitive fervour cooled, and all who attended at Mass did not, as formerly, partake of the Holy Sacrifice, a rite was introduced of merely blessing, not consecrating, small pieces of bread, which were afterwards distributed to those amongst the people who did not receive the Eucharist, as a symbol of mutual love and religious communion. The bread so blessed, though quite distinct from the Eucharist, was denominated Εὐλογία, Eulogia, or Blessing, a term originally employed to signify the Blessed Sacrament itself. In the Greek Liturgy, whenever the Eucharist is consecrated, the Eulogia is still distributed ; and a similar custom is observed in France at the parochial Mass, but instead of Eulogia it is called by the French *Pain bénit.* That the people, therefore, may not break their fast by eating the Eulogia, the Greeks do not consecrate the Eucharist on fasting days. By their Mass of the Presanctified they demonstrate that, in opposition to Protestants, they, as well as Catholics of the Latin Church, believe not only in the real and corporeal, but permanent presence of Jesus Christ in the Blessed Sacrament.

[1] LEO ALLATIUS, *De utriusque Ecclesiae Occidentalis atque Orientalis perpetua in dogmate de Purgatorio consensione.* Romae, 1655, p. 867, *Epist. ad Nihusium.*

[2] Haec Liturgia Praesanctificatorum toto maximi ieiunii tempore, exceptis Sabbatis, Dominicis, et die Annunciationi sacro, diebus singulis a volentibus peragitur, ergo toto eo tempore Sacerdos celebrans, et administri altari inservientes, et quicumque alius religionis causa communionem accipiens, sub sola specie panis, cum panis ille sanguine tinctus non est, vel si tinctus, species vini, et consequenter etiam sanguis evanuerint, communicant.—*Ibid.*, p. 876.

Churches of the Greek schismatical denomination, the Eucharistic species under the form of bread, reserved for the Mass of the Presanctified and the communion of the people, is never sprinkled with the Sacred Blood.[1] Moreover, in the Greek Church, the Viaticum or Eucharist given to the dying is administered on all occasions, and at every season of the year, under the sole form of bread alone.[2] Of the Maronites and other Oriental Christians, Abraham Ecchellensis, himself a Maronite, testifies that amongst them the Blessed Sacrament is administered under one kind only — that of bread — to the sick, to the country people, and to such as on account of the distance of residence cannot come to church for Communion.[3] With regard to the Latin Church, it is an historical fact that during many centuries Communion was

---

[1] Leo Allatius, *Ibid.*, p. 874.

[2] Magna Feria quinta quilibet Sacerdos, ritu a me iam alio in loco descripto, quos censet pro infirmis et morientibus necessarios futuros panes consecrat, eosque postmodum collectos, et in pyxide vel alio vasculo repositos in Sanctuario, donec necessitas fuerit, conservat. Eos quemadmodum et de Praesanctificatis dictum est, alii cochleari Sanguine Christi madido tangunt, alii non tangunt. Cum opus est inter annum, ex eo vasculo micam panis arreptam, et reverenter ad infirmum deportatam, in aquam vel vinum si est in cochleari immergunt, ut mollior facta, facilius deglutiri possit a valde debilitatis, et tum infirmo, recitatis ad hoc praescriptis precibus, porrigunt. Et hoc est Graecorum aegrotantium, morientiumque viaticum. Sed hic nullae species sanguinis sunt, neque separatus sanguis. Ergo Graeci morientes per totum annum in sola specie panis communicant.— Leo Allatius, *Ibid.*, p. 879.

[3] Bona, *Rer. Lit.* lib. II, ch. XVIII, num. 2.

generally, though not exclusively, administered under both kinds to the faithful, both men and women, who assisted at the public celebration of the Holy Sacrifice, at which they had made their offering of bread and wine to be consecrated.[1]

XI.—COMMUNION UNDER ONE KIND OF APOSTOLIC INSTITUTION.

That from the time, however, of the Apostles, Communion has been administered under one kind only—that of bread—in the manner which is now practised throughout the Latin Church, is attested by all antiquity. In the first ages, when the faithful suffered such grievous persecutions, it was customary to entrust the Blessed Eucharist, under the form of bread, to their pious care, for the purpose of being conveyed to the sick, and to those confined in prison for the faith; or to be privately received by themselves at home, when the danger of being apprehended should prevent them from attending the celebration of the holy mysteries in the catacombs, or other places of assembly.[2] In his exhortations to a Christian

---

[1] BONA, *Rer. Lit.* lib. II, ch. XVIII, num. I.

[2] The Acolyte S. Tharsicius was arrested by the Pagans as he was carrying the Blessed Sacrament on one of these occasions, and stoned to death because he would not betray it to them. Romae via Appia sancti Tharsicii acolythi, quem Pagani cum invenissent Corporis Christi Sacramenta portantem, coeperunt disquirere quid gereret : at ille indignum iudicans porcis prodere margaritas, tam

woman not to marry a Pagan husband, Tertullian observes: 'Will he not know what you receive in secret, before you take any food?'[1] And if he shall perceive bread, will he not believe it to be what it is called?'[2] The same author, in another part of his writings, to obviate the difficulty which was started by some scrupulous persons against receiving the Blessed Eucharist upon a fasting day, lest the fast should be broken by the Communion, suggests that 'they take the Body of the Lord, and reserve it, and thus participate of the sacrifice, as well as comply with the obligation of fasting.'[3] The testimony of S. Cyprian is equally lucid on the same subject. That illustrious Bishop of Carthage relates an astonishing event which happened to a Christian woman, who, having been guilty of an act of idolatry at a

---

diu ab illis mactatus est fustibus et lapidibus, donec exhalaret spiritum.—*Martyrologium Romanum*, 18 *Kal. Sept.* To the memory of this martyr were composed the following verses, which are ascribed to Pope S. Damasus, anno 366 :—

> Tarsicium sanctum Christi Sacramenta gerentem,
> cum male sana manus peteret vulgare profanis,
> ipse animam potius voluit dimittere caesus
> prodere quam canibus rabidis caelestia membra.

[1] This proves the primitive Christian custom of receiving the Blessed Sacrament fasting.

[2] Non sciet maritus, quid secreto ante omnem cibum gustes? Et si sciverit panem, non illum credit esse qui dicitur?—*Ad Uxorem*, lib. II, cap. 5.

[3] Accepto corpore Domini et reservato, utrumque salvum est, et participatio sacrificii, et executio officii.—*De Oratione*, cap. 19. Tertullian flourished about the year 194.

Pagan altar, immediately afterwards presumed 'to take in her unhallowed hands and endeavour to open her ark or little box which contained the Sacrament of the Lord, but was so terrified by a burst of fire flashing from within, that she dare not lay hold on it.'[1] S. Dionysius, Bishop of Alexandria about the year 247, in his letter to the Roman pontiff Fabianus, relates that a certain old man, called Serapion, when at the point of death, despatched a youth for the priest, who happening also to be confined to his bed by sickness, sent to the dying Serapion a particle of the Blessed Eucharist by the messenger, whom he directed first to moisten the Sacrament with a little water, and then put it into the mouth of the old man, who expired just after receiving the Holy Communion.[2] S. Gregory Nazianzen testifies of his sister Gorgonia, in the funeral oration he pronounced at her obsequies, that she always kept the Body of the Lord—the Blessed Sacrament—in her chamber. The Anchorites, who retired into the desert that they might become more perfect by leading a solitary life, used to communicate themselves under the form of bread.[3] To afford the sick the consolation of participating

---

[1] Cum quaedam (mulier) arcam suam, in qua Domini sanctum fuit, manibus indignis tentasset aperire, igne inde surgente deterrita est ne auderet attingere.—*Lib. de lapsis*, § XXVI. S. Cyprian suffered martyrdom in the year 258.

[2] EUSEBIUS, *Hist. Eccl.*, lib. VI, cap. 44.

[3] MARTENE, *de Ant. Eccl. Rit.*, lib. I, cap. 5, art. I.

in the Sacrament, and to provide the Viaticum [1] in
cases of emergency for the dying, particles of the
Eucharist, under the species of bread, were reserved in a pyx, as is the present custom, in the
church. The pyx was either enclosed within a
golden vessel, made in the form of a tower or of
a dove and suspended by a chain over the altar; [2]
or was deposited in one of the two chambers
which, in ancient churches, stood on each side

---

[1] Viaticum signifies a provision and preparation for a journey
into the other world. By the First Council of Nice, celebrated in
325, it is decreed, 'That all penitents shall have their final and
necessary Ἐφόδιον, or viaticum, when they are about to die.'
In the life of S. Basil by the Pseudo-Amphilochius, it is related
that that saint, after a vision that appeared to him whilst celebrating
Holy Mass, divided the Host into three parts, one of which he
placed in a golden dove hanging over the altar.—AMPHILOCHIUS,
Vita S. Basilii, cap. 6.
Περὶ δὲ τῶν ἐξοδευόντων, ὁ παλαιὸς καὶ κανονικὸς νόμος φυλαχθήσεται καὶ
νῦν, ὥσε, εἴ τις ἐξοδεύοι, τοῦ τελευταίου καὶ ἀναγκαιοτάτου ἐφοδίου μὴ ἀπο-
στερεῖσθαι.—*Canon* 13, *apud* LABBEUM, *Concil. Gen.*, tom. II, col. 673.
[2] MARTENE, *de Ant. Eccl. Rit.*, lib. I, cap. 5, art. III. S.
Amphilochius, or whoever was the author of the life of S. Basil,
remarks concerning the illustrious prelate, that once, after having
consecrated and elevated the Sacred Host, he divided it into three
parts; one of which he received with much fear—the second he
reserved for his funeral—and the third he enclosed within a golden
dove, and suspended over the altar. Amongst the various accusations preferred against Severus, the heretical Bishop of Antioch, by
the clergy and monks of that city at the Council of Constantinople
held in 536, one was, having appropriated to his own private use
not only the treasures of his church, but the gold and silver doves
which were suspended over the baptistery and at the altar. Τὰς γὰρ
εἰς τύπον τοῦ ἁγίου πνεύματος χρυσᾶς τε, καὶ ἀργυρᾶς περιστερὰς κρεμαμένας
ὑπεράνω τῶν θείων κολυμβηθρῶν, καὶ θυσιαστηρίων, μετὰ τῶν ἄλλων ἐσφετε-
ρίσατο.—*Concil. Constant.*, Act. 5, *apud* LABBEUM, tom. VIII, col. 1039.
The place at the altar where the dove used to be suspended was
called 'Peristerion,' from the Greek word περιστερὰ, or dove. The

of the altar,[1] and were called Pastophoria;[2] or was placed, as at this day in England, upon or immediately behind the altar itself, within an ark or tabernacle surmounted by a cross.[3]

Christian poet Sedulius refers to these doves in the following verses :—

Sanctus Columbae
Spiritus in specie Christum vestivit honore.

The same custom of reserving the Eucharist in a suspended dove prevailed in many churches in France until a few years ago.

[1] See CIAMPINI, *Vetera Monimenta*, tab. XI, vol. I, for the ichnography, or ground plan, of S. Clement's Church at Rome, one of the most ancient and venerable monuments of Christian antiquity in existence.

[2] From the Greek πασтοφορίον, or inner chamber. Anciently there were two small recesses, one on each side of the tribune or sanctuary. In the first of these chambers the Blessed Eucharist was kept; and hence, no doubt, arose the pious custom, now so general in Catholic countries, of having a special and richly decorated chapel for the Blessed Sacrament. In the second of these chambers were deposited the Holy Scriptures, the liturgical books, together with the sacred vessels, and the vestments of the priests and ministers, who used to robe themselves within this recess, and retire thither to pray in private, and make their act of thanksgiving after the Holy Sacrifice. While these chambers answered all the purposes of our modern Sacristy, they were also denominated Secretarium, Vestiarium, Scenophylacium, and Cimelia. S. Paulinus of Nola, in the graphic description (*Epist. XXXII, ad Severum*) which he has bequeathed to us of his church, informs us that it had two Secretaria, one on the right, the other on the left-hand side of the apse; over the entrance to the first were inscribed these verses :—

Hic locus est veneranda penus qua conditur, et qua
promitur alma sacri pompa ministerii.

and the two following over the second :—

Si quem sancta tenet meditanda in lege voluntas,
hic poterit residens sacris intendere libris.

[3] The Second Council of Tours, held in 567, enacted : 'That the Body of the Lord should be placed upon the altar, not amid the row of images, but beneath the figure of the Cross.'—Ut Corpus

From these, and numerous other testimonies which might be accumulated from ecclesiastical history, it is evident that from the earliest periods Communion was very often administered under one kind only.[1]

XII.—WHEN AND WHY GENERALLY ADOPTED BY THE LATIN CHURCH.

Towards the commencement of the twelfth century an alteration took place in the administration of the Sacrament, which then began to be administered, in public as well as in private, under one kind only—that of bread. The reasons for such a variation were the several accidents and abuses which happened through awkwardness and inattention in partaking of the consecrated

---

Domini in altari, non in imaginario ordine, sed sub crucis titulo componatur.—*Concil. Turon. can.* III, *apud* LABBEUM, tom. v, p. 853. MABILLON (*de Liturgia Gallicana*, lib. I, cap. 9, and *Tractatus de Azymo*, cap. 8) interprets this as forbidding the Blessed Sacrament to be kept in a chamber, or in a recess in the wall of the apse, which was usually adorned with figures painted or carved, but under the title of the cross, which surmounted the ciborium over the altar.

[1] The various facts enumerated in the text demonstrate that Catholics of the present time precisely agree in faith and practice with Catholics of the primitive ages, since, like them, they believe not merely in the real but permanent presence of Jesus Christ in the Blessed Eucharist. Luther, therefore, by admitting but a transitory presence of Christ, which he limited to the moment when the communicant receives the Sacrament, not only differed with the Church at his day, but with the Church from all antiquity, and was, in consequence, guilty of a notorious innovation.

cup.[1] A becoming reverence towards the Blessed Eucharist demanded such a change in discipline; and the belief that Christ was wholly present under one as well as under both species, prevented the faithful from erroneously imagining that such a practice could in any wise deprive them of a portion of the Sacrament. Nothing, however, was authoritatively promulgated by the Church concerning this regulation until the year 1414, when the Council of Constance, in opposition to John Huss in Bohemia and his partisans, who erroneously asserted that the use of the cup was absolutely necessary, decreed that, as the Body and Blood of Christ were wholly contained under each species, the custom, introduced for weighty and just reasons, and long observed in the Church, of communicating in one kind, should be received as a law which no one, without the authority of the Church, might reject or alter.[2] In this instance we cannot too loudly applaud the wise economy of the Church, which has more than once opposed error in faith—and such was that of the Hussites—by an article of discipline

---

[1] The Abbot Rodulf, who lived in the year 1110, thus dissuades the use of the cup amongst the laity :—

> Hic et ibi cautela fiat, ne presbyter aegris
> aut sanis tribuat laicis de Sanguine Christi.
> Nam fundi posset leviter, simplexque putaret,
> quod non sub specie sit totus Iesus utraque.

[2] *Concil. Constantiense, apud* LABBEUM, tom. XII, p. 100.

or a ritual observance; and no doubt, if circumstances required it, she would not only change this discipline again, but do as Pope Gelasius[1] did, and insist upon Communion being received by all the faithful not under one, but both kinds, if there were any of her members who, like the Manichæans, at the time that pontiff occupied the see of S. Peter, abstained from the cup through superstition.[2]

XIII.—AGREEABLE TO SCRIPTURE.

That Communion under one kind, that of bread, is authorised by the words of Christ Himself may be easily demonstrated. In the sixth chapter of S. John, where the mystery of the Holy Eucharist is promised, not only is there made a separate mention of eating; but precisely the same promises of future life which are announced to those who both eat and drink are also given to such as eat only. 'If any man,' says our Divine Redeemer, 'eat of this bread, he shall live for ever;

---

[1] *Apud* GRATIANUM, *De Consec.*, Diss. 2.

[2] Pope S. Leo the Great, in one of his sermons, after animadverting on the extravagant opinions concerning the creation of some kinds of matter by the evil spirit advocated amongst the Manichæans, testifies that one of the many superstitious practices dictated to those heretics by such an error was an abstinence from the Eucharistic cup: Cumque ad tegendam infidelitatem suam nostris audeant interesse conventibus, ita in sacramentorum communione se temperant, ut interdum, ne penitus latere non possint, ore indigno Christi Corpus accipiant, Sanguinem autem redemptionis nostrae haurire omnino declinent.—S. LEO MAGNUS, *Sermo* XLII, *De Quadragesima iv.*

and the bread that I will give is My Flesh, for the life of the world.[1] He that eateth Me, the same also shall live by Me.[2] He that eateth this bread shall live for ever.[3]

S. Paul, in speaking of the Eucharist, represents it under one kind only, for he says: 'Whosoever shall eat this bread, *or* drink the chalice of the Lord unworthily, shall be guilty of the Body and of the Blood of the Lord.'[4]

XIV.—OBJECTION FROM SCRIPTURE ANSWERED.

It is in vain to pretend that Christ ordained Communion under both kinds when He said, 'Drink ye all of this,'[5] for who were the 'all' actually present when Christ pronounced these words, and who 'all' drank of the chalice?[6] Not an indiscriminate crowd of the faithful; not the seventy-two disciples with His Blessed Mother, but the Apostles only—those chosen few to whom only Jesus, in the same place, and on the same occasion, delivered this mandate: 'Do this for a commemoration of Me.' He who contends that by these words, 'Drink ye all of this,' Communion under both kinds was enjoined by our Redeemer upon

---

[1] *S. John*, VI, 52. [2] *Ibid.*, 58. [3] *Ibid.*. 59.

[4] I *Corinthians*, XI, 27. The Protestant version of this passage is corrupted by putting '*and* drink' instead of '*or* drink.' Such a translation is warranted neither by the Latin Vulgate, 'vel biberit,' nor by the Greek ἤ πινη, that is, 'or drink.'

[5] *S. Matthew*, XXVI, 27. [6] *S. Mark*, XIV, 23.

all, must, by a similar process of argument, likewise necessarily admit: first, that the sacrament may be given to Turks, and Jews, and Pagans, for they constitute an integral part of 'all' men; secondly, that all persons, not only men, but women —even children—are, like the Apostles, to become priests, and are commanded to consecrate the bread and wine. By parity of reasoning this would become indisputable; for the same individuals to whom it was said: 'Drink ye all of this,' were also commanded thus: 'Do this for a commemoration of me.' It is, however, allowed on every side that the consecration of the sacramental species was intended by our Saviour to be performed by those only who should succeed to the powers and the functions of the Apostles, because to these, and through them to their ministerial successors, such a commission was exclusively directed. Precisely in the same manner, it must be acknowledged that the injunction of drinking of the cup was delivered as a precept, not to the faithful in general, but exclusively to the Apostles and their lawful successors, to be observed by them whenever they should offer up the sacrifice of the Mass, and thus fulfil the commands of Christ, who said: 'Do this for a commemoration of Me.'

The Eucharist is both a sacrifice and a sacrament. In the sacrifice it is, by Divine institution, necessary for the sacrificing priest to consecrate and drink of the chalice in order to complete the sacrifice—the mystic oblation of Christ's Body, and the shedding of His Blood upon the Cross. In the sacrament this is not required of the communicant.

There it is sufficient for him, in order to participate in its substance and its grace, to receive, in a worthy manner, the Body and Blood of Christ hidden under the appearance of only one outward sign. This sign exists in the appearance of bread. But as Christ is now immortal and impassible, His Blood cannot be separated from His Body, nor His Body from His Blood ; he, therefore, who receives His Body, must necessarily receive His Blood, and *vice versa.* It should not be forgotten, moreover, that at the Last Supper Christ took bread, and blessed it, and broke it, and distributed to each Apostle a distinct and separate portion ; He did not present them with one whole sacramental bread to be divided amongst them all. Not so with the cup; He blessed and gave but one and the same chalice for them all to drink from. His command that all should drink of it was naturally suggested by this very circumstance; He said to them, therefore : 'Drink ye all of this,' that He might admonish those who were the first to partake of the consecrated cup that there were others to participate of it also ; and hence it was to be shared amongst them all in such a manner that each one might be able to receive a portion. For as He then imparted the power, nay, issued His commands to

them all, to 'do for a commemoration of Him'
what He had just done—converted bread and wine
into His real Body and His real Blood, and mystically immolated in sacrifice that very Body which
was given for us,[1] and that very Blood which was
shed for us;[2] He wished them to receive under
both kinds, *then*, that afterwards, when reiterating
that same sacrifice in the Mass, they might comprehend the import of those words: 'Do this for
a commemoration of Me.' Hence it must be
acknowledged, to borrow the words of the Council
of Trent,[3] that 'the whole and entire Christ, and
the true sacrament, are taken under either kind;
and therefore, as to the fruit, that they who thus
receive are deprived of no necessary grace.'

XV.—UNLEAVENED BREAD USED AT THE LAST SUPPER.

Whether the bread employed at the sacrifice of
the Mass be leavened or unleavened is a circumstance of pure discipline which does not touch
the essence of the Eucharist. That our Divine
Redeemer, however, used unleavened bread at its
institution is a fact concerning which no doubt
can be for a moment entertained; for the Evangelists particularly notice that Christ instituted the
Blessed Sacrament on the first day of the Azymes,

---

[1] *S. Luke*, XXII, 19. [2] *Ibid.*, 20.
[3] Sessio XXI, *De Communione sub utraque specie*, cap. III.

or of the unleavened bread,[1] and after He had, with His Apostles, partaken of the Paschal lamb, at which sacrifice it was unlawful to make use of any other than unleavened bread.

XVI.—UNLEAVENED BREAD USED BY THE LATIN CHURCH, BY THE MARONITES, AND ARMENIANS.

Throughout the Latin Church unleavened bread is used at Mass, as more in conformity with the example furnished by our Redeemer. It is made thin and circular, and bears upon it either the figure of Christ, or the Holy Name, IHS. The Maronites and Armenians also always observe the same practice; the Ethiopian Christians consider it proper to employ unleavened bread at their Mass on Maunday Thursday. The Greek and other Oriental Churches, orthodox and schismatical, use unleavened bread, which, however, is not common household bread, but made with much more scrupulous attention, and stamped with a multitude of crosses and an inscription.

XVII.—THE SACRAMENT HINTED AT IN THE APOCALYPSE.

The Sacrament of the Blessed Eucharist under the appearance of bread is beautifully alluded to by S. John in the second chapter and seventeenth

---

[1] *S. Matthew*, XXVI, 17 ; *S. Mark*, XIV, 12 ; *S. Luke*, XXII, 7.

verse of his Apocalypse, where it is said: 'To him that overcometh I will give the hidden manna, and will give him a white counter,[1] and in the counter a new name written, which no man knoweth but he that receiveth it.'

It is necessary to premise that amongst the ancient Greeks it was a custom to vote, on public occasions, with white and black pebbles[2] gathered on the sea-shore or the banks of a river. In process of time these little stones were exchanged for small circular pieces of wood or ivory, fashioned like our modern counters. At the election of the magistracy, each citizen inscribed the name of his favourite candidate upon the pebble or the counter supplied for such a purpose, and thus gave his suffrage in his support. While the application of such a usage to the Eucharist is so happy, it cannot be satisfactorily explained, excepting by a belief in the real presence, and a

---

[1] The Protestant version renders the Greek ψῆφος by the term 'stone,' the Catholic by the word 'counter.' The latter translation is to be preferred, as more conformable to the manners of the period in which S. John wrote, and consequently better calculated to express his meaning. As little pebble stones were originally used in Greece to announce a public sentence, afterwards it happened that whatever might be casually substituted in their place, although of wood or ivory, as well as the vote or sentence itself, was indiscriminately denominated by the term ψῆφος, a pebble. Hence this word is employed in the Acts of the Apostles (XXVI, 10) to signify a judicial sentence, and is translated in the Protestant version by the word 'voice,' and not 'stone.'

[2] Mos erat antiquus, niveis atrisque lapillis
his damnare reos, illis absolvere culpa.—OVIDII *Met.*, lib. xv, 42.

reference to the Catholic form of celebrating that tremendous mystery.

According to the doctrine of the Church, it is here the victor over sin is given to feed upon the Body and Blood of Jesus Christ, the real manna, hidden, it is true, but for that very reason truly present under the appearances of bread and wine. The sacramental host resembles, in colour and in form, the white counter of the ancients; and bears upon it the impress of the sacred name which no man rightly estimates or can accurately know except the true believer. If in the sacrament there were nothing but a common piece of bread—not transubstantiated into the Body of our Lord—but quite unchanged, dead, inanimate bread, not that living bread which came from Heaven—how could the Christian's manna, the Flesh and Blood of Jesus, be hidden under it? How could a new name be written on such bread when it still continued to remain what it was before; or what name would it be?

The Catholic doctrine of the Eucharist can alone give sense and meaning to this passage, which, at the same time that it derives its true interpretation from such a tenet, reciprocally renders an important suffrage in favour of this mysterious article of faith.

XVIII.—CIRCULAR FORM OF THE HOST VERY ANCIENT.

The custom of forming the Eucharistic host flat and circular may be traced back to the remotest periods of Christian antiquity. The holy pontiff S. Zephyrinus, who flourished in the third century, denominates the sacramental bread a crown or oblation of a spherical figure : 'Corona sive oblata sphaericae figurae.'[1]

Honorius of Autun in France,[2] about the year 1130, and Duranti,[3] towards 1286, both assign to this orbicular form of the host a mystic signification.

The Greeks prepare their hosts occasionally square as well as circular,[4] for which the following mystic reason is furnished. The circle is allusive to the divinity which the bread and wine receive when they are transubstantiated; the square expresses that, by the sacrifice of Christ upon the Cross, salvation is imparted to the four quarters of the earth, to east and west, and north and south. Whether the host be round or square, the allusion to it in the book of Apocalypse, under the designation of a counter, is equally appropriate.

---

[1] BENEDICTVS XIV., *De Sacrificio Missae* lib. I, cap. VI, § 4.
[2] *Gemma Animae*, cap. XLI, num. 8.
[3] *Rationale*, lib. IV, cap. 30, num. 8.
[4] GABRIEL PHILADELPHIENSIS, *Apologia pro Ecclesia Orientali.*

The Corban or Eucharistic Bread
used by the Copts.

Form of the Eucharistic Bread
in the Latin Church.

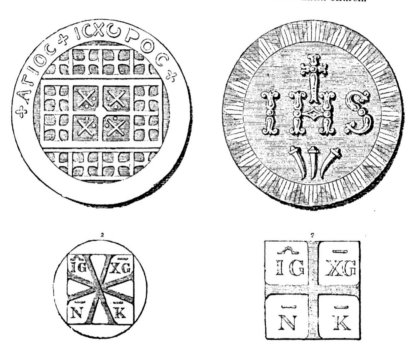

Forms of the Eucharistic Bread in the Greek Church.

CHAPTER III.

ON THE TERM MASS.

THE unbloody sacrifice of the new law, predicted with so much emphasis by Malachias when the Prophet says : 'From the rising of the sun even to the going down, My name is great among the Gentiles, and in every place there is sacrifice, and there is offered to My name a clean oblation,'[1] has been designated by a variety of expressions at the several periods of the Christian era. It has, however, been for more than fifteen hundred years denominated almost exclusively by the word Mass[2] throughout the Latin Church; and for the same period has gone under the appropriate term of Liturgy amongst the Greeks.

I.—MEANING OF THE WORD MASS.

The Latin word *Missa* is derived from *Missio,* which signifies a dismissal or permission to depart

---

[1] *Malachias,* I, 11.

[2] In the first edition of the Book of Common Prayer the Communion service is entitled 'The supper of the Lorde, and the holy Communion, commonly called the Masse.'

as soon as the sacrifice is completed. Such abbreviations are not unusual with profane[1] as well as ecclesiastical writers.

II.—ORIGIN OF IT.

The origin of denominating the holy Eucharistic sacrifice by the term Mass or dismissal arose from a ceremony which in the earliest ages of the Church was observed on two several occasions, and still continues to be practised once, during its celebration.

Immediately after the reading of the Gospel, and the delivery of the sermon by the Bishop, the Deacon turned about to the assembly, and in an elevated tone of voice admonished the different persons who composed it that the initiated only might remain, and consequently the unbaptized and unbeliever were required to depart.

The formula common to the Greek as well as to the Latin Church, employed on this occasion, was to the following effect: 'The Catechumens

---

[1] The classic reader will have noticed examples of this in the writings of Cicero, Vergil, Ovid, and Suetonius. In the works of the Fathers may be discovered similar expressions. Tertullian and S. Cyprian use 'remissa' for 'remissio.' The first observes: Diximus de remissa peccatorum.—TERTULLIANI lib. IV *adversus Marcionem*, cap. XVIII. The Bishop of Carthage says: Dominus baptizatur a servo; et, remissam peccatorum daturus, ipse non dedignatur lavacro regenerationis corpus abluere.—S. CYPRIANI *de bono Patientiae*, § VI. In both these passages 'remissa' is used instead of 'remissio,' like 'Missa' for 'Missio.'

are dismissed; the faithful shall remain.'[1] Hence it was that the portion of the Liturgy or common service which preceded the Creed and Offertory was denominated 'the Mass of the Catechumens,'[2] since those who were distinguished by such an appellation were dismissed from the church,[3] and not permitted to assist at the sacrifice which was then beginning.[4]

As soon as the Eucharistic sacrifice was terminated, the Deacon proclaimed to the congregated faithful that they might withdraw. This he announced by a form of speech which to the present day remains in use: Ite Missa est—'Go,

---

[1] This we gather from S. Isidore, who wrote in the year 595: 'Missa,' says that writer, 'tempore sacrificii, est quando catechumeni foras mittuntur, clamante levita: *Si quis catechumenus remansit, exeat foras,* et inde missa, quia Sacramentis altaris interesse non possunt qui nondum regenerati noscuntur.'—*Etymologiarum* lib. VI, cap. XIX, § 4.

[2] The Catechumens were such as had abandoned the synagogue, or passed over from Gentilism to become Christians; and, as their name implies, were under a course of catechetical instructions previously to their being admitted to the sacrament of Baptism.

[3] They were dismissed with the following formulas by the Deacon in the Latin Church:—Catechumeni recedant: si quis Catechumenus est, recedat; omnes Catechumeni recedant foras. The style of the Greek Church was similar. The Deacon first of all intimated to all heathens and heretics to withdraw: Μή τις τῶν ἀκρομένων μή τις τῶν ἀπίστων (*Constitutiones Apost.*, lib. VIII, cap. 5). Then were recited the prayers over the Catechumens and public penitents. Afterwards the Deacon proclaimed to all who were not communicants to retire: οἱ ακοινώνητοι περιπατήσατε.—*Constitutiones Apost.*, lib. VIII, cap. 12.

[4] Here commenced the more solemn part of the service, in which were included the prayers of the faithful, Εὐχαὶ πιστῶν, as they are called by the Council of Laodicea (*Can.* XIX).

leave is given to depart.'[1]   Hence arose, in the
earliest ages amongst our venerable predecessors
in the faith, a custom of denominating the second
part of the sacred Liturgy 'the Mass of the
Faithful.' From this we gather that the whole
of the Liturgy or public service was by the
ancients comprehended under two general divi-
sions, to each of which they assigned a distinctive appellation. The first was termed the Mass
of the Catechumens, 'Missa Catechumenorum;'
the second the Mass of the Faithful, 'Missa
Fidelium.' In order to express these two portions
of the Liturgy in the language of the present
time, we should denominate the one, Ante-
communion service, the latter, the Communion
service. When the discipline of the secret fell
into disuse, and public penance was abolished,
an exclusion from the sacred mysteries, and
consequently the distinction between the Mass
of the Catechumens and the Mass of the Faithful,
ceased to be observed; and the entire form of
prayer, from the beginning to the end, employed in offering up the Eucharistic sacrifice,
was denominated by the one term, Mass, as at
present.

That the whole of the Liturgy should have received its name from an incidental ceremony will

---

[1] The 'Ite Missa est' of the Latin Church corresponds with the
ἀπολύεσθε and προέλθετε in the Greek Liturgy.

cease to awaken our surprise when we remember
that reasons almost similar have determined those
appellations which usage has affixed to certain
other functions of the Church. The service
chanted at the solemn obsequies for the repose
of a departed soul is called a Dirge, from the
antiphon of the first nocturn at Matins, which
begins with the word 'Dirige.' The Thursday in
Holy Week, which is more generally known by
the appellation of Maunday Thursday, received
its name from a corresponding circumstance, as
the ceremony of the washing of feet commences
with the chant of the anthem: 'Mandatum,' etc.

III.—THE ANTIQUITY OF ITS USE.

Of the antiquity of the word Mass it may be
observed, in respect to England, that the employment of this appellation is coeval with the re-
introduction and establishment of the Christian
faith in Britain during the sixth century, through
the zeal of the Roman pontiff S. Gregory the
Great, and the labours and the preaching of the
monk S. Augustine and his Roman brethren.
This is attested by almost every document belonging to the earliest periods of our ecclesiastical or
civil history, as well as by the canons extant of
those national and provincial Councils which have
been celebrated amongst us. In reference to
Rome, to whom we are indebted for our earliest

knowledge of the faith of Christ; in reference to Italy, and to the Western Church in general, we have authorities that certify the employment of the word Mass to designate the public Liturgy as far back as the second age. Pius, the first of that name who filled the chair of S. Peter, addressed a letter, about the year 166, to the Bishop of Vienne, in Gaul. The Roman pontiff commences his epistle by observing to the Gallican prelate: ' As you well remember, our sister Euprepia conveyed over to the poor her house in which we are now residing, and where we celebrate *Mass*.'[1] In the year 254 Pope Cornelius also addressed a letter to Lupicinus, another bishop of the same city, and informs him such was the fury of the persecution then kindled against the Christians at Rome, that they durst not venture to offer up *Mass*, even in the catacombs which were anywise noted.[2]

In the acts of S. Stephen it is mentioned that this holy Pope and martyr went about celebrating Mass in the catacombs of Rome.[3]

---

[1] Soror nostra Euprepia, sicut bene recordaris, titulum domus suae pauperibus assignavit ubi nunc cum pauperibus nostris commorantes, Missas agimus.—Pii I. *Epist. ad Iustum Episc. Viennen. Apud* LABBEUM, *Concil. Gen.*, tom. I, col. 677.

[2] The pontiff thus begins his letter : Scias, frater carissime, aream dominicam vento persecutionis acerrime commoveri . . . unde publice neque in cryptis notioribus Missas agere Christianis licet.—CORNELII *Epist. ad Lupicinium. Apud* LABBEUM, *Concil. Gen.*, col. 829.

[3] During the persecution lighted up by Valerian in the year 257, S. Stephen was beheaded in the catacombs by a band of soldiers sent

Writing in the year 385 to his sister Marcellina, and detailing some disturbances which took place at Milan on Palm Sunday, when an attempt was made to seize upon a church, S. Ambrose says: 'The next day, which was Sunday, whilst I was expounding the Creed, information was brought me that officers had been deputed to seize the Portian Church; nevertheless, I continued to perform my duty, and began *Mass*.'[1]

In the year 390 was celebrated the second Council of Carthage, which had been assembled by Genethlius, and was composed of all the prelates of the Church through Africa. In the third amongst those thirteen canons enacted by that synod we find it was prohibited for ecclesiastics who were simply priests to receive again to the communion of the Church and to reconcile any-one at public *Mass*.[2]

---

to apprehend him. This pontiff was discovered in the act of offering up the Eucharistic sacrifice, which was scarcely concluded when he was thrust into his pontifical chair, and his head severed from his body. This chair is still preserved at Pisa.

[1] Ego mansi in munere, Missam facere coepi.—S. AMBROSII *Epist.* XX, *Marcellinae sorori.*

[2] Reconciliare quemquam publica Missa, presbytero non licere, hoc omnibus placet.—LABBEI *Concil. Gen.*, tom. III, col. 693.

CHAPTER IV.

ON THE USE OF LATIN AT MASS.

THOUGH the Church has never pretended that it was necessary to write and celebrate the Liturgy in a language not understood by the people, she has never considered it as imperatively requisite that her service should be performed in the vulgar tongue, and that the language which she speaks in her public service should follow the changes and variations incidental to the vernacular idioms of those several nations which compose her household. This Babel-like commixture, variety, and dissonance would have been productive of much confusion and serious inconvenience.

I.—AN UNKNOWN TONGUE USED IN THE JEWISH TEMPLE.

In this respect the spouse of Christ has imitated the example furnished to her by the ancient synagogue. From the commencement of the Jewish dispensation, up to the conquest of Jerusalem by Nabuchodonosor,[1] genuine Hebrew, the language in which the Pentateuch and most of

---

[1] 4 *Kings*, xxv.

the old Scriptures are written, was the only tongue familiar to the Israelites. The sacred volume was recited and the service of the Temple was performed in the language common to the nation. But during their seventy years' captivity the Jews forgot their ancient Hebrew, and adopted the Syriac, or Chaldaic, as their ordinary language. On their return, however, to Jerusalem, no change was made in the language of the sanctuary. The Law and the Prophets were still read in pure Hebrew to the people assembled in the synagogues, and the public service of the Temple was celebrated before them in the same language, although they did not understand it.

A practice so religiously observed after the Babylonish captivity is continued with the same scrupulous exactitude to the present day amongst the Jews, who have their ritual performed and recite their prayers in ancient Hebrew, in whatever country they happen to reside.

II.—NOT BLAMED BY CHRIST, WHO PRAYED IN AN UNKNOWN TONGUE.

Had there been any blame attached to the custom of praying in a strange or unknown tongue, Christ would undoubtedly have enumerated this amongst the other accusations which He so unhesitatingly advanced against the Scribes and Pharisees. Not only, however, did

He tacitly approve of such a practice, as He did not pass a stricture on it, but He exhibited His public approbation of its use by frequenting the Temple on occasions when it was observed ; and more than this, the very moment He was offering up Himself a bloody sacrifice upon the Cross, He prayed, and prayed aloud, in the hearing of the multitude around Him, in a language which they did not understand : 'Eli, Eli, lama sabacthani,' He ejaculated, as He yielded up the spirit ; and the people, mistaking the pure Hebrew word Eli for the name of one of the prophets, said : 'This man calleth Elias.'[1]

III.—REASONS WHY THE CATHOLIC CHURCH USES LATIN AT MASS, ETC.

The Catholic Church has been induced by several persuasive reasons to celebrate the holy sacrifice of the Mass in the Latin language throughout almost all the nations of Europe.

1st. Latin was the ancient language employed by S. Peter when he first said Mass at Rome ; and such was the language in which that Prince of the Apostles drew up the Liturgy which, along with the knowledge of the Gospel, he, or his successors the Popes, imparted to the different people of Italy, of France and Belgium,

---

[1] *S. Matthew*, XXVII, 46, 47. Eli, in Hebrew אֵלִי, is a compound of אֵל, *God*, and the suffix of the first person י, *of me*.

of Spain, of Portugal, of England, Ireland, and Scotland, of Germany, of Hungary, and of Poland.[1]

2nd. From the time of the Apostles Latin has been invariably employed at the altar through the western parts of Christendom, though their inhabitants very frequently did not understand that language. Hence the Catholic Church, through an aversion to innovations, carefully continues to celebrate her Liturgy in that same tongue which apostolic men and saints have used for a similar purpose during more than eighteen centuries.[2]

3rd. A uniformity in public worship is thus

---

[1] LE BRUN, *Explication des Prières et des Cérémonies de la Messe*, tome III, pp. 137, 138.

[2] The inhabitants of the British isles and of all the northern parts of Europe knew nothing of the Latin language when they were converted to the Christian faith. This, however, did not prevent their religious instructors from always celebrating the Mass and administering the sacraments in Latin, though the people could not understand it. In reference to this subject Dr. Lingard makes the following remarks in his valuable work, *The History and Antiquities of the Anglo-Saxon Church*, vol. I, p. 308: 'Both the sacrificial service and the canonical hours were performed in the Latin language. For the instruction of the people, the Epistle and Gospel were read and the sermon was delivered in their native tongue, but God was publicly addressed by the ministers of religion in the language of Rome. . . . It was the language to which the missionaries, Italians, Gauls, and Scots, had been always accustomed in their own countries; they would have deemed it a degradation of the sacrifice and of the Liturgy to subject them to the variations and caprice of a barbarous idiom; and their disciples, who never felt the thirst of innovation, were content to tread in the footsteps of their apostles.' The practice of the Catholics of England at the present day perfectly coincides with that followed, a thousand years ago, by their Anglo-Saxon ancestors.

more securely preserved, since a Christian, in whatever country he may chance to be, will encounter no inconvenience with regard to his attendance at church; for he still beholds the service performed in every place according to the self-same rite, and in precisely the same language, to which he has been accustomed at home from his early childhood.

Supposing it were the practice of the Church to celebrate her Liturgy in each of the several languages common to those respective nations that dwell within her widely extended pale, instead of possessing, as at present, the advantages of understanding the offices of religion when a thousand miles from home, the Englishman, for example, would find himself a stranger at their celebration in more than one spot within the narrow circuit of the British Islands; and would perceive it to be as difficult to comprehend the service when performed in Irish in Ireland, in Welsh in Wales, in the Manx language in the Isle of Man, in the Gaelic or in the Lowland tongue in Scotland, as if recited in Persian, or in any of the Oriental dialects.

Although the same order and distribution in the prayers of the Liturgy, and the same ceremonies in celebrating it, might indeed supply an index to guide the foreigner in accompanying the priest who was saying Mass in the idiom of the country, still, however, this advantage would be comparatively little. It would be more than neutralised by the distractions to which this foreigner's devotion would be almost necessarily exposed. For not only his attention must be interrupted, but his religious gravity might stand in danger of being discomposed by the novel, and, to a stranger, sometimes ludicrous sounds of those uncouth dialects which are peculiar to certain portions not only of Great Britain, but of every other empire. The same difficulty does not apply to the use of Latin. A Catholic of the Western Church, whether he be a Mosquito Indian or a Chinese, an Italian or an Icelander, never hears any other language but Latin spoken in the sanctuary. He grows up accustomed to it. To him it has nothing strange or curious; on the contrary, his ear becomes familiarised with it, and he listens to its accents with religious veneration.

4th. To avoid those changes to which all living languages, as we find by experience in our own, are perpetually exposed,[1] the Church

---

[1] This remark has been corroborated by a passage in a sermon, preached in S. Luke's Church, Liverpool, on Sunday, June 5th, 1831, by the Rev. James Aspinall, A.M., in which that gentleman, speaking on the services of the Church of England, observes: 'The omission of some obsolete words and phrases, of which time has changed the meaning, or to which it has given a stronger meaning than they bore when adopted, is a point in which criticism demands improvement' (p. 5).

has prudently determined to retain the Latin as the language of the altar; for she perceives the danger and inconvenience of altering the expressions of her Liturgy at every change and variation in language.

IV.—THE PEOPLE NOT NECESSARILY OBLIGED TO UNDERSTAND THE LANGUAGE OF THE MASS.

The same reasons which prevented the Jewish priesthood from allowing any alteration in the language of their service have at all times persuaded the whole Catholic Church, whether distinguished under the appellations of Latin, Greek, or Armenian, not to permit the slightest change or variation in the idioms in which her respective Liturgies were originally composed. During the Mosaic Law the public service of the Temple was sacrifice. In the Gospel dispensation the Mass, or public service of the Church, is also sacrifice. But in the performance of this sacred function no office is assigned to the people. The sacrifice is offered up by the priest in their name and on their behalf. The whole action is between God and the priest. So far is it from being necessary that the people should understand the language of the sacrifice, that they are not allowed even to hear the most important and solemn part of it; and in the Eastern Churches they are not permitted so much as to see either priest or altar.[1] They attend indeed, and pray, as the crowd did while Zachary was within the Temple, but they do not act; they do not say the prayers of the priest; they have nothing to do with the actual performance of the holy sacrifice.

V.—LATIN AT MASS NOWISE PREJUDICIAL TO THE PEOPLE.

It cannot be prejudicial to the poor Catholic who is ignorant of Latin that the Mass is celebrated in that tongue. Because, in the first place, the Pastors of the Church are very careful to comply with the injunctions of the Council of Trent,[2] and to instruct their flocks in the nature of that great sacrifice, and to explain to them in what manner they should accompany the officiating priest with prayers and devotions best adapted to every portion of the Mass. In the second place, the faithful in the old Law could derive much edification, and exhibited a great deal of real piety, when assisting at the service of the Temple, though they could neither understand the words, nor oftentimes so much as observe the actions of the officiating minister. No one but the high-priest, and he but once a year, might

---

[1] The Greek and Oriental Liturgies direct the sanctuary to be separated from the body of the church by a partition wall in which there are three doors. As soon as the more solemn portion of the Mass, the Canon, commences, veils are drawn over these doors, so that the priest and his assistants remain unseen.

[2] *Concilium Tridentinum*, Sessio XXII, *De sacrificio Missae*, cap. VIII.

enter into the sanctuary, which was within the veil before the Propitiatory; and it was particularly enjoined that no man should be in the Tabernacle at the time, as may be learned from the sixteenth chapter of Leviticus. In the first chapter of S. Luke we read that 'all the multitude of the people was praying without, at the hour of incense, while, according to the custom of the priestly office, it was Zachary's lot to offer incense, going into the Temple.' In a similar way a devout Christian may assist, with much profit and fervent devotion, at the celebration of the great Eucharistic sacrifice of the new Law—the Mass—though he may not understand the language of the prayers which the priest is reciting. Imagine, reader, you, or any other faithful believer in Jesus, had been present on Mount Calvary at the time our Divine Redeemer was immolating Himself upon the Cross, a sacrifice for the sins of the whole world; supposing that you had the same lively faith in Christ which animates you now, would not the view of all that painful scene have been sufficient to awaken in your soul the most lively sensations of the love of God, and have made you utter thanksgivings for such tenderness of mercy, at the same time that you avowed a detestation of your former sinfulness, though indeed you were not able to catch one word from the lips of Christ, your High Priest, or if you did hear His prayer on the Cross, like the surrounding Jews, could not understand its language?[1] Just so in the Mass, which is the self-same sacrifice as that which Christ presented to His Father on the Cross, because both the Priest and the Victim are the same. It is abundantly sufficient to kindle the devotion of the people that they be well instructed in what is going forward, and that they excite in their souls appropriate acts of adoration, thanksgiving, and repentance, though they may not understand the prayers which the priest is uttering.

VI.—GREEKS, SYRIANS, COPTS, AND ARMENIANS USE AN UNKNOWN TONGUE AT MASS.

From the days of the Apostles the Liturgy of the Mass has been celebrated in Greek and in Latin, in Syriac and in Coptic. Since the fourth century it has also been solemnised in Ethiopic and Armenian.

The language of those liturgies was never changed, although the people for whom they were originally drawn up, and amongst whom they still continue to be celebrated, have entirely transformed their ancient language, and are perfectly incapable of understanding it at the present time in its original form.

Hence it follows, as a consequence, that the Latin Church acts only in the spirit of all the

---

[1] *S. Matthew*, XXVII, 46, 47, 49.

ancient Churches from the days of the Apostles, since, like them, she refuses to exchange her ancient for a modern language.

VII.—OBJECTION ANSWERED.

Against the practice of saying Mass in Latin the fourteenth chapter of the first Epistle to the Corinthians, in which S. Paul condemns the use of some unknown tongues in the assemblies of the Church, is not unfrequently quoted. But on this subject it may be observed, in the first place, S. Paul does not utter one single word, from the commencement to the conclusion of this letter, concerning the Liturgy of the Church. In the second place, the purport of the Apostle in this portion of his writings is only to reprehend the abuse of the gift of tongues, a fault committed by some amongst the Corinthians, who out of idle ostentation affected to deliver exhortations, and to pour forth extemporary prayers, at their assemblies, in a language entirely unknown, which, for want of an interpreter, could furnish no edification to the rest of the faithful. Such, however, is far from being the practice of the Catholic Church, where all exhortations, sermons, and similar instructions are delivered to the people in a language which they understand; where no unknown, extemporary, or modern prayers are recited, but an ancient public Liturgy is performed, which, by daily use, has

not only become familiar, but is well known, at
least as to the substance, to all the faithful;
where in fine there is no want of interpreters,
since the people have the Church service translated for them in her ordinary prayer-books, and
the pastors are commanded to explain to them
the mysteries and doctrines comprehended in
the Mass.[1] In the third place, S. Paul, far from
reprehending the use of an unknown tongue,
when employed with devotion and humility, approved of it in the clearest manner—nay, absolutely requires that no one should prohibit such
a custom—for the Apostle in the thirty-ninth
verse of that same chapter commands: 'Forbid
not to speak with tongues.'

VIII.—STRICTURE ON THE PROTESTANT VERSION OF THE WORDS OF S. PAUL.

Before dismissing this subject, it may be proper
to remark the disingenuous conduct resorted to
by the authors of the authorised English version
of the Scriptures, in their translation of the four-
teenth chapter of S. Paul's first Epistle to the
Corinthians. It should be sedulously kept in
view that a reference is made in this chapter to
certain languages unknown to the people, which
S. Paul condemns some amongst the Corinthians

---

[1] *Concilium Tridentinum*, Sessio XXII, *De sacrificio Missae*, cap. VIII.

for employing at their public assemblies; and to other languages equally unknown, but the use of which is entirely approved of by the Apostle. The Protestant translators have superadded to the original Greek text the word 'unknown' in verses 2, 4, 13, 14, 19, and 27; but in verses 18 and 39, where the use of a language, though it be unknown to the people, is approved of, notwithstanding precisely the same phrase occurs in the Greek original, they have not inserted the word 'unknown,' as in the other verses.

It would appear from history that the English Protestant Church is not entirely hostile to the celebration of her Liturgy, when convenience or caprice may suggest it, in a language unknown to the people, for Dr. Heylyn informs us that, in the reign of Queen Elizabeth, the Irish Parliament passed 'an Act for the uniformity of Common Prayer, etc., with a permission for saying the same in Latin, in such church or place where the minister had not the knowledge of the English tongue. But for translating it into Irish there was no care taken. . . . The people by that statute are required, under several penalties, to frequent their churches and to be present at the reading of the English liturgy, which they understand no more than they do the Mass; by which means . . . we have furnished the Papists with an excellent argument against ourselves, for having the Divine service celebrated in such a language as the people do not understand.'[1]

'The universities of Oxford and Cambridge, together with the colleges of Eton and Winchester, obtained permission from the head of their Church to celebrate the Divine service in the Latin language.'[2]

In the *Sun* newspaper appeared the following paragraph : 'The clergy, as usual on the opening of a Session, assembled yesterday morning in convocation at the Chapter-house in S. Paul's Churchyard, whence they went in procession to the Cathedral. The Archbishop of Canterbury took his seat in the dean's stall, the Bishop of London on his throne, and the Bishops of Salisbury and Bangor in the prebendal stalls to the right of His Grace. The latter then, as the junior bishop, read the Latin Litany. A Latin sermon was delivered by Dr. Burton, of Christ Church, Oxford ; at its conclusion, "Gloria in Excelsis" was chaunted by the choir, after which the Archbishop dismissed the congregation with the usual blessing, also in Latin, and the procession returned to the Chapter-house.'[3]

---

[1] P. HEYLYN, *Hist. of the Reformation.* London, 1661, p. 128.
[2] WILKINS, *Concilia*, tom. IV, p. 217.   [3] *Sun*, Oct. 28, 1830.

CHAPTER V.

ON THE INVOCATION OF SAINTS AND ANGELS.

The Catholic Church teaches that 'the Saints, reigning with Christ, offer up their prayers to God for men; that it is good and profitable suppliantly to invoke them, and to have recourse to their prayers and assistance, in order to obtain favours from God, through His Son Jesus Christ our Lord, who is our *only* Redeemer and Saviour!'[1]

From announcing in her own language this tenet of the Church of Christ concerning the invocation of the angels and saints, we will now proceed to enumerate some few of the many passages from Scripture which so forcibly confirm this doctrine, and at the same time endeavour to arrange these proofs in such a way as to establish the necessity of its belief, while we overthrow

---

[1] Mandat sancta Synodus omnibus episcopis, et caeteris docendi munus, curamque sustinentibus, ut, . . . fideles diligenter instruant, docentes eos, Sanctos, una cum Christo regnantes, orationes suas pro hominibus Deo offerre; bonum, atque utile esse, suppliciter eos invocare; et ob beneficia impetranda a Deo per Filium Eius Iesum Christum, Dominum nostrum, *qui solus noster Redemptor et Salvator est*, ad eorum orationes, opem, auxiliumque confugere. *Concilium Tridentinum*, Sessio xxv, *De invocatione, veneratione, et reliquiis Sanctorum.*

those objections raised against the Divine truth of this dogma in the same order which its impugners follow in assailing it.

I.—IMMEASURABLE DISTANCE BETWEEN THE WORSHIP GIVEN TO GOD AND THE REVERENCE SHOWN TO THE SAINTS.

It has been unwarrantably assumed by Protestants that the Catholic, by invoking, must necessarily worship the saints and angels as divinities, and therefore, as often as he entrusts his prayers to any one amongst them, transfers to the creature that divine and superior homage which belongs to God alone. But this is false; and as the premises, so the consequences deduced from them are equally erroneous. The Catholic believes that the most flagitious of all crimes would be to exhibit the slightest particle of that respect and adoration pertaining to the Divine Being towards any creature, however pre-eminent for sanctity amongst his fellow-men, or highly exalted in heaven amid the hierarchy of angels or the choir of blessed saints. The Catholic, however, can easily point out a difference between Divine worship and the honour he manifests towards the saints. There is a supreme and sovereign homage, which belongs exclusively to God, by reason of His deity and infinite perfections. The exhibition of this sovereign homage constitutes Divine worship, which may not at any time, or for any reason, be yielded to any other being whatsoever. Such supreme religious homage has in the language of the Schools been denominated Latria.[1] There is an infinitely inferior honour which may be lawfully rendered to many of God's creatures. By an express and separate injunction of the Decalogue we are directly commanded to honour our father and our mother, and, indirectly, to show all becoming honour and deference to our superiors, both spiritual and civil. We honour all those whose rank and dignity challenge, or whose virtues and whose talents induce us to yield them our spontaneous tribute; and yet in all these instances we neither transfer the honour which belongs to God to a creature, nor defraud Him of any portion of that reverence and worship which belong to Him by Divine right. There is something intermediate between Divine perfection and human excellence; for instance, grace and the glory of the saints. These are supernatural and most transcendent gifts; and the Church, to express her gratitude towards God for such unmerited benefits, pays an honour and a reverence infinitely inferior to Divine worship, but more elevated than human respect, to all those departed servants of Heaven, who have been distinguished by such favours and hallowed with such extraordinary

---

[1] From the Greek λατρεία, the worship due to God only—from λατρεύω, to serve, to worship.

sanctity. In other words, instead of honouring the creature, she honours those rays of grace and holiness which emanate from the throne of the Creator, and are reflected in those mirrors of virtue and righteousness—His saints. Such a reverence is called 'Dulia.' [1]

II.—A RELIGIOUS RESPECT MAY BE RENDERED TO SAINTS AND ANGELS.

That we may manifest our inferior, though religious veneration towards the angels and the saints is demonstrated by the most unequivocal authorities in Scripture, and warranted by the example of the most faithful and the holiest servants of Heaven. 1st. It was God Himself who first directed man to reverence the angels, as He thus addressed the Israelites through Moses: 'Behold, I will send My angel, who shall go before thee, and keep thee in thy journey, and bring thee into the place that I have prepared. Take notice of him, and hear his voice, and do not think him one to be contemned; for he will not forgive when thou hast sinned, and My name is in him.' [2] 2nd. We behold the patriarchs and the saints of old bowing down before the angels and rendering

---

[1] Δουλεία, service, an inferior kind of respect or homage.
[2] *Exodus* XXIII, 20, 21.

them the most profound respect. Abraham, on receiving the three angels into his tent, fell prostrate at their feet.[1] Lot, on seeing the two angels that came to Sodom, rose up and went to meet them, and worshipped prostrate on the ground.[2] Josue displayed an equal reverence towards the angel-spirit whom he beheld, when 'as he was in the field of the city of Jericho, he lifted up his eyes, and saw a man standing over against him, holding a drawn sword, and he went to him, and said: Art thou one of ours, or of our adversaries? And he answered: No, but I am prince of the host of the Lord, and now I am come. Josue fell on his face to the ground, and worshipping, said: What saith my Lord to his servant? Loose, said he, thy shoes from off thy feet: for the place whereon thou standest is holy.'[3]

Protestants, to escape the pressure of these passages, observe that it was God Himself, under the form of an angel, that appeared to these ancient saints on these several occasions. This is quite a gratuitous assumption, not warranted by any part of Scripture, and directly contradicted by its internal evidence. God had never taught those venerable men to anticipate a visit from Him in this manner, and the angels did not announce it; on the contrary, God suggested to them quite an opposite belief; for first of all He

---

[1] *Genesis*, XVIII, 2.   [2] *Genesis*, XIX, I.   [3] *Josue*, V, 13-16.

promises the Israelites that He will send His angel to precede them,[1] then immediately declares that He Himself will also go before them,[2] thus tracing out a marked distinction between His angels and Himself. The homage, therefore, that they exhibited to the angels, must have been intended for the angels as created beings and messengers of God, and not immediately for God Himself. Again, the angel who spoke to Josue does not claim any attribute of the Godhead, but on the contrary, by declaring himself to be the prince of the host of the Lord, signifies that he is not the Lord Himself, but the servant, the mere minister of Heaven. Moreover, in the Hebrew text of the quotations from the books of Genesis and Josue, whenever the Deity is intended to be spoken of, the uncommunicable term Jehovah— in English, Lord—is employed, as the appropriate name of God, and expressing a title of the Divinity. When, however, the angels, and consequently creatures, are mentioned, then the appellation with which Abraham, Lot, and Josue severally salute these messengers from Heaven is Adonai, likewise translated Lord — a term applied to men, and employed here to indicate that dignity and delegated power with which creatures are invested.

The servant, who was sent by Abraham to bring

---

[1] *Exodus*, XXIII, 20.   [2] *Exodus*, XXXIII, 14, etc.

home a wife for his son Isaac, thus prayed as he halted with his camels in the evening : ' O Lord (Jehovah) the God of my master—or *Lord* (Adonai) —Abraham,' etc. The same servant when he found Rebecca, is described as having bowed himself down and adored the Lord, saying : ' Blessed be the Lord (Jehovah) God of my master—or *Lord* (Adonai)—Abraham.' [1]

The substantive מַלְאָךְ, or messenger, the word by which those spirits who visited the patriarchs and holy men of old are designated, clearly indicates that they were not apparitions of the Deity under human form, since God is not a messenger. Thus the sacred text expressly notifies that those angels that appeared to Abraham and Lot, to Josue, to Balaam, and to Daniel, were mere creatures, who were honoured by men with a religious veneration on account of Him who sent them, and who accepted of such an inferior homage instead of refusing it, which they would have done had it been unlawful. We may likewise be certain that these spirits were real and created beings, not visible manifestations of the Godhead under human form, since on some occasions two, on others, three angels appeared at the same time. God would never have chosen to reveal Himself in a manner most directly calculated to convey the notion that there was

---

[1] *Genesis*, XXIV, 26, 27.

not one God but many Gods, an idea which the Decalogue most studiously endeavoured to banish from among the Jews.

III.—THE ANGELS AND SAINTS MAKE INTERCESSION FOR MEN.

That the angels and saints have manifested their concern for the spiritual happiness and earthly prosperity of men is evident from Scripture, independent of the proof to be deduced from the public and practical belief of the Church and the doctrine of her pastors.

We gather from the prophecy of Zacharias how earnestly the angel of the Lord interceded for the Jews: 'O Lord of hosts, how long wilt Thou not have mercy on Jerusalem, and on the cities of Juda, with which Thou hast been angry?' [1]

The Angel Raphael told Tobias: 'When thou didst pray with tears, and didst bury the dead . . . I offered thy prayer to the Lord!' [2]

The angel (probably Gabriel) who came to make a revelation unto Daniel [3] thus addressed that prophet: 'But the prince of the kingdom of the Persians resisted me one and twenty days:

---

[1] *Zacharias*, I, 12.

[2] *Tobias*, XII, 12. For the canonicity of this book, see Appendix II. at the end of the volume.

[3] Gabriel appeared twice before to Daniel. See VIII, 16, and IX, 21.

and behold, Michael, one of the chief princes, came to help me, and I remained there by the king of the Persians.'[1]

The Psalmist, speaking of the man who dwelleth in 'the aid of the Most High,' attests that God 'hath given His angels a charge over thee; to keep thee in all thy ways.'[2]

Jeremias announced to the Jews that the Lord had said: 'If Moses and Samuel shall stand before me, my soul is not towards this people.'[3] God, therefore, must have given the Israelites to understand such was His wrath against them, that though Moses and Samuel were actually to intercede in their favour, still He would cast them from His sight. That Moses and Samuel could, therefore, pray for the Jews—that those holy men did pray for them—is positive, unless indeed we be willing to suppose that the Eternal Truth and Wisdom held out idle and unmeaning threats.

Judas Machabeus[4] related a vision, in which he saw how 'Onias, who had been high-priest, a good and virtuous man, holding up his hands, prayed for all the people of the Jews, and after this there appeared also another man, admirable for age and glory, and environed with great beauty and majesty. Then Onias said: This is

[1] *Daniel,* x, 13. [2] *Psalm* xc, 11. [3] *Jeremias,* xv, 1.
[4] As to the canonicity of the books of Machabees, consult Appendix II.

OF SAINTS AND ANGELS.

a lover of his brethren, and of the people of
Israel : this is he that prayeth much for the
people, and for all the holy city—Jeremias the
prophet of God.'[1]

Not only the Old, but the New Testament can
bear witness to this doctrine. It was thus that
our Blessed Redeemer closed one of those parables which He delivered to the multitude :
'Make unto you friends of the mammon of
iniquity; that when you shall fail, they may
receive you into everlasting dwellings.'[2] There
is no one so ignorant as not to know that by the
'mammon of iniquity' is signified riches.[3] Alms-
deeds are, therefore, strongly recommended by
our Divine Redeemer in this passage; and we
are taught to secure the future friendship of the
poor and indigent by our munificence towards
them at the present moment; while we are instructed such will be the efficacy of our charities,
that the poor, whom we are thus enabled to
secure as friends, will have it in their power to
serve us after they have departed from this world,
and become inhabitants of the everlasting dwellings of the heavenly kingdom, where they will
receive us, though we ourselves 'should fail'
without their assistance. As only God is the

---

[1] 2 *Machabees*, XV, 12–14.   [2] *S. Luke*, XVI, 9.
[3] Mammona apud Hebraeos divitiae appellari dicuntur. Con-
gruit et Punicum nomen : nam lucrum, Punice mammon dicitur.—
S. AUGUSTINI *de Sermone Domini in monte* lib. II, cap. XIV.

distributor of grace, the orphan, the widow, and
the miserable whom we have benefited by our
alms on earth, possess no other means of rendering us a return for our liberality than at present
by offering up their petitions in our behalf to
Christ, and making intercession for us afterward
in Heaven, when they shall be among its blessed
inhabitants.

S. John expressly tells us that the saints above
present our prayers before the mercy-seat, and
thus become our intercessors. Whilst relating
his vision of the heavenly Jerusalem, the beloved
Disciple describes how 'the four and twenty
Ancients fell down before the Lamb, having every
one of them harps, and golden vials full of odours,
which are the prayers of saints.'[1]

IV.—INFERRED FROM THE COMMUNION OF SAINTS
IN THE APOSTLES' CREED.

That the saints in Heaven should intercede for
us, their mortal brethren in the faith, is agreeable
to reason as well as to religion.

1. How we can really believe, while we recite
that specific article of the Creed which teaches
a 'communion of saints,' without acquiescing
in the truth of this assertion, would be difficult
to explain. That this communion exists only
between the faithful and the righteous upon earth,

---

[1] *Apocalypse*, v, 8.

without comprehending the saints above within
its limits, is diametrically opposed to the doctrine of S. Paul, who tells his Hebrew converts:
'You are come to Mount Sion, and to the city
of the living God, the heavenly Jerusalem, and
to the company of many thousands of angels, and
to the Church of the first-born, who are written
in the heavens, and to God the Judge of all, and
to the spirits of the just made perfect.'[1]

V.—FROM THE CHARITY WHICH ANIMATES THE SAINTS.

Charity is a virtue—a principle of ardent love
towards God, and good-will to men, which unceasingly inclines such as are endowed with it
to glorify Heaven and to do good towards others.
'Charity never falleth away;'[2] and consequently
the saints above, who are glowing with the purest,
holiest fervour of this virtue, must not only
love their brethren whom they have left below
as they love themselves, but also study how to
procure for them a participation in that beatific
happiness which they themselves are enjoying.
The only way they can command of effectually
contributing to realise the desires of their charity
is prayer, through which they intercede in our
behalf. The man who refuses to acknowledge
that among the spirits of the blessed such in-

[1] *Hebrews*, XII, 22, 23. [2] I *Corinthians*, XIII, 8.

terest is taken about mortals, surely entertains no very exalted opinion concerning the intenseness and extent of action belonging to that celestial charity which animates the inhabitants of Heaven; at the same time that he tacitly, though necessarily, admits that the influence of this love of our neighbour can be, since it has been, exerted in a more praiseworthy manner, even by the damned themselves, than by the blessed spirits. —'The rich man died: and he was buried in Hell; and addressing himself to Abraham, he said: Father, I beseech thee that thou wouldest send Lazarus to my father's house, for I have five brethren, that he may testify unto them, lest they also come into this place of torments.'[1] This single authority from Scripture would warrant the docile peruser of its sacred contents to presume that the saints in Heaven feel for the living quite as much charity as any damned soul in Hell can possibly experience; and therefore, as Dives interceded for his brethren, so Abraham and Lazarus and all the saints continually present their prayers, with unwearied charity, in behalf of every true believer.

Having proved that the angels and saints do interest themselves in our behalf by praying for us, we will now proceed to establish by an appeal to the Sacred Volume that on our part it is good

---

[1] *S. Luke*, XVI, 22, 27, 28.

and profitable suppliantly to invoke the angels and the saints, and to have recourse to their prayers and assistance.

VI.—THE INVOCATION OF ANGELS PROVED FROM SCRIPTURE—FROM THE PSALMS—FROM GENESIS—FROM THE APOCALYPSE.

While reading the Psalms, everyone must be struck with those beautiful invocations to the angels uttered by the royal Prophet. 'Bless the Lord,' he exclaims, 'all ye His angels: you that are mighty in strength; . . . bless the Lord, all ye His hosts: you ministers of His that do His will.'[1] David was aware that the sun, and moon, and stars, and other portions of inanimate nature, could neither hear his voice, nor chant the praises of the Creator; but he knew that the angelic spirits were hovering around him, and capable of mingling their songs of jubilation with his own; for he assures us that 'the angels of the Lord shall encamp round about them that fear Him and shall deliver them.'[2] 'God hath given His angels charge over thee, to keep thee in all thy ways.'[3]

Just before his death, the Patriarch Jacob, after he had called upon God in favour of the two sons of Joseph, Manasses and Ephraim, thus invoked an angel's benediction over them: 'The angel that delivereth me from all evils bless these

[1] *Psalm* CII, 20, 21.   [2] *Psalm* XXXIII, 8.   [3] *Psalm* XC, 11.

boys.'[1] Jacob consequently addressed a prayer of intercession to an angel.

That the charitable assistance of the angels may be lawfully requested by the true believer is evident from the words and the example of an Evangelist. S. John, in writing to the seven Churches, greets them in the following manner: ' Grace be unto you and peace from Him that is, and that was, and that is to come, and from the seven spirits which are before His throne;'[2]—a form of benediction which, while it assures us that we may have recourse with much profit to the kind entreaties of the spirits which stand around the Majesty of Heaven, in order to obtain grace, the spiritual gift of God, at the same time exhibits an example for our imitation; for the Apostle, by desiring that grace might flow from the seven spirits, assuredly invoked them to obtain by their entreaties such a favour from Him, before whose throne they were, since God only is the author and distributor of grace.

VII.—INVOCATION OF SAINTS PROVED FROM SCRIPTURE.

Those several extracts from the Holy Scriptures that constitute such an immovable foundation for establishing the doctrine of the invocation

[1] *Genesis*, XLVIII, 16. [2] *Apocalypse*, I. 4.

of angels, are equally available as a solid basis to uphold the invocation of saints.

This is obvious from many other portions of the Holy Volume. Christ himself assures us that the saints in Heaven 'are equal to the angels, and are the children of God.'[1] Like the angels, they receive a power over the kingdoms of the earth and their inhabitants; for our Blessed Redeemer thus declares: 'He that shall overcome, and keep My works unto the end, I will give him power over the nations;'[2]—and it is observed by S. Paul, that 'We see now through a glass in an obscure manner; but then face to face. Now,' says the Apostle, 'I know in part; but then I shall know even as I am known.'[3] The language of S. John is still more remarkable, for he says: 'Dearly beloved, we are now the sons of God; and it hath not yet appeared what we shall be. We know that, when He shall appear, we shall be like to Him; because we shall see Him as He is.'[4] The power, therefore, and the knowledge, with which the angels are endowed, and the same solicitude and charity for man which animate them, are equally attributable to the saints, who are now enjoying the beatific vision with the angel-spirits, and participate with them in all the privileges of Heaven—discharge the same kind

---

[1] *S. Luke*, xx, 36.　　[2] *Apocalypse*, ii, 26.
[3] I *Corinthians*, xiii, 12.　　[4] I *S. John*, iii, 2.

offices of brotherly affection towards us poor mortals, and are equally entitled to receive the tribute of our honour and our reverence; and, like them, may be profitably invoked to assist us by their intercession at the throne of mercy.

VIII.—HOLY MEN HAVE, EVEN IN THIS LIFE, BEEN INVOKED BY OTHERS.

It is an occurrence which is very often noticed in the Old as well as the New Testament, that the servant of God who had rendered himself conspicuous for his virtues and his piety was, whilst living, continually solicited by his admiring brethren to intercede with Heaven in their favour. Thus it was that the children of Israel entreated holy Samuel: 'Cease not to cry to the Lord our God for us, that He may save us out of the hands of the Philistines.'[1] The Lord Himself directed Eliphaz and Baldad and Sophar to go to His servant Job, and to request the favourite of Heaven to pray for them.[2] With S. Paul it was perpetually the practice to solicit a remembrance in the prayers of the faithful. 'I beseech you, brethren,' writes the Apostle of the Gentiles to the Romans, 'through our Lord Jesus Christ, and by the charity of the Holy Ghost, that you help me in your prayers for me to God.'[3] A

---

[1] 1 *Kings*, VII, 8.   [2] *Job*, XLII, 8.   [3] *Romans*, XV, 30.

similar request he urges in his Epistles to the Ephesians,[1] to the Thessalonians,[2] to the Colossians,[3] and to the Hebrews.[4]

It is certain that the Apostles were sedulous to discharge in their turn this debt of Christian kindness, which they so earnestly solicited from the charity of others for themselves, since S. Paul repeatedly announces to his converts that he did not cease to pray for them,[5] and S. John reiterates the same assurance.[6] Whilst, therefore, the Apostles and those who had been initiated into the mysteries of the Faith of Jesus by their labours, demonstrated in their daily practice that they believed that the prayers of the 'just man availeth much,[7] although in many things we all offend,[8] and even the just man falleth seven times;[9] and if we say we have no sin, we deceive ourselves;'[10] they must have been persuaded that the prayers of the saints above—of those who dwelt 'in Heaven where nought defiled can enter,'[11] and where they do not, cannot fall into the very smallest sin—were gifted with far more efficacious virtues, and availed much more, than the prayers of any

---

[1] *Ephesians*, VI, 18, 19.
[2] I *Thessalonians*, V, 25, and 2 *Thessalonians*, III, I.
[3] *Colossians*, IV, 3.   [4] *Hebrews*, XIII, 18.
[5] *Colossians*, I, 9, and 2 *Thessalonians*, III, I.
[6] 3 *S. John*, I, 2.   [7] *S. James*, V, 16.
[8] *S. James*, III, 2.   [9] *Proverbs*, XXIV, 16.
[10] I *S. John*, I, 8.   [11] *Apocalypse*, XXI, 27.

mortal being, however righteous. Independently, therefore, of the doctrine of the infallible Church of Christ, that has invariably insisted on this dogma from the moment of her birth up to the present period, we may conclude from these various reflections that we are as much authorised at present to beg of S. Peter, and S. Paul, and of every other saint, to pray for us, as was either of these glorious servants of the Lord to request that his fellow-brethren should pray for him, or the primitive believers to supplicate their martyred teachers — those glorious Apostles — to remember them in Heaven, and to offer up their daily supplications in behalf of their necessities. Whole pages might be laden with weighty extracts from the writings of those early Fathers who have so eloquently attested the belief of the apostolic times concerning the invocation and intercession of the saints ; and the reader who may wish to satisfy his curiosity on this portion of the subject is referred to a learned work which has already been pointed out to his notice.[1]

There are, however, two eminent early Christian writers, whose testimony on this and other points

---

[1] J. Berington and J. Kirk, *The Faith of Catholics on certain points of controversy, confirmed by Scripture and attested by the Fathers of the first five centuries.*

Dr. Adam Clarke, in his *Concise View of the Succession of Sacred Literature*, London, 1830, admits that Origen, a writer of the Greek Church (185-6, 253-4), insists, in his treatise concerning prayer, on the mediation of saints in Heaven.

of doctrine is so lucid and conclusive, that they must not be passed by without being introduced to the acquaintance of the reader, whose attention will be again directed to them in other parts of the present volume. These writers are S. Paulinus of Nola[1] and Prudentius.[2]   If the words or

---

[1] Pontius Meropius Paulinus was born at Bordeaux, A.D. 353 or 354, and very early in life was selected to discharge the most dignified functions in the Roman Empire. In 393 he received the priesthood, and towards the end of the year 409, or early in 410, was elected to the episcopal chair of Nola. His literary acquirements were such that S. Jerome (*Epist.* 101, 102,) writes of him : 'Everyone admired the purity and elegance of his diction ; the delicacy and elevation of his thoughts ; the strength and sweetness of his style ; and the playfulness of his imagination. His works that have been hitherto collected consist of letters, some of which are interspersed with original verses ; of short poems, mostly on religious subjects ; and of hymns, or rather birthday odes, in honour of S. Felix, for whose memory Paulinus cherished the most devout respect.

[2] Aurelius Clemens Prudentius, who is justly regarded as the most eminent and elegant of the ancient Christian poets, was born in the north of Spain, near the Pyrenees (Περὶ Στεφάνων, VI, 146), in 348 (*Praef. in librum Cathemerinon,* v. 24 ; cf. *Apotheosis,* v. 449). He was twice honoured with the office of governor, perhaps of the province of Tarragona, or that of defender of the city. Though a particular favourite of the Emperor (Theodosius or Honorius), he quitted the imperial presence to retire from the world. During a visit of devotion which he paid to Rome he saw a great many martyrs' tombs, at which he prayed for the cure of his spiritual wounds. Amongst his poems may be mentioned his Psychomachia, or combat of the soul against vice ; his Cathemerinon, or book of hymns ; his Apotheosis, or defence of the Deity and the Divine attributes. But the most celebrated portion of the writings of Prudentius is his book Περὶ Στεφάνων, or *On the crowns of the Martyrs,* containing fourteen hymns. The works of this author have a particular value about them, for, independently of the charms of poetry, they testify to the religious belief and practice of Spain and Italy at the period when they were composed, by the peculiar and minute manner in which they describe the then existing ecclesiastical monuments and pious customs of the Christian world.

VOL. I.   X

the fervent example of an enlightened and holy pastor of the Church, as far back as the close of the fourth century, can produce any effect, then we must admit, not only that it is lawful to invoke the intercession of the saints departed, but also that their prayers are highly efficacious in our behalf.   In his third ode in honour of his favourite patron S. Felix, after proclaiming the joy he felt at the annual celebration of his festival, the pious prelate thus addresses that saint and martyr :—

> Hic amor, hic labor est nobis ; haec vota tuorum
> suscipe, commendaque Deo, ut cum sedula cura,
> servitium nostrum longo tibi penderit aevo,
>
> .   .   .   .   .   .
>
> Quem bonitate pium, sed maiestate tremendum,
> exora, ut precibus lenis meritisque redonet
> debita nostra tuis, cum tu quoque magna piorum
> portio, regnantem Felix comitaberis Agnum :
> posce ovium grege nos statui, ut sententia summi
> Iudicis hoc quoque nos iterum tibi munere donet,
> ne male gratatis laevos adiudicet hoedis.
> *De S. Felice Natal. Carm. III, v. 120 et seq.*

> This is our labour, this our work of love,
> receive our vows and offer them above.
>
> .   .   .   .   .   .
>
> That God of fearful majesty whose sway
> is mercy-guided, Felix, for us pray,
> that unto prayers and merits such as thine,
> for all our faults He would a pardon sign.
> And when to thee amid the sacred band
> 'tis giv'n around the spotless Lamb to stand,

oh, sue that we amongst His sheep be placed,
not 'mid the banished left-hand goats disgraced ;
and thus shall we, a second time, be blessed
by Heav'n's mild sentence, at thy kind behest.

In other odes composed in honour of the same S. Felix, Paulinus manifests his devotion to him in language equally clear and energetic, and declares how confident he feels of receiving benefit through that martyr's intercession :—

Concurramus ad hunc spe conspirante patronum ;
suscipiet nostras placida pietate querelas,
et dum natalem ipsius celebramus ovantes,
ille preces nostras meritis pius adseret altis,
inque vicem flebit nobis, quia mente dicata
nos laetamur ei.   Non est cura haec nova sanctis
exorare Deum pro peccatoribus aegris.
De S. Felice Natal. Carm. VIII, v. 211 *et seq.*

With hope to him as patron let us fly,
and, pity-touched, he'll list our plaintive cry ;
and as his feast we keep with holy rite,
to our poor prayers his merits he'll unite.
In sweet reverse for us he'll weep, the while
we joy in him with souls devout, and smile :
unto the saints 'tis not a recent care
for sin-struck man to pour the pious prayer.[1]

----

[1] Sentiments similar to these are expressed in the consolatory poem which S. Paulinus addressed to Pneumatius and Fidelis on the death of their son Celsus :—

Sed tamen et nobis poterit tua gratia longum
    vivere, si nostri sis memor ad Dominum.
            .   .   .   .   .

Celse, iuva fratrem socia pietate laborans,
    ut vestra nobis sit locus in requie.
            .   .   .   .   .

Prudentius, by the sentiments of tenderest devotion which he has so happily interwoven with his verses, and the energetic language in which he gives expression to his homage, attests with a force, as strong as that of S. Paulinus, his own and the age's belief in the invocation of saints. That such a credence was not peculiar to his particular nation, nor a novel fabrication of the times during which he lived, is certified by the triumphant manner in which the poet notices that the saints were recognised as the patrons of the world by every people professing Christianity, amongst whom such as were induced at any period to supplicate their intercession had experienced its efficacy. In his hymn in honour of the martyrs SS. Hemeterius and Celedonius, he says :—

> Exteri necnon et orbis huc colonus advenit :
> fama nam terras in omnes percucurrit proditrix,
> hic patronos esse mundi, quos precantes ambiant,
>   Nemo puras hic rogando frustra congessit preces :
> laetus hinc tersis revertit supplicator fletibus,
> omne, quod iustum poposcit, impetratum sentiens.
>   Tanta pro nostris periclis cura suffragantium est,
> non sinunt, inane ut ullus voce murmur fuderit :
> audiunt, statimque ad aurem Regis aeterni ferunt.
>   Inde larga fonte ab ipso dona terris influunt :

> Innocuisque pares meritis, peccata parentum
> infantes, castis vincite suffragiis.
>
>   .   .   .   .   .   .
>
> Ut precibus commune tuis miserante habeamus
> praesidium Christo nos quoque, Celse, tui.
>   *De obitu Celsi pueri*, v. 593.

supplicum causas petitis quae medelis irrigant.
nil suis bonus negavit Christus unquam testibus :
    Testibus, quos nec catenae, dura nec mors terruit
unicum Deum fateri sanguinis dispendio :
sanguinis sed tale damnum lux rependit longior.
        Περὶ Στεφάνων *liber, Hymn. I, v.* 10 *et seq.*

The stranger hither hies with pious haste,
for sounding fame all earth around has paced,
and told, the patrons of the world were here,
that we should, trusting, supplicate their prayer.
For man these advocates ne'er came to try,
but home returned with joy-enkindled eye
and tears dried up—to tell to all around
his just request was with a blessing crowned.
Such, 'gainst our evils, is their saintly care,
no plaints we sigh are wasted on the air ;
but straight they heed them ;—hurrying they bring
our supplications to the heav'nly King ;
from whose deep fountains copious blessing flows,
and yields a cure to every suppliant's woes :
for nought has bounteous Christ e'er yet denied
to prayer of martyrs—saints who've testified
the true belief in one eternal God,
in galling fetters, 'neath the flaying rod,
while fiercest death stood by with brandished dart ;
then wrung the life-blood from the fearless heart.[1]

---

[1] Prudentius has repeatedly mentioned, in various other parts of his poems, the then prevailing religious practice of invoking the aid of the saints, and has eloquently asserted the efficacy of their intercession in behalf of those who address themselves to their fraternal charity. The invocation of saints is clearly pointed out in the following verses :—

    Adesto nunc, et percipe
    voces precantum supplices,
    nostri reatus efficax
    orator ad thronum Patris.

    .   .   .   .

IX.—INVOCATION OF SAINTS IN THE PRIMITIVE CHURCH PROVED FROM ANCIENT INSCRIPTIONS.

In favour of the belief and practice of the invocation of saints by the primitive Church, there

Miserere nostrarum precum,
placatus ut Christus suis
inclinet aurem prosperam,
noxas nec omnes imputet.
           Περὶ Στεφάνων lib., Hymn. V, v. 545 et seq.

Talking of the tomb of S. Agnes at Rome, he says :—

Servat salutem virgo Quiritium :
necnon et ipsos protegit advenas,
puro ac fideli pectore supplices.
           Περὶ Στεφάνων lib., Hymn. XIV, v. 5.

In noticing the protection to be derived from the intercession of the saints, Prudentius gratefully observes of the city of Calahorra :—

O triplex honor, O triforme culmen,
quo nostrae caput excitatur urbis,
cunctis urbibus eminens Iberis !
Exsultare tribus libet patronis :
quorum praesidio fovemur omnes
terrarum populi Pyrenearum.
           Περὶ Στεφάνων lib., Hymn. VI, v. 145.

Le Clerc, an eminent French Protestant writer, passes the following remark upon the Peristephanon of Prudentius : 'It is very evident from various passages in these hymns, that Christians invoked the martyrs at that period, and believed that they had been assigned by the Almighty as the especial patrons of some particular places. Certain Protestant writers, who admit that along with the Scripture should be united the tradition of the first four or five centuries, have denied that prayer was ever made to the saints before the fifth age of the Church. They should, however, not have erected such an imaginary system without having first of all investigated facts, since it is easy to refute their supposition by several parts of the writings of Prudentius.'—*Bibliothèque universelle et historique de l'année* 1689, p. 167.

is a species of proof which has been seldom, perhaps never before, introduced to the notice of the English reader. The Roman catacombs are perpetually exhibiting such lucid evidence upon this article of apostolic doctrine as to dispel the faintest shadow of doubt or uncertainty from about the subject. For whenever that burial-place of the primitive and persecuted witnesses to the faith is explored, it almost invariably happens that an inscription is discovered over some martyred saint, in which the prayers of the Christian champion who sleeps within are desired by those who with religious reverence interred his mangled body and composed his epitaph.[1] In the year 1694 was discovered, in the cemetery of SS. Gordian and Epimachus,[2] the grave of the holy martyr Sabbatius, along with the following inscription on a marble slab which closed up the oblong niche in the wall or sepulchre containing the martyr's bones : [3]—

---

[1] The religious zeal which prompted many of the faithful to expend large sums of money, and even risk their lives to rescue the bodies of the martyrs from insult, and to possess themselves even of the earth which was sprinkled with their blood, will be noticed in the next chapter ; see vol. II, pp. 7–16.

[2] This cemetery is on the Latin Way, and about a mile from Rome.

[3] See note, vol. II, p. 14, for a description of the manner in which the graves were made in the catacombs. Concerning these ancient cemeteries, the reader is referred to Appendix IV.

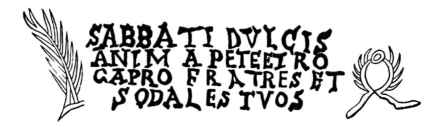

SABBATI DVLCIS ANIMA PETE ET ROGA
PRO FRATRES ET SODALES TVOS.[1]

*O Sabbatius, sweet soul, petition and
pray for thy brethren and companions.*

---

[1] Grammatical inaccuracies are of frequent occurrence in ancient
inscriptions, hence we must not be surprised to find 'pro fratres'
instead of 'pro fratribus,' etc.   This inscription was afterwards presented by Cardinal di Carpegna to the learned Florentine senator
Buonarruoti, who has inserted it in his interesting work entitled,
Osservazioni sopra alcuni frammenti di Vasi Antichi di vetro, where
the reader may see it at p. 167.   In the works of the poets and the
orators of Paganism, a palm-branch and wreath were emblematical
of victory.   The sacred writers also have noticed the palm-branch as
a symbol of the triumph gained by the martyr and the true believer
(*Apocalypse,* VII, 9), and the crown or garland as indicative of that
eternal glory which the saints enjoy in heaven (*Isaias,* XXVIII, 5 ; I
Corinthians, IX, 25 ; 2 *Timothy,* IV, 8 ; *S. James,* I, 12 ; I *S. Peter,*
V, 4 ; *Apocalypse,* II, 10).   Hence it is that a palm-branch and a
wreath of laurel are usually traced in the mortar, scratched on the
tile, or sculptured on the marble slab, which may have been severally
employed by the first Christians to seal the martyrs' graves in the
catacombs.   Both these types of victory are mentioned by the
Christian poet Prudentius, who lived so near to the times of persecution.   In his hymn in honour of S. Vincent he says of that
illustrious martyr :—

> 'Tu solus, o bis inclyte
> Solus brabii duplicis
> Palmam tulisti : tu duas
> Simul parasti laureas.'
> Περὶ Στεφάνων *lib., Hymn. V, v.* 537 *et seq.*

The palm-branch and the laurel crown, which accompany the inscription, unitedly testify that Sabbatius was martyred for the faith.

The following sepulchral inscription was extracted from a tomb in the cemetery of Callistus :—

ATTICE SPIRITVS TVS

IN BONV ORA PRO PAREN

TIBVS TVIS

O Atticus, thy spirit is in good, pray for thy parents.[1]

Another inscription, found in the cemetery of Cyriaca,[2] is to a similar effect :—

IOVIANE VIBAS IN DEO ET

ROG   (*id est ROGA.*)

In the cemetery of Priscilla[3] was discovered the following :—

ANATOLIVS FILIO BENEMERENTI FECIT

QVI VIXIT ANNIS VII. MENSIS VII. DIE

BVS XX. ISPIRITVS TVVS BENE REQVIES

CAT IN DEO PETAS PRO SORORE TVA.

The two succeeding inscriptions were inedited until a few years ago, when they became the sub-

---

[1] MURATORI, *Novus Thesaurus vet. inscrip.*, p. 1833, num. 6. F. BIANCHINI in his learned work entitled, *Demonstratio Historiae Ecclesiasticae quadripartitae comprobatae monumentis*, places this inscription in the first table of the first century of the Christian Church.

[2] This cemetery is on the Tyburtine Way, and has its entrance at the Church of S. Laurence outside the Walls.

[3] This cemetery is on the Salarian Way.

ject of a particular dissertation, and were published by an Italian antiquary :[1]—

SIMPLICIO
VENEMEREN
TI. FILIO. TE —
IN PACEM
P.T. PR. N.S.

that is :—

SIMPLICIO BENEMERENTI FILIO
(*Suscipiat*) TE (*Christus*) IN PACEM
PeTe PRo NobiS.[2]

The second is preserved in the Church of the Blessed Trinity at Velletri :—

ΑΝΑΤΟΛΙCΕΜωΝΠΡωΤΟ
ΤΟΚΟΝΤΕΚΝΟΝΟCΤΙCΗ
ΜΕΙΝΕΔΟΘΗCΠΡΟCΟΛΙΓΟΝ
ΧΡΟΝΟΝΤΕΥΧΟΥΠΕΡΗΜωΝ

*To Anatolius, our first-begotten son, (thou) who
wast given to us for a short time, pray for us.*

The following inscription, which may be found inserted in the works of one of the most celebrated

---

[1] C. CARDINALI, *Intorno un antico Marmo Christiano.* Bologna, 1819.

[2] In ancient inscriptions the V is frequently substituted for B; and to those who are anywise versed in the lapidary style of writing, it is well known that very often words are so abbreviated that their consonants only, sometimes no others than the first and last, are inscribed. See FABRETTI, *Inscriptionum antiquarum explicatio,* c. III, p. 164 ; MAZZOCHI, *de Epist. Hilarii,* p. 11, *in notis.*

scholars in lapidary writing,[1] is equally demonstrative of the belief and practice of the primitive Church with regard to the invocation of departed saints :—

ROGES· PRO· NOBIS· QUIA· SCIMUS· TE· IN· CHRISTO.[2]

At Rome, in 1758, in an excavation at the Church of S. Agnes outside the Walls, was discovered an epitaph composed by S. Damasus, who was elected Pope in 366, in honour of that youthful martyr and illustrious virgin. The pontiff concludes his verses with this invocation of S. Agnes :—

O VENERANDA MIHI SANCTVM DECVS ALMA PVDORIS VT DAMASI PRECIB.   FAVEAS PRECOR INCLYTA MARTYR.[3]

The following inscription, from the church of S. John at Ravenna, records a vow discharged by the religious empress Galla Placidia and her children towards the year 440, when, as it would appear,

---

[1] Gaetano Marini, who expended forty years in studying and transcribing the Christian inscriptions discovered in the Catacombs. Those valuable monuments of ecclesiastical antiquity, with others relating to the civil history of Pagan Rome, to the number of many thousands, were collected and classified by Marini, and now incrust the walls of the first corridor of the Vatican gallery. They form a body of documents which, to use the expression of Marini himself, 'è una raccolta la più grande e la più dotta che sia al mondo.'— M. MARINI, *Anedotti di G. Marini.* Roma, 1822.

[2] G. MARINI, *Iscrizioni antiche delle Albani,* p. 37 ; and *Atti e Monumenti de Fratelli Arvali,* p. 266.

[3] J. MARANGONI, *Acta S. Victorini,* Appendix, p. 138.

the imperial family experienced the efficacy of the intercession of S. John the Evangelist in their behalf during a tempest at sea :—

SANCTO AC BEATISSIMO APOSTOLO
IOANNI EVANGELISTAE
GALLA PLACIDIA AVGVSTA
CVM FILIO SVO PLACIDIO VALENTINIANO
AVGVSTO
ET FILIA SVA IVSTA GRATA HONORIA
AVGVSTA
LIBERATIONIS PERICVLO MARIS
VOTVM SOLVIT.[1]

X.—INVOCATION OF SAINTS IN THE ANGLO-SAXON CHURCH.

It will not, the writer presumes, be considered by the British reader as an intrusion on his patience, if a few extracts from an elegant and learned work on our native history be presented to his notice, in proof of the perfect conformity in belief and practice concerning the invocation of saints which subsists between the Anglo-Saxons and the present Catholic inhabitants of the British Islands.

'But a short acquaintance with the literature of the time,' observes Dr. Lingard, 'will prove that

---

[1] MURATORI, *Novus Thesaurus veterum inscriptionum*, p. 1878, num. 2.

our ancestors were too well instructed to confound
man with God. They knew how to discriminate
between the adoration due to the Supreme Being
and the honours which might be claimed by the
most holy among His servants ; and while they worshipped Him as the author of every blessing, they
paid no other respect to them than what was
owing to men, whom they considered as *His*
favourites, and *their* advocates. Whoever shall
attentively peruse the works of the Saxon writers, or
the acts of the Saxon councils, from the era of their
conversion to what is deemed the darkest period
of their history, will observe this important distinction accurately marked and constantly inculcated.
When the poet sang the praise of his patron, he
sought neither to interest his mercy, nor to deprecate his justice ; to obtain the assistance of his
intercession, to be remembered by him at the throne
of the Almighty, was the sole object of his petition.[1]
If the preacher from the pulpit exhorted his hear-
ers to solicit the prayers of their more holy brethren,

---

[1] See ALCUIN's *Address to the Virgin Mary*, at the end of his 'Life
of S. Willibrord' :—

> Tu mundi vitam, totis tu gaudia saeclis,
>   tu Regem caeli, tu Dominum atque Deum
> ventris in hospitio genuisti, Virgo perennis :
>   tu nobis precibus auxiliare tuis.
>   *Vita S. Willibrordi*, cap. XXXIV.

Also S. ALDHELM, *De laudibus Virginitatis*, cap. LX, and the Ven.
BEDE's prayer at the end of his *Vita metrica S. Cuthberti*.

he was careful to inculcate that they should adore God alone, as their true Lord and true God.[1] If the Christian, when he rose from his bed, was accustomed to beg the protection of the saints, he was yet commanded, in the first place, to worship with bended knees the majesty of his Creator.[2] These distinctions were too easy to be mistaken. The idea of intercession necessarily includes that of dependence; and to employ the mediation of His favourites is to acknowledge the superior excellence of the Deity.'[3]

XI.—CONTAINED IN ALL THE LITURGIES.

The unhesitating belief of our Anglo-Saxon ancestors in the intercession of the saints, and the religious ardour with which, as is attested by a

[1] The Saxon homilist is very accurate in his expressions : 'Him alone shall we adore. He alone is true Lord and true God. We beg the intercession of holy men that they would intercede for us to their Lord and our Lord. But nevertheless we do not pray to them as we do to God.' (*Homil. Sax. apud* WHEL., p. 283.) 'Nulli martyrum,' says the manuscript, quoting a passage from S. Augustine, 'sacrificamus, quamvis in memoriis martyrum constituamus altaria.' *Ibid.*

[2] 'Having worshipped his Creator alone, let him invoke God's saints, and pray that they would intercede for him to God ; first to holy Mary, and then all the saints of God.'—*Lib. Leg. Eccles. apud* WILK., p. 272.

[3] Thus, in the Saxon homilies, the preacher points out the difference between the intercession of the saints and the mediation of Christ, when he exhorts his auditory to solicit the intercession of the Virgin Mary with Christ her Son, her Creator, and her Redeemer.—*Serm. in Annunc. S. Mariae, apud* WANLEY, p. 2. See LINGARD, *The History and Antiquities of the Anglo-Saxon Church,* vol. II, pp. 84–86.

variety of monuments, they invoked their prayers, demonstrate the genuineness of their religious credence, and its consequent identity with that of the universal Church, whether in the East or West, on this important article of faith. That such a doctrine was in fact most studiously inculcated by the Apostles and their immediate successors may be readily ascertained by referring to the liturgies that have been in use from time immemorial in those several Churches which those first preachers of the Gospel, or their immediate disciples, founded.[1]

XII.—OBJECTIONS ANSWERED.

If it be idle or illicit to call upon the saints to pray for us, then the impropriety and unlawfulness of our invocations must arise from some of the following causes: namely, because the saints are unwilling or incapable of praying for us; or, because they cannot hear our prayers; or, if they can, because the offering of them up would be an injury perpetrated against the Godhead, and a particular derogation from the mediatorship of Jesus Christ.

XIII.—CHARITY ENGAGES THE SAINTS TO PRAY FOR US.

I. With respect to the unwillingness of the saints to present our petitions at the throne of

---

[1] Extracts from the Liturgies in use throughout the East are given in Appendix II.

mercy, we cannot for a single moment contemplate even the possibility of its existence : for, though faith shall have a termination when we shall see God as He is ;[1] though hope will one day win the object of its longings ;[2] charity never falleth away,[3] but glows brighter and purer, and acts more unceasingly within the bosom of the saint in heaven than in the breast of the most righteous man that ever lived upon earth.

If, therefore, charity impels each Christian, whose pretensions to piety are of the very humblest order, inwardly to remember his brethren, his friends, and all fellow-creatures in his daily prayers, the same virtues must possess an impulse incomparably more active in stimulating the blessed souls in heaven to intercede for those whom they have left upon earth.

XIV.—THEY HAVE THE POWER OF DOING IT.

II. Concerning their ability to perform this charitable office for us, it is to be observed that if the saints, while they themselves were wanderers in the desert of this world, could present their supplications to Almighty God in our behalf, it is inconceivable why they cannot exercise the same

---

[1] 1 S. John, III, 2.

[2] 'But hope that is seen is not hope. For what a man seeth, why doth he hope for ?' Romans, VIII, 24.

[3] 1 Corinthians, XIII, 8.

kindness now that they have entered into the en-
joyment of the promised land of heaven ; and how,
in the plenitude of their actual happiness, the power
of doing good, and of moving according to the
spirit of God's own love, should be circumscribed
within much narrower limits than those assigned
for its action while on earth.

XV.—THEY KNOW WHAT PASSES UPON EARTH.

III. But, perhaps, it may be argued that they
do not know what passes here below, and that,
as they cannot hear our prayers, it is consequently useless for us to beg their intercession.
What authority have those who differ from the
Catholic Church for such an objection? None
whatever; for instead of being warranted by any
passage in the Scriptures, or countenanced by
reason, it is, on the contrary, most easily removed
by calling in the aid of Scripture and reason. If
it be asserted that the saints of themselves, or by
any quality inherent in their nature, cannot hear
our prayers, nor penetrate the secret enclosure of
our hearts to read the thoughts and watch the
motions that are stirring there, we most readily
assent to such a declaration; but this does not
overthrow the dogma respecting the prayers of
the saints. To accomplish this, it must be demonstrated that Almighty God cannot impart to them
such a knowledge: to refuse, however, to recognise such a power in the Deity would be blasphe-

mous.   God has communicated to the prophets the knowledge of events that were not to happen for many hundred years.   Eliseus witnesses, as though he were personally present, the scene that takes place between Giezi and the Syrian general Naaman : 'Was not my heart present when the man turned back from his chariot to meet thee?   So now thou hast received money, and received garments, etc. . . . But the leprosy of Naaman shall also stick to thee and to thy seed for ever.'[1]   The same prophet was acquainted with what passed in the council-chamber of the Syrian king, who imagined that some amongst his friends had betrayed his secret confidence : 'And calling together his servants, he said :   Why do ye not tell me who it is that betrays me to the king of Israel? and one of his servants said : No one, my lord, O king, but Eliseus the prophet, that is in Israel, telleth the king of Israel all the words that thou speakest in thy privy-chamber.'[2]

To S. Peter was revealed the deception of Ananias and Sapphira.[3]   Surely, if the Divine Being could convey to His servants while on earth a perfect knowledge of transactions which eye could not see, nor of which the ear could receive the faintest information, He must be equally able to impart similar communications unto the spirits of

---

[1] 4 *Kings*, v, 26, 27.   [2] 4 *Kings*, vi, 11, 12.
[3] *Acts*, v, 3.

the blessed, who are now much more susceptible
of receiving these revelations. It was from afar
off, from hell itself, that the rich man put up his
prayer to Abraham; but neither the great chaos
which was fixed between them, nor the difference
of place and state, prevented that holy patriarch
from hearing and replying to the supplication.[1]
If a prayer can be heard in limbo from the depths
of hell, assuredly our petitions can penetrate from
earth to heaven. Abraham, moreover, was aware
that Moses and the prophets had existed, and
had put on record the laws and admonitions of
Almighty God;[2] the same Omnipotence that communicated this to Abraham imparts to His blessed
servants a knowledge of those prayers addressed
to them by mortals here on earth. This will enter
more readily into our conception, when we call
to our remembrance that now the saints possess
advantages which were not enjoyed by Abraham
while in limbo; for they are installed in the actual
fruition of beatific glory—are in heaven, and see
God face to face. Our Divine Redeemer assures
us that there shall be joy in heaven upon one
sinner doing penance;[3] but who are they who
participate in this holy jubilation? the whole
court of heaven; and consequently the saints as
well as the angels, the universal body of the

---

[1] S. *Luke*, XVI, 24, 25.   [2] S. *Luke*, XVI, 29.
[3] *Ibid.*, XV, 10.

studious the Church is in teaching the unlawfulness of asking anything of the saints as if they
were the authors of Divine benefits and the dis-
pensators of glory and of grace, or could impart
to us any of the means required for securing our
salvation. He illustrates this portion of the creed
of his Church by a reference to the formularies
of public prayer which she employs in her services, and to those authentic and doctrinal expositions which she exhibits as the standard of her
faith.

XVII.—MANNER OF ADDRESSING GOD THROUGH THE SAINTS.

The form of prayer used in the solemn and
public worship of the Church will, in the clearest
manner, testify her doctrine on the invocation of
saints.[1] Throughout the Missal[2] and the Bre-
viary[3] there is not one single prayer or collect

---

[1] Pope S. Celestine, who ascended the pontifical throne in the
year 431, observes, in his letter to the bishops of Gaul: 'Obsecra-
tionum sacerdotalium sacramenta respiciamus, quae ab Apostolis
tradita, in toto mundo atque in omni Ecclesia catholica uniformiter
celebrantur, ut legem credendi lex statuat supplicandi.'

[2] An appellation given to the volume which contains the Liturgy
of the Mass, together with the whole order of Divine service to be
celebrated on the Sundays, festivals, and saints' days throughout
the year.

[3] A book which contains the form of daily office or devotion to
be recited in public or private by every Catholic minister from the
moment he is initiated into holy orders until the hour of his death.
Such a duty is equally incumbent on the Pope, as well as the
humblest sub-deacon.

addressed to any saint whatever; but every one of them is directed to God alone. They begin with one or other of the following invocations to the Deity: 'Omnipotens sempiterne Deus,' etc., Almighty, eternal God; 'Intercessio nos quaesumus, Domine,' May the intercession, O Lord, etc.; 'Praesta quaesumus, omnipotens Deus,' Grant, O Almighty God, etc. They end with this conclusion: 'Through our Lord Jesus Christ, Thy Son.' The following strophe includes the sense of these lines in which each hymn chanted in the public office closes :—

> Father of mercies! hear our cry;
> hear us, co-equal Son!
> who reignest with the Holy Ghost
> while ceaseless ages run. Amen.

XVIII.—SIMILARITY OF CATHOLIC AND PROTESTANT PRAYERS.

Whoever will take the trouble to compare the Collects appointed to be read during the service of the Church of England on all Sundays of the year with the Collects that are set down in the Roman Missal for the same occasions, will be probably surprised to discover such a perfect accordance between them, in almost every instance, as to convince him that the 'Book of Common Prayer' is indebted to the Mass of the Catholic Church for every beautiful invocation to the Deity. The coincidence is peculiarly observable on the Feast of S. Michael and all Angels, when Protestants employ a prayer the very same in sense, and a literal translation of the Collect which the Catholic Church recites upon the same occasion.[1]

Though the Christian possesses only one Mediator of redemption, Christ Jesus, who alone has reconciled us through His precious Blood,[2] and after having wrought the work of our redemption, and having 'entered once into the Holy of Holies,'[3] always lives to make intercession for us;[4] it does not by any means follow as a necessary consequence that it is unlawful to solicit the intercession of angels and the saints; for, were it so, neither S. Paul would have recommended himself with so much earnestness to the prayers of the brethren on earth;[5] nor would S. James have thus exhorted us to 'pray for one another that you may be saved;'[6] for assuredly the prayers of

---

[1] ORATIO.

Deus, qui miro ordine angelorum ministeria hominumque dispensas: concede propitius, ut a quibus Tibi ministrantibus in caelo semper assistitur, ab his in terra vita nostra muniatur. Per Dominum nostrum, etc.

FROM THE BOOK OF COMMON PRAYER.

O everlasting God, who hast ordained and constituted the services of angels and men in a wonderful order: mercifully grant, that as the holy angels always do Thee service in heaven, so by Thy appointment they may *succour* and *defend us* on earth: through Jesus Christ our Lord. Amen.

[2] *1 Timothy*, II, 5.   [3] *Hebrews*, IX, 12.   [4] *Hebrews*, VII, 25.
[5] *Romans*, XV, 30, and *Hebrews*, XIII, 18.   [6] *S. James*, V, 16.

a mortal man upon earth, however just and pure
he may be from human imperfections, must dero-
gate from the glory of Jesus as our Mediator, and
deteriorate the price He paid for our redemption,
quite as much as the intercession of the glorified
spirits in heaven.   The Apostles did not consider
it to be injurious to the mediatorship of Christ to
ask the saints to pray for them; why, therefore,
should we?

XIX.—INCONSISTENCY OF SUCH AN OBJECTION.

Men of every religious denomination are mutually solicitous to obtain the prayers of one another;
and they do not hesitate to promise or request this
reciprocity of Christian brotherhood; but what are
we?   Alas, the best among us are poor miserable
creatures, with a load of sins and imperfections
on our shoulders; and yet many will request the
prayers of each other without scruple, at the same
instant that they would regard it as a heinous
crime to beg the intercession of the pure and
spotless saints in heaven, and pronounce it injurious to the mediatorship of Jesus to address to
His chosen faithful servants, who now wear robes
of glory brilliant and purple with His saving
blood, the selfsame invocations—the identical
requests they make to sinners.

It is difficult to conceive how a rational and
thinking Protestant can possibly object to that re-
lative and inferior honour which Catholics exhibit

towards the saints, when he himself is punctual in observing certain rites and ceremonies which cannot be ultimately referable to anything but this same practice.

1. There is scarcely one Protestant church, of however modern erection, which is not dedicated to God under the appellation of some particular saint: for one sacred edifice which bears the title of the Trinity, there are a hundred denominated after S. Mary, S. Peter, S. Paul, or some other saint.

2. In the ritual of the Church of England certain days are appointed for the especial celebration of festivals in honour of the saints, when their names are introduced with all becoming reverence in the Collect of the day.[1]

3. Instead of selecting an adjunct to his surname from the catalogue of heathen worthies, the Protestant assumes at baptism the appellation of some saint, and thus, in imitation of the Catholic, manifests his preference as well as reverence towards the glorified inhabitants of the heavenly Jerusalem.

[1] Such for instance are S. Andrew's day, the feast of S. Thomas the Apostle, the Conversion of S. Paul, the Presentation of Christ in the Temple, or the Purification of the Virgin Mary, S. Matthias's day, the Annunciation of the Blessed Virgin Mary, S. Mark's day, S. Philip and S. James's day, S. Barnabas the Apostle, S. John Baptist's day, S. Peter's day, S. James the Apostle, S. Bartholomew the Apostle, S. Matthew the Apostle, S. Michael and all Angels, S. Luke the Evangelist, S. Simon and S. Jude, and All Saints' day.

We will close our observations on this subject by a concise though comprehensive abstract of the Catholic doctrine on the intercession and invocation of the saints, furnished by a work of public authority in the Church, the Catechism of the Council of Trent, which says: 'We do not address God and the saints in the same manner: God we implore to grant us the blessings of which we stand in need, and to deliver us from the dangers to which we are exposed; but the saints, because they are the friends of God, we solicit to undertake the advocacy of our cause with Him, to obtain for us, from Him, all necessaries for soul and body. Hence, we make use of two different forms of prayer: to God we properly say, "*Have mercy on us; hear us*," but to the saints, "*Pray for us.*" The words, "Have mercy on us," we may also address to the saints, for they are most merciful; but we do so on a *different principle:* we beseech them to be touched with the misery of our condition, and to interpose, in our behalf, their influence and intercession before the throne of God. In the performance of this duty, it is strictly incumbent on all not to transfer to creatures the right which belongs exclusively to God; and when, kneeling before the image of a saint, we repeat the Lord's Prayer, we are also to recollect that we beg of the saint to pray *with us*, and to obtain for us those favours which we ask of God in the petitions of the Lord's Prayer;

in fine, that he become our interpreter and inter-
cessor with God.   That this is an office which the
saints discharge we read in the Apocalypse.'[1]

---

[1] J. DONOVAN, *The Catechism of the Council of Trent.*   Dublin,
1829, p. 467.

END OF VOL. I.

PRINTED BY BALLANTYNE, HANSON AND CO.
EDINBURGH AND LONDON

Breinigsville, PA USA
14 September 2009
224051BV00001B/10/A

9 780766 135499

citizens belonging to the celestial Jerusalem : no
one is and no one can be excepted ; for we are
told by Christ Himself that the saints in glory are
like to the angels.[1] The brightest angels have
not a peculiar faculty or power by which they can
ascertain what passes or is said on earth independent of the interposition of the Deity ; how,
therefore, do they become acquainted with the
sinner's repentance ? Whatever medium the Protestant assigns for the conveyance of terrestrial
knowledge to the angels, the Catholic will ascribe
as the method by which the saints become informed of our requests to engage their prayers
and supplication in our favour.

XVI.—THEIR INTERCESSION NOT DEROGATORY TO THE MEDIATORSHIP OF CHRIST.

IV. But it will be further objected, that although
the saints may be able to hear our invocations,
still it is injurious to the mediatorship of Christ to
call upon them. In reply, the Catholic observes
that he by no means elevates the saints whom he
calls upon to the dignity of mediators of redemption, or distributors of graces : he merely invokes
their charity ; he solicits them to be the bearers
of his supplications to the throne of his and
their Saviour Jesus, the true—the one—the only
mediator of redemption ; he attests how earnestly

---

[1] *S. Matthew*, XXII, 30, and *S. Luke*, XX, 36.

ELEMENTS OF
ARCHITECTURE

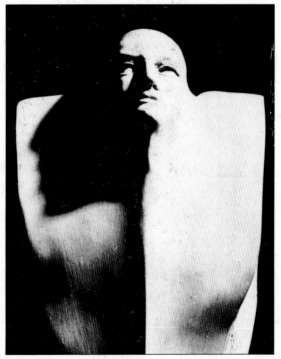

ROB KRIER, SCULPTURE

The most obvious, perhaps even the most archaic, building technique is to lay stone and thus to form an homogeneous constructed mass. A long wall must either be thick enough to stand alone or it needs to be supported by a system of pillars, ribs and terracing, outer covering or network.